Livia Andrea Piazza
The Concept of the New

Livia Andrea Piazza

The Concept of the New
Framing Production and Value in Contemporary Performing Arts

Budrich UniPress Ltd.
Opladen • Berlin • Toronto 2017

All rights reserved. No part of this publication may be reproduced, stored in or introduced into a retrieval system, or transmitted, in any form, or by any means (electronic, mechanical, photocopying, recording or otherwise) without the prior written permission of Barbara Budrich Publishers. Any person who does any unauthorized act in relation to this publication may be liable to criminal prosecution and civil claims for damages.

You must not circulate this book in any other binding or cover and you must impose this same condition on any acquirer.

A CIP catalogue record for this book is available from
Die Deutsche Bibliothek (The German Library)

© 2017 by Budrich UniPress Ltd. Opladen, Berlin & Toronto
www.budrich-unipress.eu

    ISBN   **978-3-86388-737-7 (Paperback)**
    eISBN   978-3-86388-300-3 (eBook)

Das Werk einschließlich aller seiner Teile ist urheberrechtlich geschützt. Jede Verwertung außerhalb der engen Grenzen des Urheberrechtsgesetzes ist ohne Zustimmung des Verlages unzulässig und strafbar. Das gilt insbesondere für Vervielfältigungen, Übersetzungen, Mikroverfilmungen und die Einspeicherung und Verarbeitung in elektronischen Systemen.

Die Deutsche Bibliothek – CIP-Einheitsaufnahme
Ein Titeldatensatz für die Publikation ist bei Der Deutschen Bibliothek erhältlich.

Budrich UniPress Ltd.
Stauffenbergstr. 7. D-51379 Leverkusen Opladen, Germany

86 Delma Drive. Toronto, ON M8W 4P6 Canada
www.budrich-unipress.eu

Jacket illustration by disegno visuelle kommunikation, Wuppertal – www.disegno-kommunikation.de
Picture credits: Livia Andrea Piazza, Gabriele Marino
Editing: Alison Romer, Lancaster, UK
Technical editing: Anja Borkam, Jena – kontakt@lektorat-borkam.de
Printed in Europe on acid-free paper by Books on Demand GmbH, Norderstedt, Germany

Table of Contents

Introduction	7
1. The New in Social Sciences	15
1.1 The New as Unknown: the Notion of Innovation	15
1.2 The Production of Innovation and its Temporal Dimension	18
1.2.1 The Purpose of Innovation and its Critique	21
1.2.2 Critical Innovation Studies	24
1.3 Perspectives from Sociology of Art	26
2. The New in the Humanities	37
2.1 Difference and Obscurity: The Notion of the New	37
2.2 The Production of Difference and the New	41
2.2.1 The Time of the New	51
2.2.2 The Spaces of the New	57
2.3 Duration and Value	59
2.3.1 The Problem of Value	61
3. The Present Time and the New	66
3.1 Some Notes on the Avant-Garde	66
3.2 Postmodernism and the Future	73
3.3 The Affirmation of Creativity	79
3.3.1 The Critique to Creativity and its Limits	82
4. On the Traces of the New at the Theatre	87
4.1 Theatre across Reality and Fiction	87
4.2 The Institutional Critique yet to Come	92
4.3 Open Conclusion on Theory and Practice: Where to Start	97
5. Empirical Research on the New: Methodology	100
5.1 Balancing Theory and Empirical Research	100
5.2 Objectives and Research Questions	102

5.3 Sampling and Data Collection	105
5.4 Data Analysis	109
6. The Concept of the New in the Theatre of the Present	116
6.1 The Concept of the New in Practice	116
6.1.1 The Difference of the New	118
6.1.2 The New as Incomplete	121
6.1.3 Eternity and Ephemerality	123
6.2 From the Concept of the New to its Production	125
6.2.1 A Coexistence of Differences	127
6.2.2 Suspension and Self-Betrayal	129
6.3 The Theatre System and its Value(s)	134
6.3.1 System Reproduction and Disorganisation	141
6.4 Art and Politics: Values and Roles	146
7. The Production of the New in the Theatre of the Present	151
7.1 Art Institutions as Frames	151
7.2 The Collective Cultivation of Difference	155
7.3 Curating Obscurity	157
7.4 Roles and Rules: Impossible Possibilia	159
7.5 Works in Progress and Failure	162
7.6 Theatre Production in the Meantime	165
Conclusions	170
Further Research	177
Reference List	183
Appendix I	187
Appendix II	190
Appendix III	192
Acknowledgements	193
Index	195

Introduction

"What if?" This is a question that, while at first apparently inoffensive, also has seemingly nothing to do with production, pointing in the direction of indeterminacy rather than of creation. This question drives the present research on the production of the New.

Both the concept of the New and the one of production are to be enriched by a perspective that links them together, and one of the most interesting domains to explore this connection in the contemporary landscape is that of art, in particular the one of postdramatic theatre. Here the "what if?" can be fully embraced as an instrument to navigate the borders between reality and imagination. Although the concept of art production has been widely studied in many different disciplines, it can be reconfigured by rethinking the New, which had been otherwise set aside to be replaced by some concepts related to it–such as innovation and creativity–that had gripped scientific research and policy making. Not by chance, such concepts came to the fore in recent times: their connection with the latest stage of capitalism is also a major topic in today's research.

As value shifts into the immaterial, the idea of production is shaken and notions based on process and partiality, like creativity or innovation, develop as objects of attention and critique. Although the intimate link between capitalism and innovation is surely not new, the attention dedicated to the latter today is legitimate, as are its critique. This is particularly true in the realm of the arts, which is paradoxically defined by having to produce the New in the context of capitalism that is premised itself on the exploitation of novelty. The most illustrative mechanism in this sense might be of creative destruction popularised by Schumpeter (1934), who equated innovation with progress, and critically analysed by Harvey (2006), to mention one among many, who underlined that the production of the New, by means of value destruction, is a fundamental instrument for capitalism to reproduce itself. Such reproduction is sustained at the same time by a narrative ensuring the legitimacy and survival of the system. Harvey's condition of postmodernity (1989) emerges as an exacerbated modernity, where the regime of flexible accumulation, requiring more and more radical innovation, is matched by postmodernism, affecting the way we conceive and represent our world.

According to Mark Fisher, we live in the epoch of capitalist realism, 'a pervasive atmosphere' influencing the way we produce and depict our reality acting 'as a kind of invisible barrier constraining thought and action' (Fisher 2009: 16). More specifically, the narrative of neoliberal capitalism operates by depicting the latter as a system devoid of fiction, and in doing so it legitimates capitalism's existence by weaving a fiction of its own, setting the current reality as the only possible one. In this way capitalist realism makes it 'impossible to imagine a coherent alternative to it' (ibid., 16), while postmodernism affects our ability to devise 'strategies to produce some radically different future' (Harvey 1989: 54).

In the context of a mode of production depicted as natural, the link between art and capitalism corroborates, operating in the material conditions of production and occupying the realm of imagination. It is in this entanglement between material conditions and the narratives behind them that the New becomes an interesting territory of research to investigate the relationship between art and capitalism: it recurs as a *leitmotif* in the production and funding mechanisms of art and resounds in the discourses around art, its functions and politics. The New emerges at the core of such entanglements in what Bojana Kunst effectively describes as *The Project Horizon*, a peculiar temporality regulating the production of performing arts within neoliberal capitalism, where:

one always has to begin again; however, the new start is not about differences but about another promise for the future; another indebted engagement to that which has yet to come [...] Paradoxically, the more creative people are preoccupied with creating proposals for the future, the more our time is deeply characterised by the impossibility of imagining other modes of political and economic life (Kunst 2012: 113).

In terms of material art production, this situation can be read in light of capitalism's turn to the immaterial; artists actively contribute to the production of the New as immaterial value in a system that needs their creativity, and yet binds them to a precarious existence softened by the illusion of control on their productive processes. In this context, postdramatic theatre, as with the arts at large, witnessed the return of political art, revealing a drive for resistance and unveiling–at the same time–another way for capitalism to produce profits from it. The debates on performance and labour and the ones on social art practices in this case constitute some examples. These are often seen as undermining, rather than contributing, to the position of the arts within neoliberal capitalism by feeding not only the value production processes but also the prevailing narratives that sustain it.

In the field of art, these appear as symptoms of a complexity that is too often reduced and emerges in different paradoxical situations: sometimes theory depicts the artist as an unaware cogwheel of the capitalist engine; it has also been common to witness artists refusing to engage with festivals and theatres from the conviction that institutions are too complicit with a system perceived as perverse and 'capitalistic'. At the same time, it has been equally unexceptional to see the very same institutions focusing their production and marketing efforts on political activism. Similar paradoxes develop around the New itself, which is sometimes refused as a concept completely appropriated by capitalism and at other times is operationalised by the art sectors themselves as a label for marketing strategies constructed exclusively on newness. The question of art's role within society has re-emerged, producing two opposite approaches to theory and practice: a plea to underline again the necessity and political value of an art detached from reality on the one hand, and a strong perspective advocating for an activist art on the other. Yet, these perspectives seem to reflect and corroborate the borders between art and life, and reality and fiction, and thus risk trapping the 'new' imaginaries they might produce into a narrative of capitalist realism that confines art and imagination in opposition to reality. As these often take on the quality of entertainment, they appear as closed spaces from where to escape the only possible world.

Such considerations drove the premises and objectives of this research, which develops by firmly refusing the pessimistic idea that the arts–and all individuals and organisations that constitute them–are, unconsciously or not, too complicit with the system to be taken seriously as agents of change. Rather, it takes the investigation of the New as a starting point to rethink the relationship between performance and politics at large, admitting the possibility of an art practice that treasures its own values and still has consequences on our world. As Pascal Gielen writes, art 'still cherishes the idea of that which can always also be otherwise imagined' (2013: 26), and could find room for action in nurturing and sustaining imagination and fiction as things not separated from reality, but rather in profound relationship to it.

Out of these premises, this research explores the possibilities of a reconceptualisation of the New in order to cast a light on the paradoxical position of the arts in the latest stage of neoliberal capitalism. The aim is not to produce another critique of creativity; rather, it aims to set aside fashionable debates on capitalism, creativity and innovation in the attempt to focus on the essential aspects of the dynamic that connects the production of the New with contemporariness. In this sense, this research explores the dimensions, possibilities and downsides of an idea of art production that puts the New and its constitutive aspects at its core, so that innovation practices could also be informed and enriched by revolving around the question 'what if?' rather than focusing on 'what it should be' (Dolan, 2005: 13).

The nature of such intents channelled the methodological premises of this work, which calls for a theoretical effort grounded in a multidisciplinary approach and an empirical investigation based on qualitative research, where theoretical and empirical sources could be considered and valued contextually. The choice of a multidisciplinary approach stems from the connection between the New, the material conditions of art production, the discourses around them and the prevailing narratives. Considering the New not only as the main object of this research but also as an operative concept that could deepen the understanding of art production in the contemporary landscape, called for its investigations across different disciplines that could enlighten the singular aspects relevant for this research. This investigation combines different disciplines and methods without aiming at their conciliation but rather at the depth of understanding that their arrangement could offer: a possible shift in perspectives that might broaden knowledge and substantially inform practice in postdramatic theatre and dance. More precisely, the work does not intend to offer a new definition of the New by means of theoretical research or to test a hypothesis through fieldwork analysis. Rather, it addresses the need for reorganising the discourse around the New and commits to the hermeneutical effort of combining theory and practice in order to suggest theoretical concepts and concrete actions for producing experimental theatre under the conditions of neoliberal capitalism.

In Chapters I and II the notions of 'innovation' and 'new' are explored, respectively, in Social Sciences and in Humanities, highlighting their constitutive differences from the conceptual and temporal perspective. The contrasts are then analysed in terms of value, highlighting the aspects of the New that were conveniently excluded from the discourse on innovation. In Social Sciences, the New is equated with the unknown and innovations are perceived as incremental improvements of what already exists (Braun-Thürmann 2005). The narrative at play here sets innovation as a progressive discovery of the unknown, in which the New is recognisable by means of comparison with what is already known (Dosi 1988), and is automatically attached to positive qualities such as progress or truth (Hutter 2010). The production of innovation establishes paradigms that can be absorbed and used in diverse markets in a process similar to the one that happened to the very concepts of the New and creativity (Boltanski and Chiappello 2005; Von Osten 2011). Here, the New is often accepted as a recombination of existing elements and change and–as in Kuhn's *Structure of Scientific Revolutions* (1962)–results from routine, tending to confirm the general structure or the dominant paradigm. Echoes of this are also to be found in the field of Sociology of Art, which stresses how the production of the New regards primarily a battle on the representation of the world and can hardly result in radical change: the New is either bound to happen only as 'partial revolutions' (Bourdieu 1980) or to become a systemic form of continuous renewal (Luhmann 2000) in a paradigm so flexible that it might never bring about a revolution.

Chapter 2 focuses on the Humanities, where the New emerges in stark contrast with that developed within the innovation discourse. It is primarily defined by the impossibility of establishing a relationship with it and its recognition works through different categories. The idea of difference remains at its core and yet it is a difference that cannot be recognised as such, calling for an approach to the New that includes the old (Benjamin 2003), freeing its definition from mere chronology. It is contemporary in its being obscure and anachronistic (Agamben 2009) and appears in the ordinary (Groys 2008), underlying how innovation might look like the New, but it is not, and how the New might look like the familiar, but it is not. Its production revolves around the ideas of difference (Deleuze 1994) and remembrance (Benjamin, 1999), and as such could inform–and help to rethink–the concept of creative destruction. The New is distinguished from innovation because it is incomplete, and as such it emerges as freed from purpose: its production is not determined to be substituted but rather triggers the production of other New, which is substantially different from itself.

The critique presented does not address innovation in itself but rather the use that has been made of it. Depicted as a fundamental mechanism of an assumed trajectory of linear progress, it projects similar ideas into the concept of art production, which are not compatible with the production of the New. If the New is not recognised as a step forward on a pre-given trajectory and the equation between innovation and progress is put in question, there might be room for conceiving radical change within art production, disentangling the connection between novelty and positive values that supports the narrative of neoliberal capitalism. Here, where the New emerges as first and foremost obscure and within the darkness that wraps its recognition and production, possibilities to look at reality as always otherwise imaginable might begin to emerge.

The investigation of what seems to be otherwise a too transparent present (Han 2015) develops from theoretical research on contemporary perspectives but includes, in Chapter 3, a reflection on the Avant-garde period, when at least two major paradoxes came to the fore, leaving a heavy inheritance on the concept of the New in terms of its very meaning and possibility (North 2013). Such paradoxes, and their implications in terms of production, are followed up to the form they take today, from the focus on reproduction at the expense of production (Harvey 1989) up to the compulsoriness of creativity (Reckwitz 2012), which seems to derive from the modern routinisation of the New (Benjamin 2003). In the space-time compression described by Harvey (1989), the New is hardly distinguishable from routine. At the same time, the rhetoric of innovation and creativity mantles it with newness, that which is only the reproduction of the same, corroborating the absorption of artistic practices into other markets. The removal of the New seems to be matched by a dismissal of the future as a category of political action: capitalist realism finds a renewed strength, as the politics of 'there is no alternative' makes its return and the neoliberal narrative of postmodernism seems to project time into a totalising present where people rush towards a future perceived as disappearing.

Yet, it is in the present time that action toward change might be undertaken, also in the working practices and fictions elaborated within the arts. In this spirit, Chapter 4 introduces the field of postdramatic theatre, retracing in the debates animating it the questions that develop around the paradoxes connected with the New as regards art production within neoliberal capitalism. Postdramatic theatre is a category elaborated by Hans-

Thies Lehmann (2006) to describe the aesthetic and poetic changes that marked experimental theatre and dance in the last thirty years. Among the possible ways of referring to contemporary theatre, this was chosen because it includes very different scenic practices highlighting, at the same time, their common ground. The latter revolves around the 'destruction of the foundations of dramatic theatre' (ibid., 23) and the resulting poetic and aesthetic transformations of its artistic practices. Being characterised, among other things, by the 'irruption if the real', it might not engage in an assertion of the real as such but in the production of the 'unsettling doubt that occurs through the indecidability whether one is dealing with reality or fiction' (ibid., 101). In the blurring boundaries between reality and fiction, art embraces the Real, which is, according to Lacan, unrepresentable, and as such constitutes what reality needs to erase in order to affirm and represent itself as such (Lacan 1998). Within capitalist realism, art could emerge as a space where reality also appears as always shaped by fiction and historically contingent, offering the opportunity to rethink the New and its political value at large.

Chapter 4 starts from this premise to introduce how the poetics of postdramatic theatre might interrupt prevalent representations by working on the dimension of time and space. It explores the debate around art institutions and privileges those perspectives that underline the fact that the current order and thus institutions in general are not natural, but built by humans and shaped by culture. These perspectives encourage looking for different practices exactly in those territories that have been most bent to the neoliberal logic in order to rethink rather than dismiss them. For instance, Inglis (2010) suggests that festivals able to resist the imposition of the creativity regime could become the place where to imagine different alternatives and nurture critical thinking. This unfolds first through an effort to change the conditions of production, but needs at same time to be grounded in a form of *Institutional Imagination* that Gielen (2013) locates at the core of an hypothetical third wave of institutional critique: art institutions might negotiate between reality and fiction differently from other institutions, such as the market or capitalism at large, and could be able to reaffirm and defend their autonomous values instead of following the market logic.

Accordingly, the research looks into the field of postdramatic theatre comprising the artists, institutions, people and discourses that form it, suggesting that a reconceptualisation of the New cannot be set aside from an empirical ground and its thorough analysis, to which the last three chapters of this research are fully dedicated. The field research considers exclusively those fringes of contemporary theatre that expressly work on experimenting and innovation, so that findings could better inform those processes in light of the reconceptualisation of the New and its production.

The complexities entailed in this topic called for a sensible balance between theoretical interpretation and illustration of the field of research, an effort best served by a purely qualitative approach, which is described in detail in Chapter 5, where the main objectives are tailored into research questions to be addressed in the field. These recollect on the one hand theoretical inputs, and design on the other the fieldwork in terms of sampling, data collection and analysis. The latter was conducted through the triangulation of different coding methods informed by an abductive approach, which provided the terrain to address the most urgent issues in the field and take the first steps towards a theory of producing the New within postdramatic theatre.

Chapter 6 describes and analyses the account provided by the field, which enriched the notion of the New and suggested directions for its production by arranging and re-arranging theoretical perspectives and concrete practices. In the field of postdramatic theatre, the New is recognised as something inhabited by difference and experienced in the impossibility of making a comparison. Such impossibility seems to be determined by the coexistence of radically different aspects in an object or idea that is entire and yet incomplete. The New is found in the overwhelming emergence from the ordinary and is searched for in what is obscure rather than clear. It is ephemeral and eternal at the same time and cannot take an indeterminate form but results as, and must remain, incomplete. The aspects marking the experience of the New singled out by the field ground the speculations on its production that, including different strategies, unfold in the cultivation of differences and, deserting the idea of utility and progress–being passionate about the utility of the useless–re-contextualise production itself in the realm of possibility. The New described by the field exceeds and puts into question the boundaries of art, which emerges as a central category for both artistic and political thought and action. The latter direction is explored with specific reference to performance itself and to the theatre system. It is then contextualised through an investigation of the value and role of art within society, as perceived in the field from the critique of the pressure on art to be useful.

Chapter 7 recollects the most relevant dimensions emerging from the analysis and explores their unsuspected relations, interweaving theoretical inputs and concrete ideas in one interpretation key that could be applied to the field of postdramatic theatre in order to envision the production of the New today. Here, art institutions emerge as privileged sites for the cultivation of differences and as the necessary frame for the production of the New. Within them, the possibility for envisioning different ways of living and working together could emerge, embracing the conflicts arising from collaboration as a fundamental dimension of the production of the New. The abstract concept of obscurity finds its concrete applications as regards curatorship and spectatorship. All these aspects depict a chance for today's theatre system to slip out of clarity and organisation, nurturing differences rather than trying to overcome them.

The New as entire and incomplete emerges only in the form of a product, triggering interesting reflections on the common practice of producing works in progress, and paves the way to rethink the temporality of a liberated production in the meantime of general rhythms. The New–as a work, as a concept or as an idea–could be rethought as an engine of production of other New different from itself that finds its way in settling and unsettling its mechanisms, calling for a production that can be conceived as the production of production, in order to think and experiment with the future as well as enlighten the practices of the present.

1. The New in Social Sciences

The concept of the New appears as central today, and represents an interesting point of departure for the investigation of art production within late capitalism. In particular, different conceptualisations of the new offer interesting perspectives on the debates currently animating the arts, both in terms of theory and practice, and call for an investigation of the concept itself. The following chapters aim at responding to the need of a better definition of the New by exploring the meanings of the words 'new' and 'innovation', which tend to be synonymous both in everyday and scientific language.

Generally speaking, novelty is the quality of being new. The word 'new' entails different meanings such as 'fresh, recent, unheard-of, different from the old' (Oxford English Dictionary) and some of them–particularly those indicating change–are fully expressed in the etymology of 'innovation' defined as 'restoration, renewal'. Accordingly, to innovate means to introduce 'new methods, ideas or products' and thus to 'make changes in something established' (Oxford English Dictionary). The absence of clear borders between the concepts of new and innovation is mirrored in scientific language, where a lack of effort to define the New has distinctively led to a shared meaning of novelty as 'innovation'. Interestingly, no clear definition of innovation corresponds to this accepted and shared meaning.

Although the definitions of 'innovation' vary across disciplines, some common aspects could be singled out. Rather than offering an overview of these definitions, a very selective literature review on innovation research in the social sciences is presented here, with the aim of underlining the differences between the notion of innovation and the notion of the New in terms of concepts, temporality and value. In particular, some perspectives from economics and sociology are explored in order to retrace the narrative around novelty built up in these disciplines, taking the latter as a point of departure for a more thorough investigation of contemporary theatre throughout this work.

1.1 The New as Unknown: the Notion of Innovation

Even though a single definition of innovation does not exist, novelty obviously constitutes the basis for all the definitions, consequently informing how innovations are recognised as such from a conceptual perspective. The first important characteristic of the new within innovation studies is that it can be acknowledged as comparable with what already exists and recognised in virtue of these differences, implying that the new is equated with the unknown.

In the field of economics, innovation today represents an increasingly fundamental parameter of analysis, but it also started to play a role due to the work of Joseph Schumpeter. His work has recently been rediscovered especially with regards to the concept of creative destruction, which he popularised, as will be explained later in this paragraph. The definition of innovation by Schumpeter is strongly connected with the figure of the entrepreneur, which he wanted to separate conceptually from the one of the capitalist, so far that innovation is defined as entrepreneurial change, which manifests itself in five instances:

> Development in our sense is defined by the carrying out of new combinations. This concept follows the following five cases: (1) The introduction of a new good–that is one with which consumers are not yet familiar–or of a new quality of good. (2) The introduction of a new method of production [...](3) The opening of a new market [...] (4) The conquest of a new source of supply of raw materials half-manufactured goods [...] (5) The carrying out of new organisation of any industry [...] (Schumpeter 1934: 66).

This definition represents a very interesting starting point to understand how novelty is conceived within the conceptualisation of innovation. As a matter of fact, it entails some of the most important aspects, which constitute the majority of the definitions of innovation, and provides insights on what the New means in this context. The first instance of innovation occurs, in Schumpeter's opinion, with the 'introduction of a new good', where 'new' is defined as 'one with which consumers are not yet familiar'. Although the same could be applied to processes, methods, sources or markets, their being new is what can be transformed into innovations. The acknowledgement of this quality happens mainly through the ability to tell the difference between the new object or process and what is instead familiar. In this sense, the New is associated with the 'unknown' and the ability of establishing a relationship to it (i.e. telling the difference) depends on the possibility of a comparison with the existing. Still, the existing here does not represent the conceptual opposite of the New, as the 'opening of a new market' is such for the entrepreneur and his activity 'whether or not this market has existed before'.

The field of evolutionary economics, often focusing on novelty and its production, is largely indebted to the work of Schumpeter and carries it on by starting from the same premises that see the new as unknown:

> Unfortunately, novelty is an amorphous concept. By definition, the informational content, the meaning of the properties of what newly emerges, cannot be anticipated (Witt 1993:92).

Besides evolutionary economics, the idea of novelty as something unknown is essential in the conceptualisation of innovation in economics at large, as Dosi (1988) underlines:

In an essential sense, innovation concerns the search for, discovery, experimentation, development, imitation and adoption of new products, new production processes and new organisational set-ups. Almost by definition, what is searched for cannot be known with any precision before the activity itself of search and experimentation, so that the technical outcomes of innovative effort can hardly be known ex-ante. Certainly, whenever innovative activities are undertaken by profit-motivated agents, they must involve also some sort of perception of yet unexploited, technical and economic opportunities (ibid. 1988: 222).

This definition also presents diverse insights into the nature of the new within social sciences that generally look at novelty in terms of innovation. Here the equivalence between *new* and *unknown* emerges even more clearly. The nature of the innovation process is driven by this conceptualisation of new, as what is searched for cannot 'almost by definition, be known' in advance. This, in Dosi's opinion, primarily connects innovation with a given character of uncertainty regarding both the object of the effort and the consequences of the process. The perception of the new as unknown and the possibility to acknowledge it in the form of innovation through a comparison with the existing holds true in the whole realm of social sciences. In the field of sociology, the multiple definitions of innovation are well represented by the following one, according to which, innovations are:

material and symbolic artefacts, which observers perceive as innovative and experience as an improvement on what already exists (Braun-Thürmann 2005: 5).

Here, the importance of the acknowledgement of innovation as such in the definition of the phenomenon is clearly stated. The possibility of establishing a relationship to the New, holding in mind what already exists, is thus a defining characteristic of what is innovative within the sociological perspective. This definition highlights another important aspect that, though implicitly present, it is openly stated here: innovations constitute an 'improvement' of the existing. This represents the second fundamental characteristic of innovation. Looking back at Schumpeter's definition, one could easily notice that the word 'development' is used as a synonym of innovation. In the wider context of Schumpeter's work, which studies innovation precisely as an engine of economic development, this comes as no surprise. Hutter notices more precisely that it is the attribution of the quality of newness that: 'usually arises in association with positively valued qualities, often supported by the inclusion of criteria such as originality, progress, or truth' (Hutter 2010:11). In his opinion, expressly indebted to Luhmann, the connection between newness and positive values could be explained by the 'functional differentiation of modern society'.[1]

---

1   Here Hutter refers explicitly to Luhmann's analysis of art as a social system, to whom newness and originality were established as values in connection with the functional differentiation of the social system of art from other systems, linked to the privileged role of self-reference onto hetero-reference used by the art system to define and produce itself.

By looking at the main characteristics emerging from these definitions, it is possible to state that the social sciences are inhabited by a conceptualisation of the New that informs research on innovation, with important consequences. This idea of the new implies that innovation is a progressive path through which the 'unknown', recognised as such, becomes 'known'. This notion of innovation consequently entails a vision of the world based on a linear trajectory in which innovation acts as an instrument for improving that which already exists. The 'new' is recognised here in virtue of its comparison with what exists and its 'discovery' entails positive values.

Notwithstanding the enormous influence and the important implications that such a conceptualisation entails, it must be taken into account that things are much more complex. Such complexity–unfolding in the interplay between routine and innovation on the one hand, and between creation and destruction on the other–appears manifestly in the research regarding the production of innovation.

1.2 The Production of Innovation and its Temporal Dimension

The opportunity of the progressive clarification of the unknown, the possibility of recognising the new by establishing a relationship to it through the comparison with what exists, and the positive values that naturally spring out of this possibility, characterise the recognition of novelty in the social sciences. Moreover, novelty appears mainly as a recombination of existing elements and innovation becomes the 'carrying out of new combinations', as already defined by Schumpeter (1934: 66). This reinforces the idea of the new as a step-forward and establishes the possibility of accepting recombinant novelty as valid:

> Innovation in the economic system-and indeed the creation of any sort of novelty in art, science, or practical life-consists to a substantial extent of a recombination of conceptual and physical materials that were previously in existence (Nelson 1982: 130).

In the extract above, which uses 'novelty' and 'innovation' as synonyms, the new is explicitly defined as a recombination of pre-existing elements. The latter aspect is very important as it determines an idea of production of the new based on the concept of transformation, which constitutes the basis of the concept of production in different approaches in economics as well as in the field of sociology of the arts. In terms of production, to accept as valid the idea of novelty as a recombination of existing elements also means to legitimate routine as one of its fundamental parts. The interplay between routine and change constitutes the base of the majority of theories on innovation in economics and on art production in sociology. The common theoretical reference is Kuhn's *The Structure of Scientific Revolutions* (1962), where radical change happens as a result of routine and the establishing of a new routine, confirming the general structure of scientific progress rather than changing it, while also raising legitimate doubts on how radical the change in question could be.[2] As North notices, Kuhn arranges 'an interdependent relationship between recombinant and revolutionary novelty. Normal science combines and recombines its basic elements until sufficient anomalies arise to cause a revolution, which then feeds these anomalies back into a new version of normal science. Thus normal science replicates itself in subtly different forms, generation after generation' (North 2013: 127).

Evolutionary economists are generally interested in this process of self-transformation, which represents a central theme of the field because, as Witt underlines, 'there is nothing invariable in the economy except its constant change' (Witt 2003: ix). Evolutionary economics seems to be indebted to Kuhn's work (or, at least, seems to start from similar premises) on how the production of change takes place, since the trajectory described here regards both the production and the accumulation of novelties (Encinar, 2006). Here, it is routine itself that can and should be recombined in the pursuit of innovation:

Innovations in organisational routine similarly consist, in large part, of new combinations of existing routines. It may involve the replacement of an existing subroutine by a new and different one that performs, in relation to the rest, the same function that the old one did (Nelson 1982: 130-31).

Moreover, in order to successfully innovate, some conditions should be satisfied; being routine should be fully 'under-control', as 'reliable routines of well-understood scope provide the best components for new combinations' (ibid., 130-31). Innovation here emerges as a reassuring process of controlling novelty.

Even more interesting are the aspects of substitution and of purposefulness, which recall the notion of creative destruction that is useful to explore the production of innovation as well as its temporal dimension. Although the idea is conceptually different from that of the transformation of pre-existing elements, creative destruction is also characterised and defined by continuous change, and differs from it because of the important role ascribed to the introduction of a new element producing the continuous

---

2   In Kuhn's theory 'normal science' is not interested in innovation or discovery and rather proceeds in the attempt to reinforce and advance its premises and its vision of the world (paradigm). Normal science is the only kind of science existing, as it would be unacceptable to conceive of a science working outside of a paradigm. Revolutionary moments are thus emerging from that routine: anomalies accumulate up to the moment in which they create a crisis of faith in the entire paradigm and thus prepare the terrain for a revolutionary discovery. The elements of the latter then re-constitute normal science again.

change that grounds the process of innovation. This important difference depends first on the different philosophical premises out of which the concepts are developed, and secondly on the fact that the concept of creative destruction was popularised by Schumpeter, who relied a lot on the individual as an agent of change. On the contrary, more recent theories, including evolutionary economics, tend generally to ascribe a predominant role to the collective aspect in the production of innovation, which will be explored in depth later in this chapter. Schumpeter, on the other hand, needed to keep the focus on the individual in order to explain novelty. In his perspective, there is the need to distinguish the concept of growth from that of development, where the latter should be understood as 'only such changes in economic life as are not forced upon it from without but arise by its own initiative, from within' (Schumpeter 1934: 63).[3] Still, to Schumpeter novelty remains in itself 'incomprehensive', as he does not explain how it is generated: 'between novelty and development, the only connection is the figure of the entrepreneur—he is the link between two disjointed worlds: the world in which novelty is generated, and the world of economics. [...] It is the label that, exogenously, introduces new data into the environment, acting as a vehicle of transmission of novelty' (Encinar 2006).

This is the premise that he bore in mind when he popularised the concept of creative destruction in his work *Capitalism, Socialism and Democracy* (2010). The concept, first used by Werner Sombart in 1913, was expressly developed out of Marx's analysis with regards to crises and cycles characterising value production within capitalism, where the destruction of over-produced value was singled out as a fundamental condition of capitalism's survival.[4]

Capitalism [...] is by nature a form or method of economic change and not only never is, but never can be stationary. [...] The fundamental impulse that sets and keeps the capitalist engine in motion comes from the new consumers' goods, the new methods of production or transportation, the new markets, the new forms of industrial organisation that capitalist enterprise creates. [...] The opening up of new markets, [...] illustrate the same process of industrial mutation [...] that incessantly revolutionises the economic structure from within, incessantly destroying the old one, incessantly creating a new one. This process of Creative Destruction is the essential fact about capitalism. It is what capitalism consists in and what every capitalist concern has got to live in (Schumpeter 2010: 72-3).

---

3 Schumpeter wrote this as a reaction to what he noticed to be the general understanding of development that entailed the ambiguity of developing and remaining identical at the same time.
4 In Marx's analysis the economic cycle is also characterised by a generative moment rather than a transformative one. The value generated in excess needs to be destroyed so that new opportunities can arise. Although the movement does not imply a transformation of pre-existing elements, it is based on a continuous change, a revolutionary rather than evolutionary process that preserves and reproduces the capitalist system.

In this extract, the well-known link between creative destruction, innovation and capitalism clearly emerges. It is worth underlining that in the original text it is the word *new* rather than the word *innovation* that is used to explain the concept, establishing a stronger link between the economical exploitation of the New, which also happens through the process of innovation carried out by entrepreneurs, and the reproduction of capitalism: the New, and more specifically its production, belong to capitalism and these dynamics entail by definition a destructive aspect. Creative destruction informs the temporal dimension of innovation, completing the conceptualisation of the New within the field of social sciences, which emerges here as something with a given duration, embodied precisely in the life expectancy of innovation which, independently from its being short or long, is always defined.

The literature on life cycles of innovation is extensive (see for example Christensen 2003; Tushman 1996; Rogers 2003). What is important to show here is that innovations have a given life expectancy, which depends exactly on creative destruction and more precisely on its destructive aspect: the duration of innovation is always defined by the fact that the following innovation will destroy the previous one. Moreover, there is another important aspect characterising innovation that emerges in connection to this. As destruction happens mainly through substitution–it being a purpose driven destruction–it is possible to say that innovations are characterised by having both a life expectancy and a degree of substitutability. Substitutability is, as a matter of fact, implied by the concept of creative destruction on the one hand, and plays, on the other, a fundamental role in those perspectives conceiving novelty more as a transformation and recombination of pre-existing elements. As the mechanism preparing the terrain for the exploitation of novelty, substitutability is also a fundamental part of its production–no matter if the latter depends on the transformation of existing elements or on the creation of new one–and this, of course, has important implications in terms of value.

1.2.1 The Purpose of Innovation and its Critique

As mentioned above, substitution, and thus innovation, is produced in relation to a specific objective, as the new object or practice substituting the old will fulfil the same function of the latter. The reduction of the New to innovation suggests an idea of production in which, by holding a clear view on what exists, it is possible to embrace the new as a step forward on the linear path of progress that characterises a vision of the world that is partially reinforced by the idea of innovation itself. In this sense, not only innovative products or practices emerge in order to solve a problem or fulfil a purpose, but also the concept of innovation in itself is an instrument that is produced in order to reach other purposes. Here, it is important to add to the original ideas by Schumpeter, the perspective coming from critical theory, according to which these other purposes may have to do more with the reproduction of capitalism than with general progress.

If it is clear that the production of the new is what 'capitalism wants and needs', it must be also stated that the purpose behind this mechanism is, for capitalism, to reproduce itself through the increase of profits that comes from the creation of new needs, as first intuited by Marx and then widely explored by different thinkers (Castells 1996; Harvey 2010). Creative destruction is a recurring interest in the work of David Harvey, who criticises the Schumpeterian approach for its lack of critical insight:

Both Karl Marx and Joseph Schumpeter wrote at length on the 'creative-destructive' tendencies inherent in capitalism. While Marx clearly admired capitalism's creativity (followed by Lenin and the whole Marxist tradition) he strongly emphasised its self-destructiveness. The Schumpeterians have all along gloried in capitalism's endless creativity while treating the destructiveness as mostly a matter of the normal costs of doing business (although they admit that occasionally the destructiveness goes out of hand) (Harvey 2010: 46).

In his earlier book *The Condition of Postmodernity*, he describes how the circulation of capital, and the time-space compression characterising capitalism, require more and more radical innovation:

The effect of continuous innovation [...] is to devalue, if not destroy, past investments and labour skills. Creative destruction is embedded within the circulation of capital itself. Innovation exacerbates instability, insecurity, and in the end, becomes the prime force pushing capitalism into periodic paroxysms of crisis. [...] The struggle to maintain profitability sends capitalists racing off to explore all kinds of other possibilities. [...] and that means the creation of new wants and needs. The resultant transformation in the experience of space and place is matched by revolutions in the time dimension, as capitalists strive to reduce the turnover time of their capital to 'the twinkling of an eye (Harvey 1989: 105-6).

It is exactly innovation, according to Harvey, that emerges as the 'primary force' driving capitalism to the destructive phase, out of which the creative one develops. In his perspective, the process is far from positive, and it is again the capitalist rather than the entrepreneur as the main subject of this action. 'The creation of new' that capitalism wants and needs in order to reproduce itself is described as the creation of new needs that comes from the exploration of other possibilities. The New is equated with the *other*, which is defined as the unknown, and acknowledged through the possibility of telling the difference with what is familiar or existing, consistently with the conceptualisation of the new in the whole realm of social sciences. Particularly important in the context of this research is the concept of space-time compression and its consequences in terms of perception of our present world. This, in connection with other dynamics characterising the production of the new in the contemporary world will be deepened in Chapter 3.

What is important to underline here is that the process of creative destruction determines and exploits the production of the new within capitalism. Furthermore, after the neoliberal turn these dynamics are exacerbated because of the shift of value production into the realm of the immaterial. The result is a major push on innovation well described by Harvey (2006) in his more recent paper, *Neo-liberalism as Creative Destruction*, where he offers interesting insights on how the creative destruction process takes an even faster pace, and on the association between the creation of the new and positive values such as progress and freedom. More precisely, he reflects on how neoliberalism was an attempt to restore class domination promoted on the exploitation of common values such as freedom. This aspect is also very present in the field of sociology of art, where the dynamics of the production of the new in art are influenced by the conflict on reality and its representation between the dominant and dominated groups, as it will be more fully described in the next paragraph. In this context, according to Harvey, justifications and explanations of obvious social and geographical injustice were produced through the idea of competitiveness:

> With the media dominated by upper-class interests, the myth could be propagated that territories failed because they were not competitive enough (thereby setting the stage for even more neoliberal reforms). Increased social inequality within a territory was necessary to encourage the entrepreneurial risk and innovation that conferred competitive power and stimulated growth. If conditions among the lower classes deteriorated, this was because they failed, usually for personal and cultural reasons, to enhance their own human capital) [...] particular problems arose, in short, due to lack of competitive strength or personal, cultural and political failings. In a Darwinian world, the argument went, only the fittest should and do survive (Harvey 2006:152)

Not by chance, Harvey describes this world as 'Darwinian', as some evolutionary dynamics are also present in the production of the new conceived as creative destruction and precisely in the vision of the world that they produce and confirm. In this extract it clearly emerges that innovation, by producing and reinforcing the idea of the world based on a linear trajectory of progress, produces at the same time the justifications to explain why this progress is not shared by all, placing the responsibility on the individuals or larger groups (companies, regions, countries) for their own failure in a system that is supposed to bring wealth and progress to everyone.

Within the discourse on innovation, the production of the new is connected to positive values such as clarity, progress and freedom in order to justify a system that depends on it in order to survive. It is then matched with the concept of competitiveness that represents further pressure to engage in it entrepreneurially, highlighting the cost of not taking part in the game. The field of critical theory offers valuable insights into the dynamics connected to the new within neoliberal capitalism, which go beyond the strictly economic consideration in order to enlarge the perspective to include the cultural dimension, which plays a fundamental role. These will also be explored with regard to the postmodernist rhetoric and its critique in Chapter 3.

1.2.2 Critical Innovation Studies

In light of what has been up to now explained, it comes as no surprise that innovation research usually studies the implementation and economic exploitation of the new without analysing the conditions of its emergence (Hutter 2010). Starting from this consideration, a stream of critical innovation studies has also recently developed within the most traditional realm of innovation research. The critique addressed at least three different aspects that characterise traditional innovation research.

First, most of recent research developed in response to those approaches that put the individual at the centre of the innovation process, emphasising the entanglements of the collective subject, or the social and technological context to explain change and innovation. The collective aspect of change, nowadays fundamental in much research regarding innovation and creativity across different fields, represents an important dimension of this research and will be soon explored by reviewing the main theories on art production coming from the field of sociology.

Second and more relevant in this context, there was shown to be an 'interest in ways of theorising change and the 'new' that do not rely on premises of a linear trajectory of development' (Suchman 2008:1). Since this aspect has been more developed in the context of the humanities, it is largely discussed in Chapter 2 and only mentioned here in order to highlight a trend also present in the social sciences.

The third stream of research in critical innovation studies is driven by the need to shift the focus of the research on the new away from a purely value-driven perspective. In order to do so, Michael Hutter (2010) proposes to combine the economic and sociological perspective of innovation research. In the attempt to integrate these two approaches, he states the importance of working on the concept of newness, rather than on Innovation or on the New. By shifting the perspective in this way, it will be possible, in his opinion, to study the emergence of the New, rather than the ways to exploit it, and to take into consideration both the aspects of *novelty* and *newness*, comprehended in the notion of *new*. The concept of newness, by holding the double meaning of the new as novelty in the sense of the product or process, and newness as quality attached to that product or process, allows for keeping in mind some important implications in terms of value and production.

First, the stress is placed on the quality of newness, making explicit the mechanism of value-increase characterising products to which the quality of newness is attached. This aspect involves a critical approach to innovation research, which it also derives from the contributions of critical theory and philosophy. On one side it is informed by the reflections developed in the context of the Frankfurt School. On the other, it takes into consideration the equation between innovation and positive values, such as clarity and progress, as critically explored by David Harvey. Moreover, although not explicitly stated, the connection between the producers of novelty and those sectors where the same novelty gets exploited, i.e. the current problems of co-optation, is mentioned:

> The central place occupied by the new, in the dual sense of "novelty" and "newness", is now also obvious [...] For example, in the mass media and in all other sectors of creative industry, products, news, advertising and entertainment are launched and simultaneously loaded and communicated with the quality of newness (Hutter 2010:11).

Then, the concept of newness as described by Hutter is also informed by the research conducted by Andrew Barry (1999, 2001), according to whom something becomes a novelty, and is recognised as such, when it opens up new possibilities. This allows Hutter to place the concept of newness in the interesting space between the recognition of the new and its production. This perspective represents an important input to the study of the new in the realm of arts, opening the reflection to the aspects of co-creation and allowing a critical discussion on the dynamics of spectatorship.

In his description of the technological society, Barry (2001) sees invention as conflated with technological innovation in a context where the society represents a source of resistance (inertia). In order to reconceptualise the new in this frame of thinking, which recalls that of Kuhn,[5] Barry distinguishes between novelty and *invention*. Inventiveness is 'an index of the degree to which an object or practice is associated with opening up questions and possibilities' (ibid., 2001: 211). Here, the inventions do not reside in novelty or newness *per se* but rather in the transformative chances that emerge 'by the arrangements within which they are located' (Suchman 2008). The concept of inventiveness by Barry is also quite influential in the context of the critique of creativity and thus will be tackled again.

The working definition of 'newness' highlights another important dimension of the concept of New in the social sciences, namely its 'irritating' impact:

> We understand newness as a concept denoting events, products, ideas, technologies, works of art, and processes of collaboration or coordination that have an irritating impact when they occur (Hutter 2010: 10).

---

5 This aspect also seems to be informed by Kuhn's philosophy of science: 'normal science' as a matter of fact resists discovery and revolution in order to confirm its paradigm, thus it also represents a form of inertia.

This very aspect of irritation underlined by the definition seems to constitute part of the common ground of research on innovation in the social sciences, and its roots could be retraced in traditional economics (i.e. the unfamiliarity of the new in Schumpeter). The most recent research trends are grounded in an awareness of the economic exploitation mechanism inherent to the production of the new, and make its immaterial aspect explicit; however, calling for a way out of economic exploitation seems to fall back into the value mechanism that characterises the experience economy and has not yet been fully articulated.

Still, the aspects emerging in the most recent research of critical innovation studies seem to suggest a change of trend in the field that calls for a deeper analysis of the phenomenon of the New, able to take into consideration its complexities and analyse them from an interdisciplinary perspective. This research aims at taking these reflections into account and placing them in the context of a wider analysis, enriched by perspectives coming from the humanities in the next chapter. Before moving to the conceptualisation of the New as it was developed in the humanities, it is worth completing some of the reflections started in this paragraph and at the same time putting them in the context of art production by looking into the field of sociology of art.

1.3 Perspectives from Sociology of Art

The field of sociology, where a lot of attention has been devoted to the term *creativity*, is indeed based on the idea of production as transformation, at least with regards to its most influential contributions on art production. These aspects will be deepened in this paragraph together with the collective aspect of art production that constitutes a fundamental dimension of the production of the new.

The first important dimension to be addressed regards the singular or plural actor behind the production of the New. As mentioned in the previous paragraphs, the entrepreneur represented the singular and fundamental actor of innovation in the work by Joseph Schumpeter, according to whom novelty is generated outside the system of economics and, more precisely, by the individual entrepreneur, who actively carries it into the system and thus produces a change of the norm. More recently, the figure of the cultural entrepreneur indebted to this idea re-emerged: 'cultural entrepreneurs are risk-takers, change agents and resourceful visionaries who generate revenue from innovative and sustainable cultural enterprises' (Aageson 2008: 96).

The visionary creator is generally disavowed in sociology of art, where a lot of research has shown the importance of collective action in the production of the new. Also in economics research, innovation evolved to include the collective dimension, as the number of works on networks demonstrates.

In sociology of art, the theories showing that the new work of art, or the new style, is necessarily the outcome of a collective process are the result of the difficulties encountered by scholars in different fields to understand the artwork exclusively as depending on the artist's activity. In this sense, not just the collaborative or conflicting aspect underlying production emerged, but some attention also was dedicated to the dynamics at play in reception, and to the context where innovation happens: no individual artistic vision leads to the production of an artwork without some relationship to its context. By the same token, it is impossible to explain art production as the result of exclusively external inputs and conditions. In this sense, the on-going debate on agency and structure represents a very fertile territory in order to investigate the production of the new in the arts. Trying to explain the interplay between the subjective artistic expressions and the conditions where they take place, the most important theories in sociology of art look at art production in the attempt to locate it between these two poles.

On the one hand, the role of individuals does not disappear completely, and even the concept of the cultural entrepreneur could be enriched in this context by bearing in mind the distinction between social entrepreneurs, who 'solve problems by disrupting existing systems' and cultural entrepreneurs, who 'solve problems by disrupting belief systems' (Witter 2011). On the other, there is the existing system, the belief of one and the collective aspect representing the core of research in sociology of art, where the most influential theories envisioned art production in terms of 'field' (Bourdieu); 'network' (Latour, Heinich); 'world' (Becker) or 'system' (Luhmann).

The tension between agency and structure is acknowledged here in the conviction that art production cannot be reduced neither to the romantic ideal of creation nor to the result of external conditions. Consequently, questions on it are voluntarily left open in the context of this research, where the main theories confronting it are analysed exclusively up to the extent to which they bring a meaningful input to address the matter in question.

Howard Becker based his study on symbolic interactionism and institutionalism, looking at the relationship between institutions and the actors of the art world, which in his theory become 'conventions'.[6] In the Beckerian perspective, the centre of gravity is represented by social relationships, avoiding both an excessive role of the individual and of the structure in determining the production of art. In the art world described by Becker, art production is based on cooperation which, functioning through

---

6   The notion of art world was first elaborated by Danto, who in his paper of 1964 underlined its necessity in order to understand contemporary art. More specifically, it is the art world that traces the line between what belongs to it and what does not.

'cooperative links', takes place every time the artist depends on someone else in order to carry out his activity.[7] The cooperative links are based on a shared set of conventions, which 'cover all the decisions that must be made with respect to works produced in a given art world, even though a particular convention may be revised for a particular work' (Becker 1974: 770). Conventions in Becker also refer to the form and meaning of artworks, and furthermore define the role of the artist and that of the audience. This is why the collective aspect, here in the form of collaboration based on conventions, makes art production and consumption possible in the first place, while also being easier and faster by inscribing it in a sort of routine.

The same collective aspect in Becker represents an obstacle to innovation, as conventions are resistant to change: 'interdependent systems of conventions and structures of cooperative links appear very stable' (ibid., 773). In this perspective producing the new means to break conventions, and this comes at a cost:

> In general, breaking with existing conventions and their manifestation in social structure and material artefacts increases the artist's trouble and decreases the circulation of his work, on the one hand, but at the same time increases his freedom to choose unconventional alternatives and to depart substantially from customary practice (ibid., 773).

To make some initial considerations on the nature of novelty that is implied here, the economic base in the analysis of Becker is also echoed in the idea of new he refers to, which presents many similarities to that conveyed within traditional economics. Although the collective aspect is stressed in every possible way, Becker maintains some entrepreneurial qualities in terms of the production of innovation, expressed mainly in the initial investment that the one (or the group) who breaks with conventions has to face, as 'change can occur, as it often does, whenever someone devises a way to gather the greater resources required' (ibid.,773). This process recalls somehow that of creative destruction: 'When new people successfully create a new world which defines other conventions as embodying artistic value, all the participants in the old world who cannot make a place in the new one lose out' (ibid.,774). Novelty is conceived here in terms of innovation, with all the consequences of production that such a conception entails.

Another question that could be raised by reading this text today concerns the value of newness in light of the immaterial turn of the economy, in which the cost of breaking a convention would indeed not represent such a deterrent

---

7 Although Becker would like to ascribe the same importance to all people involved in artistic production, he recognises that the cooperative work could not happen without the artistic idea. At the same time, he specifies that artistic work, while it could theoretically be carried out by one person performing all the necessary activity, is in practice dependent on all other involved activities.

to innovation, given that future revenue would arrive exclusively in virtue of the quality of newness.

Bourdieu, who outlined how the symbolic value obtained by refusing commercial values, would turn into economic profit in the long run, was also very critical of Becker's vision and made it clear that the 'field', contrary to the 'art world', is not reducible to individuals interacting in the form of cooperation:

> (What) is lacking, among other things, from this purely descriptive and enumerative evocation are the objective relations which are constitutive of the structure of the field and which orient the struggles aiming to conserve or transform it (Bourdieu 1996: 204-5)

Consistent with Becker, the idea of the new emerges again in the interplay between conservation and transformation, but in contrast to Becker's art world, the *field* according to Bourdieu is constituted by 'objective relationships' which orientate what happens in the field and consequently the possibility of production of the new. The objectivity of such relationships implies a predominant role of the structure, in comparison to agency, that exposed this perspective to many accusations of determinism, which cannot be at least partially denied.

Indeed, there is a very small margin left to the actors for producing a real change that in Bourdieu seems to be possible exclusively under two conditions. First a new product can enter the field and change its structure only if a 'structural lacuna' is present, so that it can be 'accepted and recognised at least by a small number of people' (ibid., 236); second, that can happen only within favourable conditions that imply the help of an external dynamic: 'conservation and subversion always depend in part on the reinforcement that one or another camp can find in external forces' (ibid., 234). The first condition somehow suggests an idea of novelty based on a recombination of existing elements. The new product, to be accepted, needs to be potentially already in the field, putting the New in a very similar position to that suggested within innovation research in evolutionary economics. The idea of the New as a combination of pre-existing elements can also be found in Becker, who describes change as possible when someone devises a way to combine different resources, as mentioned above. Setting aside the differences in terms of agency and structure, both the art world and the field of cultural production seem to suggest an idea of art production based on some kind of stability, where change emerges from that stability and ends up reinforcing it.

Sociology of art looks at the idea of novelty starting from the same premises discussed in relation to the field of economics, and ends up conceiving the new exclusively as innovation, with expected consequences in terms of production, as will be now explained. First, looking at the new in this perspective, its production is conceived only in terms of transformation. Bourdieu uses the opposition between conservation and transformation explicitly (see extract above) while Becker implies it, by defining conventions not as unchangeable, but rather subject to transformation:

> Small innovations occur constantly [...] such changes are a kind of gradualist reform in a persisting artistic tradition. Broader, more disruptive changes also occur, bearing a marked resemblance to political and scientific revolution (Becker 1974:773).

Here Becker refers explicitly to Kuhn, looking at the idea of artistic novelty within the theoretical framework of innovation. As does Bourdieu, according to whom innovation is the result of a conflict, rather than a collaboration, between the agents already present in the field who tend to use conservative strategies, and the 'newcomers' who, contrariwise, tend to engage with subversive, heretical strategies.

What emerges as particularly interesting for the purpose of this research is that the collective dimension in Bourdieu is characterised more by competition and conflict than collaboration, as the distribution of capital is determined by previous conflicts that also 'create the history of the field' (Bourdieu 1980: 289). Given the fact that this conflict depends on the newcomers' 'position in the structure that governs the characteristics and strategies of the agents or institutions', it is impossible for Bourdieu to conceive of the new as a radical change. The newcomers seem determined to reproduce the mechanism of the field–and its conventions–as it is clearly specified in the following extract:

> Thus their revolutions are only ever partial ones, which displace the censorships and transgress the conventions but do so in the name of the same underlying principles. This is why the strategy par excellence is the 'return to the sources', which is the basis of all heretical subversion and all aesthetic revolutions (ibid., 269).

Here Bourdieu, refers to revolution in its original, religious meaning of 'return to the origin', reducing even more the possibility for radical change to happen.[8] In order to soften the determinism of these premises, Bourdieu leaves some margin for something really new to happen in what he calls the 'space of possibles': 'the relationship between positions and position-takings is by no means a mechanical determination. Between one and the other, in some fashion, the space of possibles interposes itself' (Bourdieu 1996: 235). He admits that 'agents always have an objective margin of freedom at their disposal, no matter how tight the requirements included in their position may be' (Bourdieu 1993:65). Still, the obstacle to the production of the new–the new that is not determined to establish a new paradigm, to use Kuhn's words–goes well beyond how far the strategies of actors are determined by their positions, and represent the consequence rather than the cause of the idea of novelty conceived exclusively as innovation.

---

8   The concept of revolution and its meaning is tackled in Chapter 3 with reference to the Avant-guard.

Standing in the way of radical change is the position gained, and thus the power and capital by those already in the field who would lose something by letting the new in. The reason is mainly economical, as it refers to the cost in terms of time and effort sustained by those who are in the field in order to gain their position. The newcomers seem determined to reproduce the same modalities, corroborating the idea of the new as renewal of the same on one side, while making it impossible to conceive of the new in another way, re-inscribing novelty into the trajectory of innovation. A similar reasoning is proposed by both Becker and Bourdieu, who make this dynamic explicit. The cost of innovation is expressed in material and immaterial terms. In the latter, the distribution system selects those works that encounter the audience's taste, and the reproduction of the familiar is preferred to innovation because breaking a convention, as Becker underlines, means to perform an 'attack on morality':

> An attack on convention does not merely mean an attack on the particular item to be changed [...] an attack on sacred aesthetic beliefs as embodied in particular conventions is, finally, an attack on an existing arrangement of ranked statuses, a stratification system (Becker 1974: 773-774).

The premise is here that people do not 'experience their aesthetic beliefs as merely arbitrary', rather they perceive them as 'natural, proper and moral' (ibid., 774): the attack on morality is performed on this ground. The immaterial cost of innovation could be even higher in the contemporary art world, where the limits of aesthetics in defining what belongs to art and what does not have emerged clearly, as illustrated by the work of Danto (1964, 2002).[9] Consequently those willing to change the system face both an economic and cultural resistance, which does not develop exclusively in the relationship between the sphere of production and that of distribution and consumption, but also within the production sector itself, as 'the resistance to the new expresses the anger of those who will lose materially by the change, in the form of aesthetic outrage' (Becker 1974:774). Bourdieu expresses this even better:

> Specifically aesthetic conflicts about the legitimate vision of the world, i.e. in the last resort, about what deserves to be represented and the right way to represent it, are political conflicts (appearing in their most euphemised form) for the power to impose the dominant definition of reality, and social reality in particular [...] This orthodox art would be timeless if it were not continuously pushed into the past by the movement brought into the field of production by the dominated fractions' insistence on using the powers they are granted to change the world-view and overturn the temporal and temporary hierarchies to

---

9   Reflecting on Warhol's *Brillo Boxes*, Danto notices that they are almost indistinguishable from the corresponding ones distributed in supermarkets and argues that form and aesthetics do not help their discernment: since they look the same, appreciating Warhol's *Brillo Boxes* as beautiful would imply assigning the same quality to the *Brillo Boxes* in supermarkets.

which 'bourgeois' taste clings. As holders of an (always partial) delegated legitimacy in cultural matters, cultural producers-especially those who produce solely for other producers-always tend to divert their authority to their own advantage and therefore to impose their own variant of the dominant world-view as the only legitimate one (Bourdieu 1980: 284-5).

Here again the Kuhnian paradigm, 'the vision of the world', is at stake in this dynamic: in the vision of the world that these scholars have helped to build and transmit, the new conceived as innovation prevents real change to happen.

Following the need of conceiving the possibility of radical change, different scholars have worked on these dynamics and offered other perspectives. Gielen (2003) rightfully raises a question on how such a defined structure could provide us with something different than the reproduction of the same, and locates, in the tension between a position and the person occupying it, the possibility of a new action. Thus, the research on the new cannot be set aside from acknowledging that conventions–notwithstanding their resistance to change as Becker suggests and pre-existing the individuals as Bourdieu underlines–can still be changed by individuals and groups: 'to be able to 'act otherwise' means being able to intervene in the world, or to refrain from such intervention, with the effect of influencing a specific process or state of affairs' (Giddens 1984: 14). Giddens describes the structure as constituted by rules and resources; the former is particularly interesting in this context, as they embody the representation of the world mentioned by Bourdieu in the extract above, and thus places art production at the centre of the game.

According to Giddens, rules are 'techniques or generalised procedures applied in the enactment and reproduction of social practices' (ibid., 21). Rules are comparable to conventions and at the same time, come to continuously constitute the representation of the world. Still, 'they require interpretation and are constituted in interactions' (ibid., 21).

It is this double function of rules that emerges as worthy of attention in this context: building the structure through interactions and at the same time reproducing a representation of reality, rules represent a fertile terrain for reasoning on the production of the new. With respect to this, one of the main contributions from the field of sociology is the work conducted by Garfinkel, first due to his contribution on reflexivity and second because of his 'breaching experiments' (Garfinkel 1967).[10] Designed to break the most ordinary societal conventions and observe the spontaneous reactions of

---

10 Both Garfinkel and Giddens work on the concept of reflexivity. The former highlighted the fundamental role of context in terms of the production of meaning by single actions. The latter look at reflexivity as the individuals' capacity to include reality in the production of knowledge and meaning that happens through interactions, and thus at the societal level, so as to control society's development.

people, these experiments highlighted not only how individuals construct rules, but also how this process happens unconsciously within everyday interactions. Although his research does not tackle art production directly, there are at least two aspects that are relevant for it. First, breaching a convention resulted in 'immediate attempts at normalisation' (Giddens, Turner 1998: 234). Second, s and conventions circumscribe a range of possibilities, defining what is outside this range as not possible.

The first aspect recalls that the tendency to normalise what is different does not only belong to systems at large,[11] but also to individuals who contribute to the formation of the norm itself: the production of the new must be explored by taking both levels into consideration. Moreover, the experiments conducted by Garfinkel showed that breaching a rule requires an explanation: breaking a rule produced a bewildering effect that required a clarification of categories, aiming for a 'deviant' or normalising of the external element. The production of such bewilderment creates a space where it is not possible to establish a relationship, which might characterise the reception of the new in contrast to the one of innovation, which is based on the possibility to make a comparison.

The second aspect is particularly interesting as regards the role of art in shifting the borders between what is considered possible and what falls into the category of the impossible. This border represents the core of the production of the new and will be tackled in the next chapters, keeping in mind that 'a rule is a paradox. In order for a rule to exist one must claim that it is impossible to do certain things that can be done. A rule is therefore the collective and individual conception of the dyadic possibility and impossibility of possibilities' (Garcia 2014: 261). Indeed, if the battle is about a vision of the world, and consequently, on reality, some interesting questions can be raised on the role of theatre (and of the arts) in contributing to this debate, also embracing the interpretation by Gielen and the role he gives back to actors with regards to the political potential of the new and its production. Including the perspective of Giddens on s and the results provided by Garfinkel, it is possible to explore the potential of arts and the role they may play on s, not only by breaking them but also by making them visible, contributing to possible representations of reality. Interesting in this sense is the idea that 'artistic expressions come about not in spite of but thanks to the resistance conventions offer to them' (Hauser 2012: 21).

This will be done in Chapter 4, VI and VII of the present work, so that the analysis summed up here could be updated and contextualised in those art institutions that, contrary to the more traditional ones studied by Becker and Bourdieu, actively support artistic research and seek artistic innovation, and sometimes play an active part in the production of the new.

---

11 This aspect will be deepened through the work of Luhmann later in this paragraph.

Before actively engaging with these challenging questions, there is another perspective that must be taken into account, the one of Niklas Luhmann. On one side his system theory can be read consistently with the aforementioned contributions–for example, the importance of the collective aspect, the role of combinations of existing elements in building novelty, an idea of novelty as an evolutionary force within a tradition–on the other, it represents a rupture from other theories and introduces elements that must be considered in the context of this research.

First, while Becker looks at conventions as a result of social relationships between people and Bourdieu sees the field as constituted by conflicts between positions occupied by agents, the elements of Luhmann's system are communications. Through *autopoiesis*, the system constitutes its elements on the basis of the elements themselves, and thus without being triggered by the actions and intentions of the people who partake in the system. The important implication of this, besides the fact that the collective aspect is considered here on a completely different level, is that the system, producing its basic elements, also produces its basic structure and offers a model of production of the new that, in order to be consistent with these premises, must be based on the evolutionary concept of selection. Although Luhmann acknowledges that each communication is chosen out of a theoretically infinite set of possible communications for the system to work, only a given level of complexity can be tolerated, and thus the system selects what comes into existence and what does not.

This has two important consequences for the conception of the new and its production. First, all elements that are not selected by the system remain potentially present in it. Similarly to Bourdieu's explanation of novelty, a new element can enter the system exclusively in the case it was already present at the potential level. Second and more importantly, through this process of selection, the system is characterised by incremental change, where continuous renewal seems to prevent radical change from happening. Although similar considerations could be found in the theories by Becker and by Bourdieu,[12] innovation remains for them something happening or being produced within the respective worlds and fields. Whereas innovation cannot be conceptually distinguished by the system as *autopoiesis*, meaning and selection define the system itself. According to Luhmann, the evolutionary process of selection is governed by meaning, which makes communication possible 'because it generates a pre-selection of possible and meaningful observing choices'. This process is organised through a 'structure of

---

12 In Becker, the obstacle to radical change is represented by conventions, which are resistant to change but also subject to a slow process of transformation. In Bourdieu, radical change is prevented by an actor's position in the field and by their habitus, which make revolutions partial rather than radical, and encourage a return to the origins rather than the production of the new.

expectations', which takes the form of norms and, as such, can bring about either elements that reproduce the system or elements of deviance. In system theory, it is this recursive movement that can produce a new work of art, which not by chance emerges again in particular relation to reality and its representation:

> Only within a differentiated distinction between a real and a fictional imagined reality can a specific relationship to reality emerge, for which art seeks different forms–whether to 'imitate' what reality does not show (its essential forms, its Ideas, its divine perfection), to 'criticise' reality for what it does not want to admit (its shortcomings, its 'class rule', its commercial orientation), or to affirm reality by showing that its representation succeeds, in fact, succeeds so well that creating the work of art and looking at it is a delight. The concepts imitation/critique/affirmation do not exhaust the possibilities. Another intent might address the observer as an individual and contrive a situation in which he faces reality (and ultimately himself) and learns how to observe it in ways he could never learn in real life (Luhmann 2000: 143).

Although many aspects which Luhmann's theory shares with other perspectives presented here in sociology of art, it could easily be argued that its theorisation brings extreme consequences to the dynamics of recognition and production of the new described in this first chapter. Here novelty as recombination is not ascribed exclusively to the element constituting the work of art but almost to the artist himself, whose production is not a matter of individual expression but rather dependent on the collective body (in this case the system) to which he belongs. The system is indeed evolutionary and, as Luhmann explains, it is difficult in this perspective to look at the artwork as a product of the individual, not because this aspect does not count, but because in large systems, these individual expressions can be seen as 'variations' of the norm. In other words, if the population is large enough, the 'new' gains the character of a statistical normality (ibid., 223). As North effectively summarises:

> Creative novelty is still the product of the whole population, which generates the new and is different in the very process of maintaining its continuity (North, 2013: 166).

As Luhmann himself explains, the variations that may be perceived as new result from the complexity of the system on one side and, once selected by it, go to nurture that same complexity that will generate new variations. The evolutionary aspect of system theory here matches the revolutionary one of creative destruction.

The impossibility of radical change–emerging through the process by which the new is conceived exclusively as innovation–seems to be fully developed and embraced so much that one could ask whether in this continuous renewal there could be any need of radical change at all; or, to put it in more political terms, if these systems will ever witness the need of a revolution. Probably yes because, as it is now clear, the production of the 'new' in these perspectives emerges from the norm in order to reinforce it in a different state. Still, this is just one part of the story, as North also asserts: 'to think in terms limited to modern social systems is to ignore the fact that the sociality at work in language, as Wittgenstein sees it, is temporal as well as spatial [and] the rules of language always include an implicit 'and so on', which is meant not to summarise but to extend the set of possible statements.' (ibid., 213) The next chapters will explore the possibilities of a different conceptualisation of the idea of new and the consequences of operationalising such a concept in terms of art production.

2. The New in the Humanities

The previous chapter focused on the concept of novelty in the realm of social sciences and traced how the notion of the New is reduced to that of *innovation* which, in economics and sociology, is more commonly used than the ones of *new* or *novelty*, highlighting the implications of such reduction on the idea of production.

The following chapter explores perspectives on the new in the humanities, where the possibility to think the concept in other ways emerges, and sometimes develops, in stark contrast to the idea of innovation. In the following paragraphs the conceptual, temporal and value dimensions of the New are highlighted in order to find out the constitutive aspects of the concept, and to trace clearer theoretical borders between it and its more fashionable alias. In this sense, something needs to be specified: in the next chapters the reference will be made to the New for the sake of clarity and simplicity, but, since the objective of this research is not to provide an absolute definition of the concept, it still represents one possible conceptualisation of novelty. Moreover, the definition of new that will be here developed and sustained does not aim at a blind critique of other conceptualisations of novelty, but rather at underlining the importance and the potential offered by keeping in mind this difference, especially in the realm of art and contemporary theatre.

2.1 Difference and Obscurity: The Notion of the New

At the conceptual level, the New differs from the notion of innovation because of the impossibility to establish a relationship with it. In contrast with innovation, whose recognition is based on the comparison with the existing or to what is already known, and usually is automatically attached with positive values, the notion of the New can also be defined by the impossibility of making such a comparison. In this case, its recognition works through different categories. A short reflection on the idea of difference will allow for exploring and clarifying the major conceptual dimensions of the New in terms of its recognition.

The idea of difference is intimately related to the concept of New and as such also plays a determinant role in the conceptualisation of innovation. Still, the concept is more complex than the one denoting the variance, the dissimilarity between two objects of observation, between the old product and the new product, to put it in innovation terms. The complexity and centrality of the idea of difference is proved by the attention dedicated to it by many thinkers through history, and in the current cultural panorama, by the affirmation of the philosophy of difference.[13] Since the notion inhabits the whole history of philosophy, here it will be tackled only partially, in order to enlighten the idea of new beyond that of comparison with the old or the existing, and suggest insights for its production.

One of the most famous texts on the new in the field of art theory is namely *On the New* by Boris Groys (2008), who starts his reflections exactly from the notion of difference in the theorisation by Søren Kierkegaard. According to the philosopher, the New and the different are strongly contrasting concepts because recognising a difference implies the act of remembering. In very simple terms, no difference can ever be new, because if it really were new it could not be recognised as different. The real difference, the New, according to Kierkegaard, is a 'difference beyond the difference', something not recognisable in relation to a 'pre-given structural code' (Groys 2008: 29). In his argumentation, Groys tackles together the production and the reception of a new art work. The *newness* of a freshly produced artwork, is not established through the comparison with the old art, 'rather the comparison takes place before the emergence of a new artwork and virtually produces this artwork' (Groys 2008: 28). Looking at an audience at large, one could assert that everything can be new just because it is unknown. Starting from this remark, Groys requires a distinction 'between the New and the other, or between the New and the different' (Groys 2008: 28), necessary to grasp the concept and phenomenon of the New. Although the new is commonly identified as something that is both recently produced and different (Groys 2008), it is the impossibility to establish a relationship to the new artwork that marks the distance between what is New and what is different or innovative.

Accepting this definition of New also means putting the old in a different perspective, as the two concepts cannot be theorised as opposites. Upon reading this text, one could argue that what is old in virtue of its being remembered is certainly not the new, yet the strength of this perspective lies in the impossibility of establishing a relationship to the object in question, and thus calls for an approach that frees the reception of the new from a matter of mere chronology. By shifting the perspective on the (im)possibility of establishing a relationship with the object, nothing prevents the recognition of the New to happen with regards to objects that are historically old. Moreover, conceptualising the old as opposite to the new would mean to once again reduce novelty to the concept of innovation that negates the opportunity for the recognition of the New within something old or familiar. So, in the context of this research it is important to state that, on the

---

13 The concept of difference is always present in the history of philosophy. It evolved from being used to describe a relation between identities up to the ontology of difference that sees it as constitutive of identity itself.

conceptual level, the New could be in no way theorised as opposed to the old. This represents a fundamental premise in this research and as such its different facets and important consequences in terms of production will be deepened later on in this chapter.

In order to complete the perspective here suggested, the role played by memory in the impossibility of establishing a relationship with what is new must be addressed. Interestingly enough, the 'truly new' is to be found, according to Walter Benjamin, exactly through the act of remembering (Benjamin 1989). The important contributions of the philosopher on the concepts of memory, progress and novelty represent a rich source when investigating the New in the contemporary landscape, and they are not inconsistent with what is stated above. If the act of remembering marks the distance between the 'new' and the 'different', and at the same time the 'truly new' could be recognised and even produced through remembering, this is because the concept of remembrance in Benjamin enjoys a quality that the mere act of remembering can not.[14] The concept of remembrance is typified by the interesting interplay between remembering and forgetting that offers the opportunity to rework the completeness of the past into something incomplete. It is indeed constructive and destructive at the same time and, in virtue of these characteristics, it represents a pivotal concept for the production of the New. As such, it will be given the space it deserves in the next pages, together with the insights on its temporal and spatial dimensions. For now, suffice to bear in mind that the New in this research does not stand in contrast with the old, but rather embraces it in a complex relationship.

In the previous chapter it was shown, through the different definitions of innovation, how the new in the realm of social sciences is commonly equated with the *unknown*. This equation, in terms of production, implies a progressive linear trajectory, charged with positive values that naturally emerge when what was unknown becomes known through the process of innovation. Contrariwise, it is possible to state that the New, to be such, cannot be defined through these kinds of comparisons, as is well explained by Boris Groys (2008). Enriching this perspective with the reflections of Walter Benjamin, it is also possible to conceive the new outside the common idea that defines it negatively and conveniently, as opposite to the old and thus that the New is conceptually distant from innovation. It could also be stated that the New comprehends the old, which is less limiting than defining it as a step forward on a pre-given trajectory. This allows a conceptual separation between what is new and what is unknown, and some perspectives

---

14 The 'truly new' in Benjamin is a 'third opposed to both repetition and novelty' (Wilding 1996: 62-63), where the latter is 'produced as an historical illusion as a mythical experience of time at the heart of enlightened modernity' (ibid.). As such, the 'truly new' may emerge as a 'radical encounter with the past' (ibid.) through remembrance.

in the humanities develop in this direction, defining the new not just as including the old but even as ordinary, at least when it comes to the arts.

Considering that Horkheimer and Adorno find a pattern of domination at the bottom of their contemporary historical situation that is indeed produced by the irrational fear of the unknown, and by the false belief that being free would mean to reach a stage where there is no longer something unknown (Horkheimer & Adorno 2002: 11), the equation between the new and the unknown comes as no surprise, together with a concept of innovation that is equated to progress. Not by chance, this reflection is part of an analysis that shows that both myth and Enlightenment are characterised by the impossibility for fundamental change to happen. At the same time, an art world that rejects such equations may be on the right path to conceive and produce new artworks and practices freed by the paradox that inhabits them, especially in the capitalism of the present. In other words, separating the new from the unknown offers the opportunity to free the idea of novelty from some of its associated positive values, which are also used within capitalism for the reproduction and justification of the system.

As mentioned above, Groys (2008) also refers to the risk, at the individual level, of interpreting something as new just because it is unknown. Interestingly, this argumentation goes further to state that the ordinary represents the only possibility of the emergence of the New, which is to be found in what is not 'other' or 'different', but in what is or seems 'the same'. This conceptual ordinariness presents interesting consequences in terms of production of the New in its spatial dimension and casts a light on the temporal dimension that defines it; both aspects will be tackled later on in this chapter. For now it suffices to underline that while innovation is conceived as something surprising, able with its disruptive character to change that which exists and to produce an irritating impact as it occurs, the New, conceptualised as difference beyond difference, can be found exclusively in the ordinary, at least when it comes to the realm of the arts. Consequently, it is possible to argue that innovation may look like the new, but it is not, while the New may look like the ordinary, but it is not.

Given the symbolic and economic value inherent to the quality of newness that contributes to attaching positive values to innovation while disguising its unequally distributed costs, the narrative around innovation cultivates the semblance of being new and by doing so, cultivates the production of the same. Yet, the New seems to cultivate its own form of disguise which, by blurring the boundaries between the new and the ordinary, might trigger the production of difference. This form of production in disguise–which will be explored later in this chapter–starts with another important quality of the New: the dimension of obscurity, which enriches the possibility of finding the New in what is ordinary and old.

The recognition of the New, in contrast with the clarity wrapping novelty in innovation, requires a certain quality of obscurity. The possibility of finding the new in the old breaks the link with linearity, offering the opportunity of reconceptualising progress outside of a linear trajectory–as with the new conceptualised as ordinary in the realm of arts, in its being obscure and for its being obscure, as it is here clearly described by Groys (2008):

> The New functions here not as a re-presentation of the Other or as a next step towards a progressive clarification of the obscure, but rather as a reminder that the obscure remains obscure, that the difference between real and simulated remains ambiguous, that the longevity of things is always endangered, that infinite doubt about the inner nature of things is insurmountable (Groys 2008: 42).

The obscure will be a recurring theme in these pages as it curiously builds bridges with the temporal dimension of the New and allows some further considerations on the role of artistic practices in its production. Not by chance, the aspect of ordinariness and that of obscurity are often mentioned in relation to these themes and also with regards to theatre:

> On leaving the theatre one must have the impression of waking from a strange sort of sleep in which even the most ordinary things had the strange impenetrable character of a dream and which cannot be compared to anything else (Witkiewicz in Lehmann 2006: 65).

This extract describes perfectly the role of art, and of the specific space of the theatre, to mantle what is ordinary with obscurity and thus to provide not only a space for recognition of the New, but also for its production.

As it will be deepened in Chapter 4 that focuses specifically on contemporary theatre, performance and dance, constituting the empirical territory of this research, the same obscurity acts as a counterpart of the artistic research carried out in recent years. By shifting and questioning the borders of reality, it instils the doubt that the world could be otherwise, and also explores the possibilities for the production of the New in political terms.

2.2 The Production of Difference and the New

The experience of the new and its recognition emerge in the humanities in stark contrast to the same in the field of innovation research. Rather than being something that, being equated with the unknown, is recognised through a comparison with the existing, usually charged with positive values and considered surprising when it occurs, the New is to be found in what is ordinary and obscure and is recognised in virtue of the impossibility of establishing a relationship to it.

In this paragraph the temporal dimension of the New–which demarcates further differences from the notion of innovation on the conceptual level, and the possibilities for its production–is explored, in order to better explain the phenomenon that represents the centre of this research. In the previous paragraph the notion of difference in Kierkegaard and of remembrance in Benjamin were used in order to highlight some specific characteristics guiding the recognition of the New. Those characteristics represent the perfect starting point to explore its production.

As mentioned above, the notion of remembrance in Walter Benjamin highlights that the new and the old are not contrasting concepts; rather, it is exactly through the notion of remembrance that the experience of the New can be found in what is commonly conceived of as historically old. In this sense, remembrance represents an interesting concept when it comes to the production of the New. As already explained, the notion of remembrance does not correspond to that of remembering and, at a closer look, it is consistent with the reflection of Kierkegaard, according to whom no difference could be New because its recognition implies the act of remembering.

The German word used originally by Benjamin to describe the concept is *Eingedenken*. As Wilding (1996) notices, there is no direct English translation for the term, which means 'to bear in mind' and at the same time, 'memory'. The English suffix 're-' in the word remembrance may suggest a 'duplication of the past which the concept is meant to avoid' (Wilding 1996: 19). The interpretation of remembrance as duplication would be inconsistent with the production of the New, but remembrance besides not entailing the notion of duplication, is also characterised by a singular temporality and other features that do allow its inclusion among the theoretical tools to be considered in this research. In order to better understand the concept of remembrance, it is useful to start from the taxonomy of memory in Walter Benjamin: *Erinnerung* (recollection), *Eingedenken* (remembrance), *Gedächtnis* (memory), and *Andenken* (memento).[15]

The most interesting specification is the one between memory and remembrance. While memory is characterised by a passive aspect, remembrance is active. Its activity is both constructive and destructive and acts on the passive landscape of memory. This activity has to do with Benjamin's conception of the past as an open, incomplete object, which lays

---

15 In the Arcades Project, *Erinnerung* (recollection) refers to a form of memory closely related to tradition and to its conservation and reproduction; *Eingedenken* (remembrance) is also closely related to tradition and history but is characterised by a transformative and critical relationship to it. *Gedächtnis* (memory) is also used by Benjamin in this sense but it represents the more passive spatial aspect of memory, the landscape on to which remembrance carries out its destructive and constructive activity. *Andenken* (memento) refers to a particular object of memory and denotes the specific relation to the past from which a commodified form emerges.

the basis for that radical encounter with it that may lead to the production of the New.

In terms of its specific temporality, remembrance 'performs the privileged feat of opening up the past from its apparent self-sufficiency' (ibid., 20), by proceeding as 'structuring of time' that, by virtue of its orientation towards the past, 'holds the future open by paradoxically looking at the past to as yet-unrealised possibilities' (ibid., 24). With its destructive and constructive movements, remembrance frees the future from the temporality of predetermination, and thus embraces the possibility of novelty.

Through the concept of remembrance, Benjamin criticises the view of the past, characterising positivist sciences that see it as an inviolable, complete, finished object of study and by doing so actually prevent that involuntary encounter with it so necessary for the production of the New. [16] Thus, it frees time from linearity and makes incomplete what was complete. It is this incompleteness of the past that preserves it from duplication and allows the New to happen. In the words of Benjamin:

> Remembrance can make the incomplete (happiness) into something finished and that which is finished (suffering) into something incomplete (Benjamin 1999: 471).

What is particularly interesting in Benjamin's reflection, more than the possibility of seeing the past as incomplete, is the intuition of understanding the New itself as the *incomplete*. In this perspective, it is also possible to go back to the concept of creative destruction and conceive it in a different way that, by virtue of the temporality of remembrance, becomes conceivable outside of substitutability.

As a matter of fact, Benjamin needs destruction in order to give incompleteness back to the past: on the one hand, it interferes with the past's apparent closed nature and on the other, puts into question the clarity of the present, exposing the narratives underlying history and tradition. It is the destructive character that brings remembering closer to forgetting, and allows Benjamin to develop his critique to that historiography which, by eliminating this aspect, is destined to remain uncritical in its interpretation. It is also in this sense that the concept of creative destruction could be reconceptualised: as a step towards the incomplete, it emerges as freed from purpose and thus lays the basis for the production of a new that is not determined to be substituted, but rather can be a trigger of production of another New, which is substantially different from itself.

In political terms, creative destruction is freed from its only purpose, which is to reproduce the capitalist system and, as such, opens possibilities through the obscurity and incompleteness of its destructive phase to 'defamiliarise the present', and thus to its critique in its creative counterpart.

---

[16] According to Benjamin the conception of the past in positivism is best described by the notion of 'inventory'.

This is why in Walter Benjamin, the destructive aspect of remembrance is paired with its equally important constructive one, and described thus by Wilding:

> The principle of construction here is that of montage, the juxtaposition of past and present in the cause of defamiliarising or estraning the present from itself (Wilding 1996: 49).

In this sense, the constructive moment represents the critical, active engagement with history, which is of course necessary, because 'any engagement with history which was solely destructive would amount to a contradiction in terms', and then more incisively, quoting Benjamin: 'a no-saying form of historical knowledge is meaningless' (ibid., 50).

The concept of remembrance involves an interesting dialectic between repetition and novelty, which inhabits the philosophical work of Benjamin in diverse aspects. If on the one hand, he does not see any productive force in repetition,[17] then on the other hand–and consistent with the possibility of an incomplete past–there is a sort of Deleuzian repetition in difference entailed in remembrance. More precisely, the difference defined in virtue of the impossibility of comparison described in paragraph 2.1 does not just represent a dimension of the recognition of the New as such, but also suggests direction for its production. The concept of remembrance in Benjamin, besides casting an interesting light on the relationship between memory and the possibility of recognising such a difference, establishes an enlightening dialectic between it and the idea of repetition.

On this basis, it comes as natural to proceed with the exploration of the production of the New through a closer look at the work of Gilles Deleuze, who ascribes the production of the New to the interplay between difference and repetition. Although the work of the philosopher represents at large a very interesting perspective in this research, here I will focus primarily on the concepts described in *Difference and Repetition*. More precisely, I will select just a few aspects in order to highlight further conceptual characteristics of the New that also represent valuable insights in term of production and the arts context. Although the concept of difference may seem to play the main role in this discussion, one must start from what may seem its opposite.

The discussion also proceeds in this way in the original work by Deleuze, and rightfully so, because repetition and difference share an intimate link which must be explored in order to understand the dynamics of the production of the New.

---

17 On the one hand, Benjamin criticises the concept of recollection as repetition as expressed by Kierkegaard, who suggests that there is a 'repetition backwards' that is recollection and a 'repetition forward' that is affirmation. Benjamin does so logically, as Kierkegaard started from the premise of an unchangeable past. In Benjamin's view, recollection, exemplified by Proustian involuntary memory, cannot be equated to repetition because it includes forces that, by working against repetition, could offer a renewal of time and also of experience.

Repetition, rather than being in opposition to difference, emerges as the contrary of what Deleuze calls 'generality', and it is also consequently opposed to 'resemblance'. Starting from this, repetition already emerges clearly as a concept working outside the category of comparison, allowing difference, and the New, to be produced. More specifically, resemblance represents the qualitative category ascribed to generality, which is also quantitatively defined by the 'order of equivalences'. In this sense, we behave in relation to generality through the acknowledging of particulars that can be compared, exchanged and substituted. On the other hand, Deleuze writes with reference to repetition:

By contrast, we can see that repetition is a necessary and justified conduct only in relation to that which cannot be replaced. Repetition as a conduct and as a point of view concerns non-exchangeable and non-substitutable singularities (Deleuze 1994: 1).

What is first worth noticing here is the use of the word 'particulars' while defining the behaviour of humankind in relation to generalities, as opposed to the word 'singularities', used by Deleuze with reference to repetition. The New is conceived here as 'altogether different' in contrast to innovation, where novelty can also emerge as a combination of pre-existing elements. It is the partiality of its particulars that helps to tell the difference through the act of comparing. This aspect will be deepened later, as now it is even more interesting to focus on what comes next:

If exchange is the criterion of generality, theft and gift are those of repetition. There is, therefore, an economic difference between the two. To repeat is to behave in a certain manner, but on relation to something unique which has no equal or equivalent (ibid., 1).

Within conceptualising the New outside the frameworks of innovation and creativity, it is important to state that the New also emerges in stark contrast to innovation when it comes to its production and value. While creative destruction characterises the production of innovation for a certain degree of substitutability, repetition characterises the production of the New for the impossibility of being replaced. Creative destruction is based also on the idea of substitution, while repetition characterises things that are not substitutable. As Deleuze himself notices, what separates the two is not just a conceptual but also an economic difference.

The concept of repetition may be spontaneously equated to that of habit, but this is absolutely not the case. Deleuze logically ascribes habit to the category of generality and states: 'Habit never gives rise to true repetition' (ibid., 5). In the case of a habit that has not been acquired, the action changes as the intention stays the same, bridging habit to the order of resemblance. When the habit has been acquired, the action stays constant, motivated by diverse intentions in different contexts, connecting habit to the order of equivalence. In both cases habit falls into the category of generality and is thus opposed to true repetition. Here, it is worth underlining that in contrast to perspectives coming from social sciences, Deleuze does not understand habit as mechanical repetition of the same, but as fundamentally creative and addressed to the future (Grosz 2013).[18] Interestingly, the perspectives of Bourdieu and Deleuze on habit present overlapping premises and come to very different conclusions. Both emphasise immanence over trascendence on the ontological level,[19] underlining that habit is contained in an individual's action itself and is not determined by something beyond it. However, while Deleuze emphasises the creative, emancipatory and empowering character of habit, 'for Bourdieu the immanence of habitus is characterised above all by inertia. Bourdieu shows how habit leads to social reproduction and works against radical social change' (Murray 2010: 190).

In order to better understand how true repetition can produce the possibility for the New to happen, the opposition between repetition and generality must be deepened. Repetition, although opposed to that of generality still needs generality in order to unleash its productive potential. Within the order of generality, repetition emerges as either a transgression or as an exception to it, and here the difference between what is particular and what is singular must be taken into account:

Repetition belongs to humour and irony; it is by nature transgression or exception; always revealing a singularity opposed to the particulars subsumed under laws, a universal opposed to the generalities which give rise to laws (ibid., 6).

Thus, repetition works by uncovering, opposing what is singular to what is general, what is universal to what is particular. This is the quality of transgression and exception ascribed by Deleuze to repetition, which by its nature: 'puts law into question, denounces its nominal or general character in favour of a more profound and more artistic reality' (ibid., 3). Repetition in this sense, may allow a production of the New that is not just freed from the determination to reproduce the system through continuous change, but endowed with a potential of critique.

The potential of repetition, of bringing back to the fore what Deleuze describes as 'artistic reality', together with the political implications that the

---

18 According to Deleuze, 'generality only represents and presupposes a hypothetical repetition' (Deleuze 1994: 4) which maintains habit as indeed creative. Still, as it will be explained with reference to the time of the New, habit is a passive form of repetition and cannot be compared to 'true repetition', which, as an active form of repetition produces difference and the possibility to produce the new. Deleuze provides a precise account of the creative possibility eintailed in habit in his re-reading of Hume, contained in the book 'Pure Immanence' (2001).

19 Jon Beasley-Murray (2010) compares Bourdieu's habitus with Deleuze's virtual and underlines that both are immanent, productive, intensive and immediate. As a matter of fact both intellectuals privilege immanence–the qualities embedded in the material aspect of life, which cannot exist separately from the subject itself–over transcendence (the quality of belonging to another sphere beyond the materiality of reality). This common ontological premise also explains the distance taken from the concept of ideology by both thinkers.

concept suggests, will be tackled later with specific reference to postdramatic theatre. Not by chance, Kierkegaard and Nietzsche–to whom Deleuze credits the merit of making repetition a fundamental category of the philosophy of the future–found in their respective ideas of theatre a fertile territory of reflection. In the work of these two philosophers, Deleuze traces the willingness of opposing repetition to both the laws of nature and moral laws. Moreover, they both oppose repetition to memory.[20] Most importantly, both Nietzsche and Kierkegaard 'make something new out of repetition itself' (ibid., 6).[21] Starting from these reflections, Deleuze proceeds in the explanation of repetition, which becomes more and more intertwined with that of difference.

A fundamental aspect of the complex relation between repetition and difference has to do with representation. Representation is defined here as the relation between a concept and the object this concept refers to. In this sense, difference, when considered as a concept, constitutes the perfect territory of representation and thus for repetition. In Deleuze's words: 'the principle of difference understood as difference in the concept does not oppose but, on the contrary, allows the greatest space possible for the apprehension of resemblances' (ibid., 14). A 'difference in concept'–a 'mere difference' in Kierkegaard's words–belongs to representation and generality, and is thus related to the concept of the new as innovation. According to Deleuze, there are both logical and natural blockages to this,[22] which allow difference in itself and thus for the New to be produced because they 'form a true repetition in existence rather than an order of resemblance in thought' (ibid., 14):

> As difference without a concept, repetition which escapes indefinitely continued conceptual difference, expresses a power peculiar to the existent, a stubbornness of the existent in intuition, which resists every specification by concepts no matter how far is taken (ibid., 15).

---

20 In their work, memory may act through recovering the particulars dissolved in generality. It is in this sense that 'Forgetting becomes a positive power' (Deleuze 1994:9), recalling the concept of remembrance in Benjamin and confirming the predominance of the possibility of forgetting and establishing a relationship in terms of both recognition and production of the New.

21 Deleuze explains that in the case of Kierkegaard the point is not extracting something new from repetition but rather 'making repetition as such a novelty; that is a freedom and a task of freedom.' With reference to Nietzsche, Deleuze sees his attempt of liberating the will from every constraint it may have by making repetition the very object of willing.

22 At the logical level, the blockage is constituted by the fact that concepts are characterised by 'infinite comprehension', which makes remembering possible on the one hand, and the their application to infinite objects by still remaining fixed in themselves on the other. The natural blockages listed by Deleuze are: the discrete extension, exemplified by the paradox of twins (nominal concepts); the virtually infinite comprehension and the paradox of symmetrical objects (concepts in nature) and finally repression and the paradox of buried objects (concepts of freedom).

It is important to specify that concepts are not rejected as such, as they can escape representation and thus generality in the moment in which they lack either memory or self-consciousness. The impossibility to establish a relationship with the New, through recognition or memory, which was explained above, is again restated in the work of Deleuze, who opposes repetition to consciousness, recognition and remembering: repetition becomes the mechanism through which difference is produced.

Particularly interesting for the production of the New in the realm of art is the aspect of self-consciousness, the lack of which also enables the production of difference in itself in concepts endowed with memory:

> When consciousness of knowledge or the working through memory is missing, the knowledge itself is only the repetition of its object: it is played, that is to say repeated, enacted instead of being known (ibid., 16).

Difference and Repetition represents an important text in the context of this research because it confirms and enriches the definition of the New at the level of its recognition and at the same time considers aspects that have to do exclusively with its production. The predominance of the *being* on the *being known* represents an interesting input for an art that is characterised by obscurity when it comes to the recognition and production of the New. The lack of memory or consciousness reinforces the concept of New defined on the impossibility of making a comparison, and sets the basis for its production outside of a linear trajectory. Moreover, the conceptualisation of New as 'altogether different' excludes the idea of partiality and process from its production, in stark contrast with the interplay between routine and change that gives rise to incremental novelty or, in other words, to innovation.

In order to put the concept of repetition at work for the production of the New, Deleuze needs to provide for it an explanation that is not 'purely negative', i.e. defined as the negative of something else. This negativity in the definition of repetition has the important downside of providing an explanation by not doing something: in the first blockage, repetition occurs by 'not comprehending', in the second by 'not remembering', in the third by 'not knowing', or missing self-consciousness. Out of this, Deleuze is urged to postulate a positive force able to explain repetition and finds it through re-reading Freud.[23] Deleuze comes to the conclusion that it is 'ultimately a question of the relation between repetition and disguise' (ibid., 18): there is no mask covering the force of repetition, rather the mask is repetition's

---

23   By looking at Freud's studies on repression and repeated behaviour, Deleuze uncovers repetition as masked: the mask, the disguise is not external to repetition but rather constitutes its 'genetic element'. Deleuze criticises Freud for not maintaining the model of repetition in itself and having solved it in the result of a compromise between conflicting elements of human psychology and by doing so, working again with conceptual differences.

constitutive element and that is the positive force that defines repetition in itself:

> Repetition is truly that which disguises itself in constituting itself, that which constitutes itself only by disguising itself. It is not underneath the masks, but it is formed from one mask to another [...] with and within the variations (ibid., 19).

This implies that the object of repetition cannot be abstracted, separated from repetition itself: the New, produced through such a repetition, emerges once again as obscure, masked, in contrast to innovation. More specifically, if the production of the new within innovation seems to go through a process of clarification, once conceptualised outside that framework, it seems to proceed in the opposite direction, not only acknowledging to the New the function of a 'reminder that the obscure remains obscure' (Groys 2008: 42), but also bringing, through repetition, obscurity and complexity to their extremes.

In light of this, Deleuze tackles repetition in terms of causality and effect. Causality, in art and in nature, does not depend on the symmetrical elements of a pattern no matter what specific pattern that is, but rather on those elements that are missing. It is also in light of this that signs are important,[24] as they allow to distinguish between two kinds of repetition that explain repetition as active:

> Signs are the true elements of theatre. [...] they signify repetition as real movement, in opposition to representation which is a false movement of the abstract. We are right to speak of repetition when we find ourselves confronted by identical elements. However we must distinguish between these discrete elements, these repeated objects, and a secret subject, the real subject of repetition, which repeats itself through them. [...] As a result, rather than the repeated and the repeater, the object and the subject, we must distinguish two forms of repetition (Deleuze 1994: 26).

Signs thus show the internal difference that is both object and subject of repetition as a positive feature: 'the negative expression "lack of symmetry" should not mislead us: it indicates the origin and positivity of the causal process. It is positivity itself' (ibid., 22). As exemplified by rhythm and rhyme,[25] the two kinds of repetition, which Deleuze defines as 'bare' and 'covered' are not independent but still very different, as it emerges from this

---

24 Difference must be symbolic because repetition cannot be otherwise; its variations are the product of an internal movement and not of an external compromise.
25 The first kind of repetition shares the characteristics of 'Cadence-repetition': it presents a regular division of time and is an 'isochronic recurrence of identical elements'. The second kind of repetition, which allows difference in itself to be produced, works like tonic and intensive values, which 'act by creating inequalities or incommensurabilities between metrically equivalent periods or spaces. They create distinctive points, privileged instants which always indicate a poly-rhythm. Here again, the unequal is the most positive element [...] rhyme is indeed verbal repetition, but repetition which includes the difference between two words and inscribes that difference at the heart of a poetic Idea, in a space which it determines' (Deleuze 1994:23-24).

list of opposites, which is almost entirely quoted here below because of the richness of inputs that will echo later in this work:

> In one case, the difference between objects is represented by the same concept, falling into the indifference of space and time. In the other case, the difference is internal to the Idea; it unfolds as pure movement, creative of a dynamic space and time, which corresponds to the Idea. The first repetition is repetition of the Same, explained by the identity of the concept or representation; the second includes difference [...] one is negative, occurring by default in the concept; the other affirmative, occurring by excess in the Idea. One is conjectural, the other categorical. One is static, the other dynamic. One is repetition in the effect, the other in the cause. One is extensive, the other intensive. One is horizontal, the other vertical. One is developed and explicated, the other enveloped and in need of interpretation. One is revolving the other evolving. One involves equality, commensurability and symmetry; the other is grounded in inequality, incommensurability and dissymmetry. One is material, the other spiritual, even in nature and in the earth. One is inanimate; the other carries the secret of our deaths and our lives, of our enchainments and our liberations, the demonic and the divine. One is a 'bare' repetition, the other a covered repetition, which forms itself in covering itself, in masking and disguising itself. One concerns accuracy, the other has authenticity as its criterion (ibid., 26-27).

The aspects that are particularly relevant in the context of this research are diverse. First, the simultaneous consideration of the two kinds of repetition must be privileged in comparison to a perspective that differentiates the repeater from the repeated, or the object from the subject. This is important because it underlines how both the recognition and the production of the New must allow a co-presence of opposite elements. In terms of recognition, the co-presence of different elements matches the conceptualisation of the New as obscure. In terms of production, this tension represents an opportunity to envision the production of the New freed from substitution. In particular the 'repetition in the cause' could be seen as the trigger of a production of the New envisioned as a production of the new that is different from itself.

The verticality that by nature belongs to this process must be kept in mind as a dimension contrasting the horizontal character that defines the production of innovation, from the spatial dimension of creative destruction to the concept of networks of innovation. This verticality places repetition in that impossibility of establishing a relationship that has characterised the New not exclusively on the conceptual level but also in its production, so far that the already known cannot be distinguished from the unknown, and this impossibility represents the territory where the New can be produced, where 'the repeated cannot be represented' (ibid., 20).

Furthermore, the qualities of verticality and asymmetry, besides being consistent with the obscurity of the New, are also interesting once this idea of the production of the New is translated to the realm of the performing arts, and especially to its institutions that as such must entail a certain degree of organisation. In this light, the fact that one repetition depends on the criterion of accuracy and the other on that of authenticity, entails speculation and empirical research into the production of the New within those theatres that focus on research and innovation.

These inputs are particularly relevant to the extent that the interaction between bare and covered repetition puts the production of difference in place: 'When a body combines some of its own distinctive points with those of a wave, it espouses the principle of a repetition which is no longer that of the Same, but it involves the Other–involves difference, and carries the difference through the repetitive space thereby constituted [...] in which the distinctive points renew themselves in each other and repetition takes shape while disguising itself' (ibid., 26).

In the next chapters, the above-mentioned aspects will be taken into consideration exactly in this light, in the conviction that they are particularly relevant in the realm of the arts, as indeed repetition and remembrance enlighten that battle over the representation of reality that emerged in connection with the production of the New within sociology of art–and they do so in a remarkable way. Agamben describes the potential role of repetition in questioning reality in relation to cinema, and his reflection could be applied to the arts at large:

> The force and the grace of repetition, the novelty it brings us, is the return as the possibility of what was [...] Here lies the proximity of repetition and memory [...] that makes the unfulfilled into the fulfilled, and the fulfilled into the unfulfilled. [...] It is that which can transform the real into the possible and the possible into the real. If you think about it, that's also the definition of cinema' (Agamben 2002: 315-316).

The ability of transforming the real into the possible and the possible into the real is indeed to be credited to all arts, and undoubtedly to postdramatic theatre. Furthermore, the same faculty of putting reality in question to open it to the possible could be attributed also to the institutions, such as theatre and festivals that can also define in this sense their role in the production of the New, as well as their legitimacy as political subjects within society.

2.2.1 The Time of the New

As already stated, it is difficult to talk about production without considering the dimension of time. It is equally problematic to consider time without mentioning space. This is why time and space were silently but strongly present in the discussion up until now, and need to be addressed directly to better distinguish the New from its alias.

Moreover, their analysis offers relevant directions of research for a reformulation of production in the realm of performing arts within neoliberal capitalism. There are at least three different significant aspects: the conception of time and history as such, and the idea of contemporariness and the problem of duration. In the previous paragraph, the importance of remembrance and repetition was explored in terms of the production of the New. Such analysis is incomplete as long as the dimension of time is not properly discussed, also shown by the fact that both Deleuze and Benjamin deal with these concepts together.

To discuss time, Deleuze starts from the consideration that repetition is commonly understood, consistent with the traditional idea of difference, as repetition of the same in two different moments, from a point of view that sees time as a succession of moments.[26] This is why going back to repetition means to address time in the light of his new definition of difference, which leads to a renewed understanding of repetition. Here it is sensible to give a very brief account of such a complex analysis in order to highlight the aspects that inform the concept of the New and its production.

Deleuze singles out three different models of time, which he calls synthesis.[27] The first model is the one of passive synthesis, which refers to cycles. Within this model repetition can just take the form of habit, which places in the present the gesture performed in the past and to be performed in the future. In the conception of time as a circle, also exemplified by the structure of tragedy, repetition happens because of an external law and not for itself. Seasons represent an instance of it, as they embody the repetition of the same over time passing through its cardinal points. This latter aspect, together with the form of habit that repetition necessarily takes in this perspective, leads to the exclusion of this model for the production of the New because it presents the typical aspects of generality and not those of true repetition.

The second model of time is that of active synthesis. In this model, there is no space for habit, because there is no space for the repetition of the same;[28] in the active synthesis of time, nothing returns and a more active force, able to produce repetition on a more profound level appears: memory. Contrary to habit, memory does not work in relation to the present but refers to a past through which it creates a form in itself, which did not exist before its active intervention. In this model, repetition presents an active role but the concept of memory, although already virtual and vertical, still works in

---

26 The second chapter of 'Difference and Repetition' is called 'Repetition for itself' and in it, Deleuze deals exclusively with time. After having discussed difference in itself, Deleuze goes back to repetition, and this means to address the dimension of time: in the common understanding of the word, 'to repeat' means to do or say the same thing twice at different moment in time, which are usually understood to be equal.
27 Starting from the assumption that the only time to be considered is the present, the models of time are of synthesis because past and future are synthesised into it. This movement is also related to the concept of repetition.
28 In order to describe it, Deleuze starts from what he thinks to be one of the main ruptures of Kantian philosophy, that of freeing time from its circular proceeding. In the opinion of Deleuze, the conception of time as a line that contains events prevents looking at events as constituting time itself through synthesis in the present moment.

relation to identities,[29] and as such is inconsistent with Deleuze's philosophical plan. Consequently it is far from being able, through repetition, to produce difference in itself, and thus the New.

Starting from this problem, Deleuze builds his third model of time establishing repetition as a form of time itself. Here repetition is considered in the light of difference in itself: if difference represents the essence of what exists, then repetition cannot be such, as long as it synthesises differences into identities. On the other side, when beings are repeated as something other than themselves, their essential difference comes to the fore. Consequently, in the third model of time, which is constituted by repetition itself, repetition cannot be repetition of the same. Here Deleuze refers to the concept of eternal return by Nietzsche, which is considered as a movement that escapes the cyclical return of the same. The Nietzschean eternal return becomes the third form of time that is repetition for itself, or in the words of Nietzsche himself, the repetition of those beings 'whose being is becoming':

> The subject of the eternal return is not the same but the different, not the similar but the dissimilar, not the one but the many' (Deleuze 1994: 126).

In this perspective, where time is conceived as repetition for itself, 'difference inhabits repetition' (ibid., 76). The third model of time represents the time of the future in Deleuze and may represent the time of the New here.

As a matter of fact, in this model, only 'that which differs from itself' is able to return. Such a conception of time opens the way for a conceptualisation of the New as generative of something new that differs from itself and as such enlightens the political opportunities for the arts to embrace novelty outside of the framework of innovation. Still, keeping a strictly Deleuzian perspective would limit the consideration connecting the concept of time with that of the New. In this short description, there is a very important aspect that should be not underestimated, which is that the only time that really exists is the present time and in every one of the models above explained there is a synthesis of past and future in the present. This aspect calls for a deeper understanding of the relationship between the New and the contemporary; terms that sometimes, especially in the realm of arts, are used interchangeably.

One of the most interesting contributions on contemporariness was recently written by Giorgio Agamben. In his short essay *What Is the Contemporary?* Agamben (2009), like Deleuze, privileges the present as time dimension: our time is contemporariness and as such it demands us to be contemporary with what we deal with, independently from the historical date of the object in question, putting the stress immediately on the level of

---

29 The aim Deleuze is pursuing in his work is that of demonstrating difference in itself as first principle, not subordinated to that of identity, which in the history of philosophy was never deeply questioned enough to give difference its ontological right.

relation. Moreover, he starts from Nietzsche, who in his *Untimely Meditations* reflects on his position in respect to his own time and places his being contemporary in a disconnection with it. Agamben accepts that 'the contemporary is the untimely' and states: [30]

> Contemporariness is then, a singular relationship with one's own time, which adheres to it and at the same time keeps a distance from it. More precisely, it is that relationship with time that adheres to it through a disjunction and an anachronism' (Agamben 2009: 41).

Agamben suggests that a certain disjunction, an anachronism, is necessary in order to be truly contemporary because it is in virtue of these attitudes that it becomes possible to see and grasp the epoch in which one lives.[31] Following the inspiring contents of the poem *The Century*, written in 1923 by Osip Mandelstam, Agamben provides a second definition of contemporariness:

> The contemporary is he who firmly holds his gaze on his own time so as to perceive not its light, but rather its darkness. All eras, for those who experience contemporariness, are obscure. The contemporary is precisely the person who knows how to see this obscurity' (Agamben 2009: 44).

It is very interesting to notice how the aspect of obscurity, acknowledged by Groys to the new artwork is here a fundamental defining characteristic of the contemporary in Agamben. Obscurity that characterises the new artwork in its recognition stands in contrast to the clarity characterising the most recent technological innovations, just to mention one example; here it gains, in the light of Agamben's perspective, a more active quality, embodied in the ability of the contemporary person to see that obscurity: also in this case time cannot be considered separately from production.

This active quality of obscurity, which is neither definable as the absence of light nor as non-vision is, for Agamben, the product of the activity of our own eyes:[32] 'to perceive that darkness is not a form of inertia or passivity, but rather implies an activity and a singular ability' (ibid., 45). The active part resides in not allowing oneself to be blinded by the lights coming from the present epoch in order to embrace the intimate obscurity between them. Then, Agamben refines his definition of darkness by turning to astrophysics, which explains darkness as the result of the farthest galaxies that move away from the earth so fast that their light can never reach it.

He writes: 'for this reason to be contemporary is first and foremost a question of courage, because it means [...] also to perceive in this darkness a

---

30 Here Agamben quotes Barthes, who in the sentence summarised his reading of Nietzsche's 'Untimely Meditations'.
31 In Agamben's words, those who coincide too much with their own time and 'are perfectly tied to it in every respect are not contemporaries, precisely because they do not manage to see it; they are not able to firmly hold their gaze on it' (Agamben 2009: 41).
32 Here Agamben backs up his argument with neurophysiology, explaining that the darkness we see is a product of the off-cells of our eyes that produces a vision that we call 'darkness'.

light that, while directed towards us, infinitely distances itself from us. In other words, it is like being on time for an appointment that one cannot but miss' (ibid., 46).

Darkness can never be separated from light; rather, the two share a more complex relationship that the contemporary must embrace with courage in order to be such. Taking up this courage is important because of its transformative power:

> The appointment that is in question in contemporariness does not simply take place in chronological time; it is something that, working with chronological time, urges, presses and transforms it. And this urgency is the untimeliness, the anachronism that permits us to grasp our time in the form of a 'too soon' that is also a 'too late'; of an 'already' that is also a 'not yet' (ibid., 47).

In light of what has been explained, it would be difficult to argue that innovation does not belong to contemporariness. However, it would nonetheless still be possible to say that the New belongs to contemporariness in a different way, in comparison to innovation. This difference lies exactly in the relationship the two concepts–or better, objects and practices derived from these concepts–have with their own time. In the case of the New, they are in relation with their own time through anachronism, disjunction and asynchrony. In Agamben's words, 'it entails a certain quality of being out-of-phase or out-of-date, in which one's relevance includes within itself a small part of what lies outside itself' (ibid., 49).

The co-presence of different, sometimes opposite, elements is stated once again as fundamental for the production of the New. To accept it as specific to the time of the New means to exclude the mechanism of substitutability from its production that reduces the power of novelty to innovation, with relevant consequences in terms of value. This perspective allows the inclusion of the old and the ordinary in the production of the New and casts a light on the reasons why those same aspects have been excluded from the realm of innovation, both in terms of concept and production. Here it is possible to state that innovation at the conceptual level, establishes a relationship based on adherence and synchrony to its own time, covering that distance that allows it to see the darkness coming from the epoch and thus to be contemporary in Agamben's terms. Such a relationship does not leave any space for critique in the conception of new within the framework of innovation.

Although the problem of critique is not directly addressed in Agamben's text, its echoes inhabit the whole argumentation. First, one could notice that the inclusion of the old and of the ordinary in the conception and production of the New is deeply related to the potential of critique that such an idea of the new could produce. As Agamben also notices–mentioning the Avant-garde and thus implicitly the New and its critique–the archaic is a fundamental dimension of contemporariness: 'the Avant-garde, which has lost itself over time, also pursues the primitive and the archaic' (ibid., 50). Second, the idea of critique is addressed indirectly with reference to the transformative potential that such an idea of contemporariness entails. The contemporary who engages his attention to what is 'unlived' in the present, is able to put in place a *caesura* within time and thus:

> He is able to read history in unforeseen ways, to 'cite' it, according to a necessity that does not arise in any way from his will, but from an exigency to which he cannot not respond' (ibid., 54).

It comes as quite easy to read hints regarding the life and role of the contemporary artist in what Agamben calls 'the life of the contemporary' and to investigate the potential of transformation that they might bring by producing the New. This kind of reasoning recalls the artistic devices put in place in the context of postdramatic theatre in the past thirty years, and first and foremost, the research on time on the border of what is real and what is not, which, as a fundamental characteristic of the theatre of the present and sometimes as political strategy, will be deepened in Chapter 4.

At the beginning of this section, the dimension of time was presented as relevant within this research for both the aspect of relation and belonging and that of duration. The latter will be tackled after some reflections on space that are now necessary to introduce. This should not be interpreted as an abrupt change of topic, since this analysis proceeds in the conviction that the dimension of space and time cannot and should be not tackled separately, but rather considered together so that a more profound, though more complex, understanding of the matter in question could be provided.

First, it must be underlined how, in the sources here presented, the past and the future have quite a spatial relationship with the present. The three models of Deleuze, in which the past and the future are always spatially synthesised in the present, are not so distant from the reasoning of Agamben. The anachronism belonging to contemporariness is of course time-based, but it presents also a deep spatial quality: the 'unlived' in the past as well as the prophecy of the future that come together in the present could be easily described, in the attitude of the contemporary, as a 'step aside'.

The approach described does not conceive of steps forward or backwards on a linear time but rather a spatial step aside that allows the contemporary to be such by virtue of the distance to his own time that lives in that space. Thus, this spatial quality of asynchrony and anachronism must be acknowledged and taken into account in the course of the analysis, also because of its relevance in the realm of postdramatic theatre both in aesthetic and political terms.

2.2.2 The Spaces of the New

According to Boris Groys, a new artwork, in order to be such, must look alive, meaning that, as it was widely explained, it must be different in the Kierkegaardian sense, presenting the 'difference beyond the difference', and thus is to be found in what is ordinary. In the course of the current chapter, it was shown how this also happens in production terms through memory and repetition, and how these concepts that are commonly related exclusively to time present an important spatial dimension. Moreover, it was anticipated that one of the most important poetic characteristics of postdramatic theatre that actually distances it from dramatic theatre is the questioning of a clear border between the real and the fictional.

Putting these aspects together, it is necessary here to underline how they cannot be tackled separately from a spatial dimension, which in this context takes first and foremost the form of the institution, a deeper analysis of which is presented in Chapter 4.

A new artwork looks really new and alive only if it resembles, in a certain sense, every other ordinary, profane thing, or every other ordinary product of popular culture. Only in such a case can the new artwork function as a signifier for the world outside the museum walls. The new can be experienced as such only if it produces an effect of out-of-bounds infinity—if it opens an infinite view on reality outside of the museum. And this effect of infinity can be produced, or rather staged, only inside the museum: in the context of reality itself we can experience the real only as finite because we ourselves are finite. The small, controllable space of the museum allows the spectator to imagine the world outside the museum's walls as splendid, infinite, ecstatic (Groys 2008: 30).

In this extract, the role of the institution emerges clearly. The museum–but it would be possible to extend this reasoning to art institutions in general, composed by all its singular and collective actors–functions as an active producer of difference beyond difference and thus of the New. It does so by producing and shifting the borders between what is real and what is not, by introducing a spatial distance that allows a different gaze on reality, in which the time dimension is also fundamental.

In fact, the 'infinity' Groys refers to, is not just spatial, rather it is primarily temporal; as in Kierkegaard the difference beyond the difference is not a difference in form but a difference in time. Namely, it is the 'imperceptible difference between the short time of ordinary human life and the eternity of divine existence' (Groys 2008: 35).

Here a step back might be necessary in order to understand this passage. Kierkegaard, in order to exemplify his difference beyond the difference in contrast to mere difference, used the figure of Christ, who could not be distinguished as different at the aesthetic level by one of his contemporaries and therefore constituted a difference without a difference, in other words a difference beyond the difference. This ordinary character of the difference beyond the difference is the same one that Boris Groys ascribes to the readymades in art, which is again a difference not in form but rather in the life expectancy, and thus in time, of the object, which once inside the museum becomes infinite if compared to the same object outside of it, and consequently looks more alive. Here, the new is produced through a change in the life expectancy of the object: the very same dimension characterising novelty within the framework of innovation.

It is in this sense that Groys argues: 'Kierkegaard could show us, by implication, how an institution which has the mission to represent differences can also create differences and thus produce the new' (Groys 2008: 35). Here it is important to remember that this particular, active role of the institution was already acknowledged by the philosopher and dramaturg Witkiewicz (1885-1939), who ascribed to the theatre the privileged function of gifting 'the most ordinary things' with that impossibility of establishing a relationship to them that is at the core of the experience of the New (see paragraph 2.1). This impossibility of establishing a relationship, which was already widely explained, is here enriched by acknowledging the role of institutions in producing such impossibility. This is also a reminder that, although the recognition and the production of the New are tackled separately for the sake of clarity, in the analysis they must be always considered together at the conceptual level, especially when it comes to theatre, where it would be hard to speak of production without considering consumption. In this perspective, the aspects that emerged as fundamental to define how the New is recognised are completed here by those characterising its production. This production cannot be analysed without taking into consideration those art institutions that, to put it in Benjamin's terms, act by making incomplete what was before complete, by gifting reality with that sense of infinity and thus of possibility, to make the unlived appear within their space, whose borders are indeed asynchronically shifted in time.

Such a production could be done exclusively from a space that is recognised as non-real, because: 'life today looks alive only when seen from the perspective of the archive, museum, library. In reality itself we are confronted only with dead differences—like the difference between a new and an old car' (ibid., 30). There are interesting implications in applying this kind of reasoning to the realm of theatre and performing arts; which are the live art *par excellence* and do not have any possibility of collection. This aspect will be tackled directly through the empirical analysis of this research.

Moreover, there are other aspects that deserve to be mentioned. As also Groys notices, a paradox emerges: 'the status of this artwork as artwork always depends on the context of its presentation as part of a museum collection. But it is extremely difficult—actually impossible—to stabilise this context over a long period of time. This is, perhaps, the true paradox of the museum' (ibid., 39). This is one of the consequences of conceiving, as Groys does, the production of the New merely as 'shifting of the boundaries between collected items and the profane objects outside the collection' (ibid., 33). This view must be partially rejected or at least reconceptualised in the context of this research, also in light of the fact that, as Groys admits: 'If I change the life expectancy of an ordinary thing, I change everything without, in a way, changing anything' (ibid., 36). Consequently, although the intuition regarding the important role of institutions and that of the category of space within the production of the New must be retained here and valued, some aspects need to be reconsidered in light of the time dimension, as the reflections on duration and value contained in the next paragraph will clarify.

2.3 Duration and Value

A second important aspect of the time dimension is that of duration, which also further differentiates the concept of the New from the one of innovation, and consequently their respective production. With regards to innovation, in the previous chapter some aspects were highlighted that define for how long something innovative can be defined as such. The number of studies on the life cycle of innovations highlight that this aspect plays quite an important role, establishing how long the label 'new' can be exploited for the production of profit in relation to a given product. What emerged as relevant in the context of the definition of innovation is that, independently from contexts, factors and effective duration, innovation is characterised by having a life expectancy. On the contrary, what is emerging here is that the same could hardly be ascribed to the New, which appears either as ephemeral or eternal.

Furthermore, it is interesting to notice how, in Groys' opinion, it's exactly a matter of life expectancy that lies at the core of the production of the New in visual arts (see 2.2.3). If the aspect of the relationship and belonging to time is intimately intertwined with the production of the New, the aspect of duration seems to share a strong link with its value dimension, and conceiving the New either as ephemeral or as eternal entails consequences in terms of value that must be taken into account. Groys considers the New as ephemeral, which is very coherent with his reasoning. To be precise, he considers the effect of newness delivered by an artwork to be ephemeral. Since the new artwork functions for him as a 'symbolic window' that allows for the gaze upon the infinite outside the museum, after a short time it must become merely different–Agamben might describe it as too adherent to its own time. To describe such a disjunction, Groys writes:

But, of course new artworks can fulfil this function only for a relatively short period of time before becoming no longer new but merely different, their distance to ordinary things having become, with time, all too obvious [...] the need emerges to replace the old new with the new 'new', in order to restore the romantic feeling of the infinite real (Groys 2008: 30).

On the other side, the New could be eternal as Deleuze states coherently with his perspective:[33]

The new with its power of beginning and beginning again remains forever new, just as the established was always established from the outset, even if a certain amount if empirical time was necessary for this to be recognised. What becomes established with the new is precisely not the new. For the new- in other words difference- calls forth forces in thought, which are not the forces of recognition, today or tomorrow, but the powers of a completely other model, from an unrecognised and unrecognizable terra incognita (Deleuze 1994: 172).

By comparing these two extracts, it is not only an opposite appraisal of the New in terms of duration that emerges, but also a fundamental distance regarding the role of time and that of recognition. In Groys, it is the passing of time that weakens the difference between the new artwork and the mere thing, leading to the need to replace the 'old' new with the 'new' new. In Deleuze this problem does not even come to the surface, because in his perspective, the difference is not just in form but first and foremost in kind: to consider recognition in the equation of the New would be incoherent with the concept of the New itself.

Notwithstanding the spatial perspective that Groys brings to the problematic dynamics characterising the production of the New, he is, according to a Deleuzian perspective, still reasoning in representation and thus producing a difference in degree, rather than in kind. This is indeed true and seems to be incoherent with the fact that Groys builds his argumentation on the premise that the difference distinguishing what is New is not a difference in form–'this difference can be explicitly thematised in the museum as obscure and unrepresentable'(Groys 2008: 38)–and as such should escape representation. As a matter of fact, the realm of representation represents the territory where the comparison between forms could be made, and as such deals with the 'mere difference' rather than with 'the difference beyond the difference'. This is because Groys looks at the new still in connection with the framework of innovation.

First, his conceptualisation of the New allows the mechanism of substitutability to happen: the 'old' new must be replaced by the 'new' new. Second, he is not interested in providing a framework for the new outside that

---

33 Here Deleuze is once again referring to Nietzsche and to the distinction he makes between new and established values. According to Nietzsche, the established values were not new at their time, nor will new values be established with the passing of time. The difference between the two is, according to Deleuze, a difference in kind.

of innovation, and that is no mystery, as his *On the New* finishes by stating: 'That is probably the reason why the museum was always—and still remains—the only place for possible innovation' (ibid., 42).

Since one of the objectives of this research is to inform innovation practices of postdramatic theatre with the opportunities of conceptualising the New outside the framework of innovation, while having no interest in rejecting the concept of innovation as such, the contributions offered by Groys will be taken into consideration. Still, while Groys does not deal with the political implications of production entailed by the two concepts, this research aims at restating the importance of making such a difference; what is left open here will be solved with the insights emerging from the empirical part of this research. It is acknowledged that the role he ascribes to institutions has indeed political implications that must be addressed, as they seem to constitute the difference between what is New and what is innovative, as in the realm of art, where innovation, though re-conceptualised, must not be condemned, but encouraged.

2.3.1 The Problem of Value

Taking the opportunity offered by leaving open the question on the duration of the New means addressing the problem of value. This cannot be done without going back to Walter Benjamin, who considers this problem exactly by analysing the complex relationship between the ephemeral and the eternal. Interestingly enough in this research, he does so in relation to novelty, whose generalisation characterises 'the modern', jeopardising on one side its production and allowing on the other its emergence. The complex debate around novelty and modernity and the inheritance it left will be tackled in the next chapter, while here they constitute just the background for the problem of value to be identified.

Benjamin based his reasoning on the reflections that Baudelaire carried out in his critique of the *Salon of 1845* and then, more thoroughly, in *The Painter of Modern Life*. In the latter, the poet gives his very famous account of modernity, characterised in his words by the 'transitory, fugitive element', which constitutes the other half of what is 'eternal and immutable' (Baudelaire 1995).[34] Here, it is already clear that Baudelaire maintains an opposition between modernity and antiquity, which Walter Benjamin, in his reading, aims at overcoming. The Painter of modern life must, in

---

34 Here the passage: 'By 'modernity' I mean the ephemeral, the fugitive, the contingent, the half of art whose other half is the eternal and immutable...This transitory, fugitive element, whose metamorphoses are so rapid, must on no account be despised or dispensed with. By neglecting it, you cannot fail to tumble into the abyss of an abstract and indeterminate beauty'.

Baudelaire's opinion, 'make it his business to extract from fashion whatever element it may contain of poetry within history, to distil the eternal from the transitory' (Baudelaire 1995: 12). Fashion also represents an interesting example in Benjamin, although it will serve as example for a different dynamic at the core of the modern, namely the generalisation of the new as a mode of experience.

As mentioned above, in his reading of Baudelaire's reflection on modernity, Benjamin is much more interested in the aspect of novelty rather than in that of transitoriness, which he analyses through the example of fashion due to its embodiment of the generalisation of the new as a mode of experience based on the repetition of the same. Within modernity, the repetition of the same is bestowed with a quality of newness that, in its repetition, becomes a generalised mode of experience, while transitoriness is a direct result of this process rather than its trigger (Benjamin 2003: 45-60). It is in this sense that Benjamin reworks the complex relationship between the eternal and the ephemeral in Baudelaire and, through reflecting on novelty, he overcomes it. The ephemeral here emerges as a direct result of the routinisation of newness, which on the other side implies the generalisation of the new as a mode of experience. In other words, in the experience of the modern, what is new appears as always the same and as a result, transitoriness itself is eternalised.

The reason for the experience of the modern to be characterised by the repetition of the same lies in its particular temporality. The experience of the modern lacks exactly what is experienced: it is characterised by a temporality devoid of duration, where time emerges as 'empty and homogeneous. The temporality of the modern is without duration. In this precise sense, the modern is a temporal space already marked by a certain *post'* (Chowdhury 2008). There are important consequences to this that develop in at least two directions, and are relevant for this research. First, Benjamin considers this in his philosophy of history, with related implications on the relationship between novelty and progress that, as already shown in Chapter 1, arises almost automatically with the acknowledgment of novelty within innovation studies. Second, the new appearing as an eternal repetition of the same presents important implications when it comes to the value aspect of the New.

With reference to the first class of consequence and thus to the relationship between novelty and progress, the experience of the modern seems on one side to prevent the possibility for the New to emerge, and on the other to open up a space for it. Starting from the consideration that Baudelaire misunderstands the New for the modern, Benjamin specifies: 'The modern stands in opposition to the antique, the new stands in opposition to the ever-always-the-same' (Benjamin 1985: 49).[35] The point here that Benjamin aims to state is that in the experience of the modern that emerges clearly in Baudelaire's work, the historical takes the form of the commodity and historical events are turned into mass-produced articles. This latter aspect is particularly relevant as it links these reflections with the second class of consequences of Benjamin's reading of modernity, those regarding the relationship between value and newness. In order to explore thoroughly the consequences of it, Benjamin leaves Baudelaire aside and refers more and more to Nietzsche and Blanqui. In Benjamin's opinion, their philosophies reflect the transformation of the New into the 'ever-always-the-same' by the commodity.

As Chowdhury (2008) notices, within the experience of the modern, the new becomes the eternal recurrence of the same and that, according to Benjamin, is also the fetish character of commodities, once again exemplified by fashion. As the idea of eternal recurrence transforms historical events into commodities, fashion represents the other side of this dynamic, by which the quality of newness is ascribed to products in order to sustain their demand and again transforms the new into the 'ever-always-the same':

> With the new production processes, which produce imitations, appearances (Schein) are crystallised into commodities. For people as they are today, there is only one radical novelty, and that is always the same: death. [...] Fashion is the eternal recurrence of the new. Are there nevertheless motifs of redemption precisely in fashion [...] Dialectic of commodity production: the newness of the products acquires (as a stimulus for demand) a hitherto un-heard of significance; the ever-always the same appears palpably in mass production for the first time (Benjamin 1985).

The eternal repetition of the new is particularly important as it entails consequences in terms of value that cannot be left aside in the context of this research. Objects or practices to which the quality of newness is attributed regain exchange value. The repetition of the new thus implies a reinvestment in terms of symbolic and economic value that also works through the process of innovation.

The New conceived as ordinary, obscure, anachronistic, ephemeral or eternal does not represent in itself a good market opportunity. Contrariwise, the new as defined by innovation research, seems to represent the ultimate

---

35 Benjamin reads between the lines of Baudelaire's poetry the possibility for the emergence of the New, where the poet has a distinctively active role, as he: 'makes the new appear within the ever-always-the-same and the ever-always-the-same within the new' (Benjamin 1985: 43). To this, poetry, in the opinion of Benjamin, was a necessary condition that Baudelaire was hostile to progress, or as Benjamin himself specifies, to the 'belief in Progress [...] as it were heresy, false doctrine, rather than a simple error' (ibid.). In Benjamin's opinion, the idea of progress must be: 'grounded in the idea of catastrophe. That things 'just go on' *is* the catastrophe. It is not that which is approaching but that which is. [...] Redemption looks to the small fissure in the on-going catastrophe (ibid.). It is in this sense that 'It is very important that the 'new' makes no contribution at all to progress'.

market opportunity through which capitalism reproduces itself. Here, the aspect of value comes to the fore as essential for thoroughly understanding the dynamics connected with the production of the New in the context of neoliberal capitalism.

There is in this respect, another contribution that deserves to be recalled in this context: the writings of Adorno, especially those contained in the *Dialectic of Enlightenment* and in *Aesthetic Theory*, that link novelty, value and progress in a complex way, here represent the starting point to analyse the same complexities in our present time with the due updates, as it will be done in the next chapter. In their revision of Marx's fetishism of commodities, Horkheimer and Adorno speak of 'exchange society' to address the fact that the exchange value now dominates every sphere of human life and, relevant to the context of this research, they regard as exemplary the culture industry. In the well-known homonymous chapter, they describe the change in the commodity character of art that is now acknowledged, and state:

> The character is not new: it is the fact that art now dutifully admits to being a commodity, abjures its autonomy and proudly takes its place among consumer goods, that has the charm of novelty (Horkheimer & Adorno 2002: 127).

When the use value of artworks has been replaced by their exchange value the focus on marketability is then predominant. This exemplifies a shift of capitalism at large that in the case of culture is put in place by the culture industry and strikes directly at art's autonomy. Putting the emphasis on marketability and exchange value, art becomes devoid of the purposelessness that was vital to its autonomy. In the *Aesthetic Theory*, where Adorno deepens the categories of the content on one side and of the social function of art on the other, stating that the two must be considered in terms of the other, he comes back to the reflections above mentioned and develops them completely, by asserting: 'Insofar as a social function can be predicated for artworks, it is their functionlessness' (Adorno 1997: 227). This last sentence, besides reminding the reader that the purposeless of art is in no way defined as the absence of a function, recalls the reasoning of Agamben on what he calls 'pure means', instruments with no given end that disclose their functional power in virtue of being functionless; in the arts: 'a medium, that does not disappear in what it makes visible [...] one that shows itself as such' (Agamben 2002: 318).

In the context of this research–as it is important to keep in mind that the culture industry wrests the 'genuine commodity character' that belonged to artworks before its advent, when their exchange value was a consequence of their intrinsic use value (Horkheimer & Adorno 2002: 129-30)–it is also fundamental to restate that the main point that Adorno underlines is that this shift does not exclusively regard artworks; rather, the commodification of artworks is a consequence of a more profound change of capitalism itself.

Considering that the original text was written in 1947, when the immaterial turn of capitalism was still in its infancy, and the term 'neoliberal' did not exist yet, questions regarding the implications of this arise today.

The processes entangling the production of the New, its value and its complex connection with the idea of progress are for sure still relevant today for neoliberal capitalism. In this sense, it would not be so difficult to argue that nowadays it is not just art that has given up its purposelessness and lost its autonomy, but it is the concept of the New itself that is instrumentalised for other purposes and, by appearing as 'ever-always-the-same', to put it in Benjamin's words, has also lost the potentiality for its political unleash.

These perspectives on value recall and complete the possibility to conceive creative destruction as freed from a purpose and thus freed from the predominance of exchange value on use value. It would also be understandable to argue, in this context, that the New should be conceptualised as a 'pure means without end' and considered as such in contrast to innovation, which is not simply an instrument with an end, but also represents the process through which novelty is given a purpose and exploited. Once again, there is no direct critique to the concept of innovation in itself, rather the need to recreate a space for the production of the New within the context of postdramatic theatre, where the need to attach art and the New art to a function emerged clearly in past decades, in the form of debates on participation or social art practices, to mention one among many. In the next chapters these will be explored, keeping in mind that in the context of neoliberal capitalism, where value lies in the immaterial, producers of the new in the arts also risk their autonomy.

3. The Present Time and the New

This chapter aims at exploring the dynamics connected to the New in the contemporary landscape. In the previous chapters the notion of the new was explored across different disciplines in order to highlight how its production is indeed informed by different conceptualisations. Here, some of the aspects that emerged will be considered again in light of the current economic and cultural dynamics so that the paradoxes inhabiting the production of the New in the present time could be stated, and some responses to them explored. In order to engage in such analysis of the present, the first thing to do is to look at the past. More specifically, the major debates on the new that animated the period of the Avant-garde will be recalled, up to the extent to which they informed the complexities that emerged in Chapters I and II, remaining unsolved, up to today. In particular, the focus is on the possibility of novelty in modernism and that of the future in postmodernism, and the problem regarding the compulsoriness of the new first and of creativity afterwards.

In the next chapters, the attention shifts to the empirical ground of this research, contemporary theatre and dance, in order to look at the same dynamics with a perspective closer to the field of analysis.

3.1 Some Notes on the Avant-garde

It would be strange to engage in the exploration of the dynamic connected to the New without mentioning the debate around novelty that animated the Avant-garde and modernity at large. Still, given the scope of the present research, the matter is tackled here with the aim on one side of highlighting the complexities that are emerging, having been informed by that period, and on the other, to provide a sound basis to engage in the analysis of the complex dynamics around the production of the New in the arts in our own time. There are in particular two aspects that are relevant in this sense. The first regards the very possibility of novelty and its duration: the question of whether the New is determined to establish a new paradigm, losing the status of novelty. The second, already mentioned as the routinisation of the new, is considered here again as it also includes, though in a different form, one of the paradoxes that characterises the production of the New today: the new becoming compulsory, expressed today through the compulsoriness of creativity, and the implications in terms of value and autonomy.

These two problems were at the core of the debate around novelty that animated modernity, which is commonly considered the epoch of the new, as also shown by the etymology of the word itself to be traced back to the Latin word *modo*, which means 'just now'. Although the attention given to the new at the time is unquestionable, it is important to consider, as North (2013) does, that the Avant-garde entailed diverse conceptions of novelty, and these were developed out of models whose basic shapes 'have been established before Plato and have not varied much since' (North 2013: 13). Although part of this research also aims at testing whether this is also true in the realm of postdramatic theatre, these two models, being the basis of the conceptualisation of the new during the Avant-garde, are considered here as the conceptual sources of the above mentioned paradoxes.

According to North, the two models represent a way around philosophy's scepticism about the possibility of novelty itself:

One of these, recurrence, has the advantage of seeming to have the sanction of nature but the disadvantage of not seeming to offer any real novelty. The other, recombination, seem to offer unlimited novelty, but only if unprecedented relations between existing elements can be considered truly new entities (ibid., 13).

Looking at this extract, they could hardly be described as 'a way around philosophy's scepticism about the possibility of novelty' as the first negates the possibility of the New, and the second needs specific premises to consider recombination as a possible source of the New. Such premises recall the conceptions of novelty in the social sciences, which have, of course, also been influenced by the debate in question and would hardly be accepted as consistent with what has been explained up to now. Still, what emerges in the historical analysis by North is the ambiguity, if not sometimes the impossibility, developed around the concept of the New that animated the debate around the Avant-garde. It is in this sense that in the context of this research, the focus is not so much on aesthetic modernism as the time of the new, but rather on the debates that exploded between the Avant-garde and the Neo-Avant-garde (Rosenberg 1959, Greenberg 1961) that cast a light on the paradoxes of the production of the New in art that are still in place today.

'The famous modern break with tradition,' it is possible to read in Rosenberg's book (1959) 'has lasted long enough to have produced its own tradition'. Its title, *The Tradition of the New*, already stated the problem. As North (2013) notices, such debate was possible because of the premises already contained in the aesthetics of high modernism itself. Particularly relevant in this sense is the fringe that saw the advent of modern art as a return to something lost in the past. With the authorisation of Christianity, according to North, these avant-garde movements were able to look at revolution as a renewal and to conceptualise it as a return to an original, lost purity. Although privileging a conception of change, which was necessarily violent and radical, this discourse ended up setting the bases for the new to legitimately become tradition, as radical change was indeed connected to the one of return to the origin, through the concept of revolution.

Notwithstanding its consistency with different aspects of the New that emerged in Chapter 2, such as the inclusion of the old, obscurity and ordinariness, this conceptualisation of radical change entails consequences–especially in the political sphere–that must be acknowledged when considering the production of the New in the arts nowadays, as this idea of revolution was not completely free of criticism at the time and nor is it today.

First, conceiving revolution as a return to the origin puts in question change itself. Second, considering revolution exclusively as a radical change presents the risk of preventing incremental change to happen, as Latour pointed out, since what is total and entire could not be 'touched unless completely revolutionised' (Latour 1993: 126).[36] Although here the matter is tackled with certain scepticism towards the postmodern attention to partiality, part of this critique is taken into account, up to the extent that 'actual change is misunderstood and reform is bungled' (North 2013: 162). The present work does not criticise the idea of radical change and the comment of Latour is here included to stress the importance of keeping this possibility in mind in the context of art production, without banishing that of incremental change (e.g. artistic research process). At the same time, it is important to restate the possibility of radical change in a world in which continuous innovation makes it more difficult to recognise real change when it occurs.

As a partial answer to this problem, other movements grouped under the label of modernism conceptualised the new as incremental change consistent with evolution. This fringe of modernism highlights one of the continuities that make it more complex to talk about a real rupture between modernism and postmodernism. Most importantly, by trying to solve the paradox of the new becoming tradition, it paved the way for the new to become compulsory. First, because of the focus on elements and recombination, of which the important implication is that, being based on the element as its constituting form, it cannot be invented in itself but just infinitely recombined. This aspect involved a vision for artistic research similar to the scientific one, which, being based on experiments–whose role is also fundamental within the arts–defuse the possibilities to envision production in a different way. Consequently, although the problems connected to conceiving the New as revolution are avoided here, it is equally hard to speak of something truly

---

36 Bruno Latour addresses this problem in *We've Never Been Modern* (1993). He criticises the modern project of pretending to completely separate nature and culture, failing to bring them together and thus allowing and forbidding at the same time what he calls 'hybrids'. In this context, Latour conceives the idea of radical change, embedded in the modern conception of revolution, as the only solution modernity could provide to explain the emergence of these hybrids, which could not otherwise be explained because of the strict categorisation imposed by modernity 'in order to avoid another monster: the notion that things themselves have a history.' The asymmetry between nature and culture is mirrored in that between past and future. In this framework, Latour reads modernity's refusal of the old, to which postmodernism represents a symptom rather than a solution.

new on such premises. Artistic novelty becomes a matter of combination of pre-given elements that not only exclude the possibility of the truly new, but also end up being conservative, as the work by Becker suggested and that by Luhmann brought to extreme consequences. It is not by chance that the latter speaks of innovation and not of new, describing it as a natural characteristic of a system whose population is large enough to transform what is extraordinary into a routine, and thus to size down the idea of change into incremental change, coming to the conclusion that the new is produced by the population in the process of maintaining its continuity (see Chapter 1).

An influential perspective on this problem was given by the analysis of modernism by Cavell who shifted the focus on the idea of paradigm, developed together with Kuhn and found in the work of Wittgenstein. The mechanism of language described by the philosopher inspires Cavell to build his model of novelty within the arts: language does not develop through the recombination of pre-given elements but, being constructed in the practice, is so open to change so that it extends the paradigm itself by generating new meanings from old words (Cavell 1979). The downside of this idea of novelty, as North notices, is that 'with a paradigm so flexible as this, there would never be any need for revolution' (North 2013: 189). Although the risk seen by Latour is avoided by such a conceptualisation, the problem of the new becoming tradition is reinforced by this model of novelty that has come to characterise modernism itself, as exemplified by Luhmann.

The paradox of the new becoming tradition entails that of the new becoming compulsory, which emerged in the modernist debate on novelty between the Avant-garde and the Neo-Avant-garde. The problem is well exemplified by what Clement Greenberg (1961) called 'novelty art', distinguishing it from modernism in his *Art and Culture*. Novelty art, in the specific case represented by the Neo-Avant-garde, is considered despicable exactly because it embodies the new that has become routine. Contrariwise, modernism represents in his opinion the New that stays new. More specifically, Greenberg and his followers accuse 'novelty art' to be too keen on innovation and thus to have primarily commercial motives,[37] consistently with the fact that these are the times in which the debate on the commodification of art was coming to the fore. It is curious that Greenberg uses the word novelty in such a negative way but at the same time praises modernism for being a system that constantly renovates itself.[38] According to

---

37 As North explains, the word 'novelty' in English is derived from the French expression *magasins de nouveautés* that was used to indicate the first malls. Because of this origin the word 'novelty' in English is still mainly associated with the commercial context. This also explains the fact that novelty often refers to plural subjects, as it was originally associated with the multiplicity and standardisation found in a store that still gave a general impression of uniqueness and newness.

38 According to Greenberg the high modernists were 'reluctant revolutionaries'. Still, the revolution is here again seen as return, renewal, rediscovery of the essential and thus the

North, 'recasting the new in terms of renewal is the time-honoured way to resolve the apparent conflict between novelty and tradition and forming them into an independent system that sustains itself'; the work by Greenberg seems to be readable in this perspective.

At the time when the New emerged as such a strong value as to become compulsory, today we are confronted with the problem of compulsory creativity within neoliberal capitalism. Criticisms of the routinisation of the new and its connected compulsoriness were harsh then and are still valid today. One of the most famous is certainly that of Adorno, who criticised the aspiration of artists to be new in order to pursue the autonomy of art as a short-sighted strategy; the fact that the reproduction of capitalism follows exactly the same strategy based on novelty suggests that this does not work. This contribution, already mentioned in Chapter 2, can now be enriched and updated by that of Badiou, who in his analysis of the Avant-garde, contained in *The Century* (2007), refers to the problem as the re-enactment of repetition that becomes a repetition of revolution, since one Avant-garde follows the other, promoting another doctrine of radical beginning.

In the light of all this, the time between the Avant-garde and the Neo-Avant-garde must be taken into account as the source of diverse problems that are still unsolved in the present. Before focusing the analysis on this and the complex dynamics it entails in terms of production of the New in the arts, it is important to understand the inheritance of the Avant-garde, whose most important unsolved issues are now listed. First, one must acknowledge that this debate left quite a heavy inheritance in terms of the possibility of the production of the New. Whereas high modernism and the Avant-garde developed by sustaining and reproducing an idea of revolution that, conceptualised as return to the origin, is bound to lead to restoration, the Neo-Avant-garde, acting in the awareness of this problem, left the idea of a paradigm so flexible that revolution is no longer needed. A good example of this is provided by the common artistic tendency of the time to work in series, which 'meant to qualify the novelty along with the uniqueness of the individual instance, but also to substitute for this vanished new another kind, derived from the very multiplicity of the series' (North 2013: 203). Out of this inheritance, the present epoch emerges as sceptical of the possibility to produce the New and this is exemplified, among other things, by the loss of interest in the topic that characterises postmodern thought.

---

new becomes the 'tradition of art that keeps itself alive through constant innovation'. In his model, novelty emerges from revolutionary moments in 'normal panting' in which the artist rejects conventions that are no longer necessary. This structure works on the premise that art is impossible without a set of conventions and that those are not just restrictive but also constitutive, and thus can give rise to the new.

This is connected to the paradox of the new becoming routine and could be seen in light of the critiques coming from very different perspectives, i.e. Latour, but also Benjamin, who foresaw the risks connected to the arts taking the form of fashion, where radical change is so common that it is difficult to distinguish it from routine. The political consequences of this are manifold, to mention one above all: the problem of absorption of artistic practices by the system that is particularly relevant for the production of the New in the arts today. The disinterest in the New and the difficulty in distinguishing it from routine did–and continues to–make the way for perceiving things that are not as equal and thus not substitutable; it corroborates the absorption of artistic practices into other markets, or generally of the new into the system. It is in this sense that today it is even more necessary to think about the New: as long as the concept of the New is still an object of confusion, it will always be bound to be some form of conservative recombination.

Although exacerbated today, this dynamic was also in place before: ironising or disclaiming the new were in itself artistic strategies used by artists as a way to resist the market's capitalisation on the New for its own sake, and to prevent the artwork from being turned into a commodity. These were exactly the practices that the market singled out as new and consequently marketed. Still, North (2013) thinks that the aesthetics of the Neo-Avant-garde were somehow able to answer the problem of novelty by escaping the circle of the new by establishing its own tradition, and this is why, in North's opinion, such an animated debate developed around it. Whether this represents a way out of co-optation is not specified, as it is probably not the case.

Not by chance, Arthur Danto defines rightfully the new art–the Neo-Avant-garde, in his case exemplified by the *Brillo Boxes* and in particular by their seriality–as ahistorical: the work of art in series reworks the concept of novelty so that it becomes open ended and endless, and thus the history of art is no longer history but rather 'a process of endless substitution' (Danto in North, 2013). There is no need here to recall that innovation is constituently defined by substitutability and how intimate the link is between it and the problem of co-optation. Rather, it is more interesting to acknowledge that, by virtue of this seriality, the Neo-Avant-garde prevented the idea of revolution reconstituting tradition to be reproduced, excluding the origin to which it is possible to go back to, and thus 'to give the entire system the unity and purpose of a cycle' (North 2013: 197). Although this represents an important aspect, it still contributed to the disavowal of the New that was passed then to today. On the other side, the production of the new based on seriality could be connected with the predominance of creativity today; more importantly for the objectives of this research, it could be questioned if it ever amounts to anything as theoretically endless, and thus if it is possible to speak of production, and if so, in which terms.

By putting in question the notion of conditions that constituted the basis for the discourse on the production of the New during high modernism, the Neo-Avant-garde embraces, consistently with the production of series, the idea that art does not depend on conditions but rather generates its own conditions, whose nature is 'to generate further conditions, new ones that extend in an essentially unpredictable way and never hit the limit that brings on revolution' (Smithson in North 2013).

The idea of such a flexible paradigm that indeed recalls the production of innovation presents, in terms of inheritance, both positive and negative aspects. Among the positive ones, one must acknowledge that, notwithstanding the closeness to innovation, there is indeed space for critique, as Rosalind Krauss notices: 'artists that put paradigms in question create new ones within the old ones' (Krauss 2011 in North 2013: 191) Still on the negative side there is always the problem of autonomy, which is today particularly relevant: if the producers of the new define themselves as such just with reference to the paradigm, these may constitute a problem and a real obstacle to the production of the New, no matter how flexible this paradigm. Here the matter is wider, as it regards the philosophical problem of the paradigm in itself that it seems to make impossible whatever it does not make possible. Although the question of whether it is possible to conceive the New outside a paradigm could be a stimulating intellectual exercise, here it cannot be treated properly because the production of the New today indeed happens under given conditions that are those of neoliberal capitalism, under which there is a much more urgent matter: as long as a way out of this circle does not come to the fore, it is no surprise that someone, like North did, may argue: 'If the production of art is a whole that perpetually reconstitutes itself so as to remain whole, how can the new even matter very much in the split between its appearance and its instantaneous reabsorption into the whole' (North 2013: 194)?

It is in this sense that the Neo-Avant-garde and the Avant-garde are the time of the new: the critical push against it was strong enough to negate its very possibility and left as inheritance a general disinterest in the topic in postmodernist thought, where it was substituted by the over attention on creativity and innovation. Such a shift happens not by chance in a time of capitalist space-time compression, where everything seems the same or at least equally substitutable. This is why it is so important today to think again about the New, to get outside the logic of the *post-* to enter that of the future, and in this the arts can surely play an important role.

3.2 Postmodernism and the Future

In this acknowledgment of the condition of modernity, it is time to address the problems connected to the condition of postmodernity, as Harvey names it in his homonymous book (1989). Given that postmodernism's view on the new is surely informed by the debate reviewed in the last paragraph, the question remains whether the present we are referring to in this chapter is indeed the result of radical break with modernity or, as Harvey puts it, just another fashionable 'twist' taken by high culture and academics that does not really correspond to a change in social conditions. The answer, in Harvey's opinion, lies in what he defines as 'space-time compression': 'processes that so revolutionise the objective qualities of space and time that we are forced to alter, sometimes in quite radical ways, how we represent the world to ourselves' (Harvey 1989: 241). The choice of the word 'compression' lies in the fact that these processes are characterised by time speeding up and distances getting smaller as the history of capitalism shows: capitalism, characterised by periodical crises of over-accumulation, leads to space-time compression to which a crisis of representation in aesthetics usually corresponds. As modernism could be read in relation to industrialisation and high modernism as the effect of the time-space compression of World War I, postmodernism can be examined as the crisis in representation linked to the shift of capitalism from Fordism to flexible accumulation. In the words of Jameson, postmodernism is indeed the cultural logic of late capitalism (1991) and as such it seems to exacerbate the problems connected not only with the New but also with the concept of production itself.

The preliminary account that Harvey gives of postmodern aesthetics–characterised by the predominance of reproduction on production and by what he defines 'depthlessness'–perfectly matches the one of flexible accumulation that embodies, to put it simply, postmodern economics. Flexible accumulation has different effects,[39] which can be summarised in the shift of value production into the realm of the immaterial; such a description is of course approximate but points at the relevance of the topic within the production of the New. There is undeniably, according to Harvey, a change in the mode of production of capitalism that leads to the aesthetic expressions of postmodernism. Still, it represents a phenomenon continuous with the conditions of Enlightenment and modernist thought rather than a radical break with it:

The experience of time and space has changed, the confidence in the association between scientific and moral judgments has collapsed, aesthetics has triumphed over ethics as a

---

39 Harvey mentions dynamics connected to the labour market which becomes more flexible, the corporate business that becomes generally faster and counts more and more on outsourcing, the integration of the financial system at the global level.

prime focus of social and intellectual concern, images dominate narratives, ephemerality and fragmentation take precedence over eternal truths and unified politics, and explanations have shifted from the realm of material and political-economic groundings towards a consideration of autonomous cultural and political practices [...] shifts of this sort are by no means new, and that the most recent version of it is certainly within the grasp of historical materialist enquiry [...] Postmodernism can be regarded, in short, as a historical-geographical condition of a certain sort (Harvey 1989: 328).

Besides offering a first partial answer to the question at the core of the book, this extract already contains the main aspects of the condition of postmodernity resulting from the time-space compression that followed the crisis of over-accumulation of the late 60s.

Time and space–and in particular their production–are considered by Harvey as powerful political dimensions.[40] Their last compression that triggered postmodernism is indeed enlightening as regards the production of the New in art, both in terms of the paradox with whom the producers of the New need to cope, and in terms of their potential as agents of change. Moreover, as it will be shortly explained in the next paragraphs, they represent two of the fundamental dimensions across which the poetics of postdramatic theatre developed, not independently from this shift of capitalism. According to Harvey, 'the first major consequence has been to accentuate volatility and ephemerality of fashions, products, production techniques, labour processes, ideas and ideologies, values and established practices' (Harvey 1989: 285). These changes in the production of space and time are linked to the change in the representation of value that, as mentioned above, is increasingly immaterial, i.e. not linked to production or to a material value.[41] In this light, the above-mentioned complex dynamics between the New, duration and value are enriched by Harvey's analysis. If during modernism the question was how far the new counts, if it was in any case determined to establish its own tradition, in the present condition the question becomes more urgent; it regards how, and for how long, the new lasts before being co-opted by the system, endowed as it is with high immaterial value:

---

40 Time and space are produced through material practices and as such they cannot be fully understood outside the context of social action. At the same time capitalism, being characterised by the revolutionary movement of creative destruction, continuously produces time and space and consequently produces the precise experience of space and time that defined modernity.

41 With regards to space, the spatial adjustments to the regime of flexible accumulation fundamentally altered the production of space itself. Harvey notices how, if on the one hand distance represents no variable in terms of costs, on the other the attention to the specific characteristics of various places increased consistently with capital becoming more mobile. In terms of time, the condition of postmodernity is associated with acceleration. The acceleration regards both production (capital turnover) and consumption (consumerism).

If there are limits to the accumulation and turnover of physical goods, then it makes sense for capitalists to turn to the provision of very ephemeral services in consumption. This quest may lie at the root of the rapid capitalist penetration, noted by Mandel and Jameson, of many sectors of cultural production from the mid-1960s onwards (ibid., 285).

With the shift of value to the immaterial, acceleration and disappearing of distances, the condition of postmodernity emerges as characterised by ephemerality and volatility, which in turn have the second important consequence of affirming the image as commodity, and thus pave the way for its absorption. It is not by chance that the debate on the commodification of art started at the end of the 50s preceding by a few years the full display of the condition of postmodernity and the related postmodernist aesthetics: 'such a system of asymmetrical money relations relates to the need to mobilise cultural creativity and aesthetic ingenuity, not only in the production of a cultural artefact but also in its promotion, packaging, and transformation into some kind of successful spectacle' (ibid., 347).

As a commodity, the image must indeed be produced. Such a production on one side means an active engagement in the production of volatility, and on the other it needs to count on the creativity of the image producers, who 'have an insecure existence, tempered by very high rewards for the successful and at least a semblance of command over their own labour process and creative powers' (ibid., 290). In this way, the co-optation dynamic reaches its full form by integrating artists into the dominative logic of capital not only by absorbing their work but also their values. The debate around the new becoming compulsory that exploded with the advent of the Neo-Avant-garde today sadly results in the acknowledgement of the fact that creativity has become compulsory.

This implies the substitution of the concept of New with that of creativity. This aspect will be deepened in the next paragraph since now it is important to focus on how the removal of the New seems to be matched by a general dismissal of the future, which emerges both in the conditions of production and consumption and at the level of the postmodernist discourse.

With reference to the production side, the time compression is translated in a speeding up of decision-making and in the difficulty of long term planning. Indeed the suffix *post-* has not so much to do with the future; rather than the production of the New, it privileges instead the reproduction of the same covered by the convenient and improper use of the concept of innovation. The idea of the future also seems to vanish on the consumption side, where ephemerality and volatility force individuals 'to cope with novelty and the prospects for instant obsolescence' (ibid., 286). This is exemplified by the increased eclecticism in commodity disposability, which according to Harvey nourishes the postmodern taste for eclecticism at large. Consequently, not only commodities but also cultural products become equal and thus subject to that substitution mechanism typical of innovation–the new as 'ever-always-the same' in modernity. One of the implications of this change, according to Harvey is the commodification of history, a concept indebted to Benjamin's analysis, which entails the dismissal of the future and thus also corrodes the spirit of agency by transforming production into reproduction. In the spirit of engaging with the production of the New, one must agree with Harvey, who enlightens the risks of postmodern thought in this perspective:

Postmodernism typically strips away that possibility by concentrating upon the schizophrenic circumstances induced by fragmentation and all those instabilities (including those of language) that prevent us even picturing coherently, let alone devising strategies to produce, some radically different future (ibid., 54).

In their book *Les Passions Tristes*, the philosopher Benasayang and the psychoanalyst Schmit refer to this by stating that the future changed its 'sign': contemporary society is defined by the shift from the unbounded trust in the future to an equally extreme wariness towards it. Contemporary society is inhabited, according to the authors, by what Spinoza defined as sad passions–such as powerlessness and social disintegration–which are useful to people in power as they defuse desires and the potential for transformation.

The distrust in the future, here conceived as perspective, also depends on the failure of the Enlightenment project—up to the extent by which it ascribed the potential to deliver human happiness to scientific progress–and notwithstanding its failure, it animates the rhetoric of innovation. Still, in the condition of postmodernity the future does not simply change sign, shifting from positive to negative, but seems to disappear as a category. In postmodern thought, the same happens to the past: the current space-time compression is characterised by a totalising present that absorbs both the category of the future and that of the past:

Accelerations in turnover times in production, exchange, and consumption that produce, as it were, the loss of a sense of the future except and insofar as the future can be discounted into the present. Volatility and ephemerality similarly make it hard to maintain any firm sense of continuity. Past experience gets compressed into some overwhelming present (Harvey 1989: 291).

The distrust in the future entails a disinterest in the New that extends to a particular attention to the past: 'eschewing the idea of progress, postmodernism abandons all sense of historical continuity and memory, while simultaneously developing an incredible ability to plunder history and absorb whatever it finds there as some aspect of the present' (ibid., 54).

In the previous chapters, an idea of the New was advocated that could include the old and at the same time could function as a productive interruption of continuity. Here, the stress is set on the postmodernist attention to the past as it projects time in a totalising present in which both the past and the future are eliminated as dimensions of action and thus politically unavailable. Yet, it is only in the present that the possibility to imagine the future might be regained. This emerged in the focus on the present plead by Agamben and Deleuze for instance, who besides sharing different aspects of postmodern thought, do not negate the future, but rather embrace the present as the time for its enactment. Harvey, who maintains that the time dimension to engage in the reactivation of the future is the present, shares the same perspective: it is in the crises of accumulation that interventions are possible. These interventions must take the form of production of time and space:

Since phases of time-space compression are disruptive, we can expect the turn to aesthetics and to the forces of culture as both explanations and loci of active struggle to be particularly acute at such moments' (ibid., 327).

In the production of time and space, artistic practices also play a fundamental role because the crises of accumulation, by being disruptive are also constructive, and thus generate new ways of producing time and space, within which rises the opportunity for new cultural forms to be produced.

As the reflection here presented does not regard the existence or absence of the future at the ontological level but its availability as a perspective of thought and action, these 'cultural forms' or artistic practices might act by producing a different narrative for the contemporary man, who often acts in the conviction that tomorrow he will be exactly like today. The acceleration described by Harvey comes to the fore as a paradox, as humanity moves faster and faster in a condition where the future as perspective, by virtue of which it should transcend the present, does not exist anymore. The resulting experience of late modernity is that of being in a rush that cyclically reproduces the present. This recalls the typical dynamics of innovation and the postmodern negation of production in favour of reproduction on one side, and on the other regards directly the temporality of production in contemporary performing arts. Bojana Kunst discusses in this regard the use of the word 'project' to address the specific temporality of production in performing arts. Artistic and creative work is caught up in a 'projective time' where 'the main paradox is that artists are constantly challenged to imagine and to form proposals for the future. To do this, they perpetually rehearse ways of imagining that which has yet to come or that which has yet to happen. Paradoxically, despite that so many creative people are preoccupied with imagining and creating proposals for the future, we are living in a time that is deeply characterised by the impotence and impossibility of imagining and creating modes of political and economic life different from the ones that we already know' (Kunst 2012: 112).

Within contemporary politics, this is mirrored by the rhetoric that negates possible alternatives–implicating the negation of the New–as a result of such acceleration that prevents ethical behaviour to root and grow. 'There is no alternative' was the slogan of Margaret Thatcher at the beginning of the neoliberal turn and it is the leitmotif of today's austerity policies. Harvey already carried out similar reflections on politics that, under the condition of postmodernity, privileges aesthetics over ethics and thus negates production to fall back into reproduction. A trace of this could also be found in slogans such as 'Yes we can', by which it is not always clear to what people are supposed to say yes, or whether the advertised change regards the actual conditions of production or its part in the narrative of innovation. The contributions here listed connect the dynamics of acceleration, the emerging of an overwhelming present of endless reproduction and the possibility of the New, locating their sources in modernity, whose disclosing was characterised by tension towards the future. This implied on the one hand the acceleration of production rhythms, and on the other the rise of the new as positive value from an axiological perspective.

Looking at the production of the New today means acknowledging that if the acceleration characterising modernity is maintained, the horizon towards which it was directed might have disappeared; the acceleration reflects even more Benjamin's thought on a frantic research of the new that is always the same, and the paradoxes that emerged during modernism, far from being solved, are exacerbated in the present age, which appears as late modernity rather than postmodernity.

If on one side these dynamics have to be traced back to the Enlightenment[42]–a theoretical corpus that in Adorno's opinion prevents any radical change–on the other, the question regarding the production of the New today is more urgent than ever, as it entails the enactment of the future as perspective and the concept of production as action in the present. This implies that, while some aspects that modernism had inherited from the Enlightenment–such as the deformation of reason and the blind trust in modernisation mentioned by Harvey–must be questioned, some other characteristics must be valued, possibly without falling back on to a blind modernism that liquidates the past *tout court*, nor in postmodernism that negates the production of the New, and thus the future. In this sense, the critique presented to the concept of innovation (see Chapters I and II), and the way it is used to produce a vision of the world based on a linear trajectory, is here juxtaposed to the refusal of the determinations it entails as well as the premises on which it is based, since they emerge as the illusion of continuous change that prevents real change to happen. Contrariwise, by rehabilitating the New as concept, it is also possible to escape the totalising present and thus to reconstruct the future as perspective.

This could be done by fighting the 'no alternative' rhetoric, also through art production. According to Alain Badiou, the present time is a moment of

---

42   This perspective is shared by the whole Marxist tradition to which Harvey belongs. Harvey in particular looks at the Enlightenment as the moment in which the theoretical possibilities for the domination of the production of space and time by the bourgeoisie were opened.

crisis and more specifically, the epoch of a second Restoration that finds in the real and the fictional its source of power:

> The real, as the obligatory correlate of thought is considered by the ideologues of restorations–and not entirely without reason–as always liable to give rise to political iconoclasm, and hence Terror. A restoration is above all an assertion regarding the real; to wit, that it is always preferable to have no relation to it whatsoever (Badiou 2007: 26).

At the same time, Mark Fisher remarked how capitalism presents itself exactly as 'a shield protecting us from the perils posed by belief' (Fisher 2009: 5), and as the most desirable world, imposing a little price to pay before the risks of terrorism and totalitarianism, which are accused of thriving in false belief and fiction. In his *Capitalist Realism*, Fisher refers to it as 'the widespread sense that not only is capitalism the only viable political and economic system, but also that it is now impossible even to imagine a coherent alternative to it [...] a pervasive atmosphere, conditioning not only the production of culture but also the regulation of work and education, and acting as a kind of invisible barrier constraining thought and action' (ibid., 16). Within neoliberal capitalism, whose focus on reality seem to serve only the purpose of weaving its own fiction, artistic practices could contribute to disentangling exactly these narratives by settling and unsettling different forms of present and future, or at large, of reality and fiction.

3.3 The Affirmation of Creativity

In the previous paragraph, it was analysed how the problems connected to the new and its duration before becoming tradition that animated the debate around the Avant-garde, translated into the negation of the very possibility of the New, and thus of the future under the condition of postmodernity.

Here, the second paradox that emerged during modernism–the new becoming compulsory–is addressed in the form it took in the contemporary landscape, that of the 'creativity regime'. David Harvey mentions the issues of creativity while addressing the problem of the image becoming commodity, that in order to be produced must rely on the 'creative capacity' of people and notices that the industry of the production of volatility is 'where there is a ferment of intense, often individualised, creativity poured into the vast vat of serialised and recursive mass culture' (Harvey 1989: 291). Creativity is indeed compulsory and as such results in a sort of mass creativity producing a contradiction in terms. The same contradiction inhabited modernism, and that debate today sadly results in the acknowledgement of the fact that creativity has become compulsory and seems to have substituted the New not just at the level of the concept, but even in its compulsoriness.

David Inglis (2010) acknowledges that innovation and creativity, independently from being thought as characteristic of a class or diffused through networks, became so great as values that it is possible to speak of them as the bulk of 'a new culture of creativity'. Like the new in modernity, creativity today is established as a value in itself so much that Osborne (2003) defines it 'a moral imperative': selling a product by virtue of its aesthetic presentation rather than its intrinsic quality is something that has long been obvious, but the 'creativity industries turn such a fact from what might be considered a matter of shame into a positive–precisely because of creative–value' (Osborne 2003: 509). It is on this basis that creativity shifted from being something that could emerge either from the individual or from the collective, according to different perspectives, to become something that could and should be produced.

The production of creativity as compulsory is useful to understand how the concept became mingled with that of the New so much to have substituted it completely. There are many similarities with what has been already explained with regards to innovation in Chapter 1. Still, while the absorption of the New in the concept of innovation has a long history, the matter of creativity emerges as characteristic of the present age, as it is clear by also looking at the critique of creativity. This became a critique at large of neoliberal capitalism, addressing both the problem at the theoretical level and in its embodiment in the material relations of production, including those connected to artistic labour, flexibility and precarisation of the workforce.

Before addressing the critique of creativity, it is worth going deeper into how creativity substituted the New and what kind of implications it presents in terms of production. Due to the complexity of the matter, only the most relevant aspects will be addressed here: the democratisation of creativity and the related resurgence of the entrepreneur on the one hand, and the concept of networks and competition on the other.

With reference to the first, some characteristics traditionally ascribed to artists are now sold as a possibility for everyone. Sentences like 'make it new' (E. Pound) or 'Everyone an artist' (J. Beuys) are reformulated in the logic of creativity with the consequence that 'old notions of art and "the artistic" are being replaced, even as they are absorbed, by the new concepts of creativity and creative industry' (Raunig et al. 2011). Once creativity is sold as 'the democratic variant of the genius', it becomes a social obligation: 'everyone is required to develop her/his creative potential. [...] The subjects comply with these new relations of power apparently by free will' (Osten 2011: 138). Such appearance could be partially explained by the adoption of the artist's life as a base for the creative worker of immaterial capitalism: 'the ambiance of this production context and the always useful enthusiasm with which [it] is embraced, and even 'scientifically legitimised' under the guise of individual independence, makes the art world especially sensitive to neoliberal value regime [...] Within these parameters work offers a unique chance for self-realisation, and that is exactly why labour is easily offered at low rates' (Gielen 2013: 24).

This may explain the resurgence of the entrepreneur, who within some innovation studies is the privileged producer of the new through creative destruction. Paradoxically, this entrepreneurial culture seems to be partially fuelled by the very source that sociology of art has widely used to criticise the idea of the creative genius and underline that creativity is inherently social. As Osborne (2003) notices, 'Mihaly Csikszentmihalyi describes the creative person as potentially a sort of "everyman" who has a great deal of energy but who is often quiet and at rest; someone who is smart yet naïve at the same time; someone with a combination of playfulness and discipline; someone who is humble yet also proud' (Osborne 2003: 508). Such generalisations help the conceptualisation of creativity as a skill to be nurtured and developed through different techniques, and one of the most celebrated is that of creative problem solving.

In this respect, Pascal Gielen argues that 'indeed, in the flat wet world, creativity is often equated with "problem solving", which is something else entirely than causing problems or rather, problematising issues, a task that was until recently reserved for the artist' (Gielen 2013: 23). Mihaly Csikszentmihalyi, on the other hand, argues for the opposite perspective: 'if the question is unanswerable in principle, why ask it? The better strategy is to recognise that in sciences as well as in the arts, creativity is as much the results of changing standards and new criteria of assessment, as it is of novel individual achievements' (1999: 321). This makes perfect sense in the work of Csikszentmihalyi, who studies creativity within a system approach. It is not criticised here as such, but rather chosen to enlighten on the one hand the ease with which 'the creative' and 'the artist' are used as synonyms, and on the other to highlight that the production of the New calls for a different approach with different criteria. Focusing on solving problems rather than creating them drives creativity closer to innovation, whose production is tied to a specific purpose which at a larger perspective is that of the reproduction of the system, which has already been shown to be a concept–notwithstanding its importance and validity–perfect for studying innovation, but useless when it comes to the New.

In the production of creativity, the central role of the entrepreneur is matched by the equally central role of networks. Since creativity is indeed deeply social, it is not studied as just a property of people but of systems and 'especially of networks' (Osborne 2003), where the latter has recently been highly criticised as one of the embodiments of the neoliberal economy. Although critiques are valid up to a certain extent, it would be exaggerated to dismiss the concept as such–like those of the New, of innovation, of creativity–just because they are appropriable by the system. In this spirit, just few aspects are mentioned here that are indeed critical in terms of the production of the New.

According to Inglis (2010), the concept of creativity, originally supposed to promote individual freedom of thought and expression by becoming compulsory, ties this freedom to economic networks of cultural production. To put together entrepreneur and networks means to produce and sustain an idea of novelty expressed by the concept of creativity that is perfectly consistent with the neoliberal turn of capitalism and its reproduction.

This has a relevant impact on the arts, since 'the neoliberal engine has set a new operational framework in motion in the art world [...] Sloterdijk calls it the shift from art production power to art exhibition power' (Gielen 2013: 20). This is the problem presented by the concept of network to the production of the New: on the one hand, by virtue of their volatility, they could corroborate the power of exhibition over that of production, while on the other they challenge the collective aspect of this production. This collective aspect is also embodied by institutions, conceptualised by Gielen as opposed to networks, which should carry out art production in a context where the values mentioned by Inglis are 'predictably exchanged for an immaterial discourse that is all about mobility and the institution dissolves in a network structure' (ibid., 20). The role of art institutions in the production of the New is considered in this research and the complexities connected to it will be explored in Chapter 4.

3.3.1 The Critique to Creativity and its Limits

The critique to creativity has exploded in recent years both in theory and in art practice. With regard to the latter, the paradoxical position felt by artists in the context described here has taken, among others, the form of *artivism* with the related recrudescence of debate on the relationship between performance and politics.[43] The very same topics that animate this debate are present in the literature: the critique to creativity is a critique at large to neoliberal capitalism and it includes reflections on precarisation, flexibility and networks.

One of the most influential and discussed texts in this perspective is *The New Spirit of Capitalism* by Boltanski and Chiappello.[44] Among the main

---

43   The neologism appeared in recent years, contextually with the last wave of international protest (e.g. Occupy movement) and is increasingly spreading in the world of art and in the academic context. The term refers to artistic practices that aim explicitly at intervening in the political sphere with reference to diverse matters, from the environment to civil rights.

44   In this book the two authors engage in the exploration of the moral grounds that capitalism must provide in order to defend and reproduce itself in the belief, stated in the introduction,

thesis presented, there is the idea that capitalism must draw from an external resource to involve humanity 'in an insatiable process' (Boltanski, Chiappello, 2005: 486) and this external resource is represented by anti-capitalist critique: 'Capitalism has discovered routes to its survival in critiques to it' (ibid., 27). Moreover, they argue that artistic and social critiques are incompatible as they draw from conflicting values, respectively those of autonomy, freedom and creativity and those of solidarity, security and equality. Creativity, once opposed to oppression, is today completely absorbed by the system, as the two authors demonstrate through the analysis of management rhetoric, and represents the very territory of oppression, as exemplified by the creative worker. Recently, the new spirit of capitalism adapted to incorporate the most recent challenges that came to it: networks, autonomy and flexibility.

The creative worker embodies the failure of artistic critique in the opinion of Boltanski and Chiappello and the failure of Boltanski and Chiappello in the opinion of those who criticise their analysis, especially with regard to the notion of 'artistic critique'. Lazzarato, in this respect writes: 'Boltanski and Chiapello have taken the artist and artistic activity as the model of the liberal economy, whereas this model was constructed on (the idea of the individual) as "human capital", as an entrepreneur of her/himself' (2011: 46). The focus on the mechanisms of self-exploitation is valued by many others (Reckwitz 2012, Han 2010) and represents a much more interesting perspective of analysis since it considers creativity as something different from art, and thus allows to envision the production of the New in the latter outside a deterministic mechanism of co-optation, in the belief that:

Artistic ways of living and working contain forces that cannot fully be controlled because they not only engender but also always take part in the dissolution of their own conditions. [...] Historical quotation of the artistic subject and aesthetic ways of living cannot serve as a source of the measurable data required by economic discourses because the production of a context of equivalency between the economical and specific forms of life is a reduction of the inherent complexities and antagonisms (Von Osten 2011: 144-145).

In the light of this, Reckwitz's *Die Erfindung der Kreativität* presents a more useful approach to the matter in question, although his critique to creativity unfolds through a harsh critique of the new. His book, on the one hand, exemplifies perfectly the confusion that is in place between the concept of the New and those of creativity and innovation. On the other hand, it provides an indirect explanation on how this confusion came into being through his critique to creativity, which is fully embraced in this research, once the due distinction between the New and the creative is kept in mind.

---

that 'capitalism will face increasing difficulties, if it does not restore some grounds for hope to those whose engagement is required for the functioning of the system as a whole' (xiiii).

Reckwitz maintains that there is nothing bad about the new, rather it should be questioned what exactly is so good about it: 'We take it for granted that the new is better than the old; that's the progressivist pressure of modernity. Naturally, a radically reactionary, anti-modern attitude isn't the solution. The point is to balance the whole [...] Does aesthetically stimulating newness keep the promise it makes? Or are the events and products that surround us really rather a matter of an "empty newness", of an excess of the only apparently new, which we soon forget' (Reckwitz 2013)?

What emerges as a too close conceptual relationship between the concept of New and that of creativity seems to spring out of the fact that Reckwitz conceptualises the new as opposite to the old, falling back into the rhetoric of innovation discourse, then inherited by the concept of creativity: 'The "new" doesn't exist objectively; it must first be determined in opposition to the "old". The new is determined in an interplay between the creator and the public' (Reckwitz 2013). In Reckwitz's view, the root to the creative apparatus is to be traced back to the figure of the modern artist, who was not only creatively active but also found in this creation the way to realise himself. Here, according to Reckwitz, but consistent with Harvey, Gielen and others, lies the real co-optation mechanism. Still, the dynamic is different from that of Boltanski and Chiappello, according to which capitalism found new instruments of repression in the concept of creativity and 'self-realisation'. According to Reckwitz, it is the reverse case. It is the economy that has been aestheticised:

The close interrelation of aestheticisation and economy is the core of the creativity apparatus and constitutes contemporary society. Above all the aestheticisation of the economy delivers the motivational "fuel". We could say that homo *aestheticus* has become homo *oeconomicus*'s best friend (ibid.)

This is because creativity became an economic hope as exemplified by the concept of creative cities, and one of its major contributors, Richard Florida, who depicts the creative turn as the only possible alternative (Florida, 2002) and connects once again the concept with competition that, already seen by Harvey as a convenient justification in his description of neoliberal creative destruction, seems to have become an integral part of the idea of creativity.

Fortunately, these critiques offer some possible paths to follow in order to unravel the knot. First, the tone of the critiques shows that a possible way of achieving a different kind of production lies in a better conceptualisation of the New. Such a production could be envisioned on the basis provided by these critiques, one above all the critique regarding the appropriation of artistic values and works by the market. An emancipation of the concept of creativity could lead to a clearer definition of the New rather than a pessimistic dismissal of it, as also Inglis (2010) pleads in the awareness that the 'Creativity Regime' can deaden exactly those capacities it apparently encourages. Creativity has been fetishised and Florida's creative class 'colonises and attempts to shape what people think of as the human being, what it is capable of, what it should do and how it should do those things'.

Always in the spirit to restore the emancipatory potential to the concept, Osborne proposes to rescue creativity through the notion of invention. Mixing Deleuze's concept of repetition and Barry's research on the category of invention, he writes:

> Invention is not just a question of novelty; or, rather, we need to broaden our conception of novelty away from artefacts and objects towards arrangements and practices. "What is inventive is not the novelty of artefacts in themselves, but the novelty of the arrangements with other activities and entities with which artefacts are situated". And what counts in an invention is not so much an invented artefact as the questioning invention itself opens up. Invention, then, is the opposite of closure (Osborne 2003: 519).

Although this category offers very interesting insights on how to free creativity from itself, it is not a useful approach in the perspective of envisioning the production of the New within neoliberal capitalism. An approach that starts from the premise that accomplishment and fulfilment 'make it more or less wholly at odds with most version of the doctrine of creativity today', risks relegating the New once again to the creative by stressing processes over products. The risk of this idea of the new already emerged during the Neo-Avant-garde, where the category of endless novelty helped the rise of the compulsoriness of the new.

Moreover, such a conception tends to cut production out of the picture to envision the new as recombinant novelty and thus falls back into creativity. Still, the idea of invention as opposed to closure is very close to the idea of the New that is emerging here. However, it must be handled carefully as, by privileging processes at the expenses of production, it risks ascribing a false liberating effect to the immaterial value, which is what Osborne indeed does: 'the creative "turn" has had quite liberating effects, in the turn, for instance, towards the study of inspiration, wonder and imagination, the affectivity of the body and, similarly, a whole field of performance studies, emerging not least within contemporary feminism, and which accords greater import to the singularity and creativity of the occasion of performance than to the settled letter of the text' (ibid., 510). Here he also quotes Peggy Phelan who, in the belief that the immateriality of performance constitutes a potential for it to work outside the market's laws based on reproduction and circulation, writes: 'What would it take to value the immaterial within a culture structured around the equation 'material equals value' (Phelan 1993: 5)?

It did not take too much: as it was widely explained, the shift of value into the immaterial constitutes the base of late capitalism and makes immaterial products the perfect prey for appropriation. In light of this, the options to give back the emancipatory effect that were once ascribed to these concepts must also consider the spaces where production takes place. It is in this sense that a more satisfactory indication seems to emerge indeed from combining the values of artistic and social critique, not to reduce the political to a short-sighted activism, but 'to teach artists that being an artist is not an individual fate, such as proclaimed by entrepreneurship, but that they can fall back on collective structures of solidarity', a task that Gielen (2013: 17) ascribes to an hypothetical new wave of institutional critique. In this light, the production of the New must indeed also be reviewed in relation to the collective aspect, and in particular to art institutions that, if on one side represent the territory where the creativity regime develops, on the other are one of the few places where these mechanisms can be reversed.

4. On the Traces of the New at the Theatre

The theatre of the present is a chorus of poetics and aesthetics so incongruously varied that it is objectively difficult to describe its porous borders, thus the category of postdramatic theatre proposed by Hans-Thies Lehmann (2006) is particularly useful in this context. It provides a specific frame and at the same time, it is open enough to include the different genres, such as experimental performance, dance, multimedia theatre and new writing that constitute the empirical ground of this research. Postdramatic theatre is a name given *ex post* in the attempt to categorise theoretically something that came into being after it already formed its production sector in practice.[45]

In this short chapter, the reflections on the New and its production are re-contextualised in this specific sector of the performing arts with the aim of providing a framework of interpretation for the perspectives coming from field research. First, the relevant aspects of postdramatic theatre aesthetics are highlighted, especially as regards the dimensions of space and time and their use as artistic devices to work on the border between reality and fiction. Second, the current position of art institutions is introduced as regards their possibility to take part in the process of rethinking the New and its production. *Institutions* refers here to theatres and festivals, and in particular the ones that, consistently with the topic of this research, not only distribute works but also engage in their production and do so with an expressed focus on innovation and artistic research. Finally, the most relevant points are collected in order to outline the state of the art and describe the point of departure of the empirical part of this research, which aims at illustrating critically the possibilities of producing the New in this specific territory of contemporary performing arts.

4.1 Theatre across Reality and Fiction

Postdramatic theatre represents a functional framework of analysis in the context of this research. First, its poetic devices are highly related to the

---

45 In Lehmann's opinion, the 'aesthetic consistency' and the 'inventiveness' characterising theatre since the '70s onwards, justify the affirmation of a 'new paradigm of postdramatic theatre' (24). In using the word 'paradigm', Lehmann is urged to specify that it 'is not intended to promote the illusion that art, like science, could conform to the developmental logic of paradigms and paradigm shifts', rather the use of the terms is justified to avoid a simple description of the 'motley costumed styles' that would result into missing the actual underlying productive process.

paradoxes emerging for the producers of the new within neoliberal capitalism. Then, the sector that developed around these works is usually seen as engaging with artistic production and financially sustained by virtue of the focus on innovation. Third, and most importantly, the *caesura* from dramatic theatre regards closely the production of the New, by virtue of being characterised by what Lehmann defines as 'the irruption of the real': 'postdramatic theatre can be seen as attempt to conceptualise art in the sense that offers not a representation but an intentionally unmediated experience of the real' (Lehmann 2006: 134). As explained below, the unmediated experience of the real unfolds through a productive doubt between reality and fiction that may constitute an interesting terrain for the experience of the New.

Moreover, the adjective *postdramatic* in comparison to postmodern allows an analysis that can indeed talk about production. The term postdramatic already entails a productive meaning, as it is not meant to describe either an epochal category or just an *after-* drama, but rather that process of 'mutual emancipation between drama and theatre' through which all elements that constitute theatre and drama were analysed and known anew as both single elements and part of a totality, rather than a unity. Indeed, the result has many characteristics that are generally ascribed to postmodern aesthetics, as the aim is not anymore unity and wholeness; there is a search for the fragmentary and the partial instead. Still, as Lehmann notices, the typical adjectives used to describe postmodern aesthetics are not helpful in describing what has come into being: 'Process, heterogeneity or pluralism in turn are true for all theatre–the classical, the modern and the postmodern' (ibid., 25).

Postdramatic theatre emerges as a poetics, characterised by the non-hierarchy of the constitutive elements of theatre and their related simultaneity. This also includes the level of the real, which, always being important in theatre, is for the first time turned into a co-player both at the practical and the theoretical level. This means that reality is not exclusively an object of reflection but becomes part of the theatrical design itself. Lehmann names this the 'aesthetics of indecidability':

In the postdramatic theatre of the real, the main point is not the assertion of the real as such but the unsettling doubt that occurs through the indecidability whether one is dealing with reality or fiction (ibid., 101).

On the premises given in Chapters I and II, this extract recalls the impossibility of establishing a relationship with the New and paves the way for its production. The 'irruption of the real' by virtue of which postdramatic theatre constitutes a good ground to study the New, lies exactly in the fact that reality and fiction are on the same level, presenting the possibility to imagine and produce the New across them.

These aspects can be better understood by looking at how two elements, not by chance space and time, become by virtue of this poetics, also dimensions of action. Here, it must be specified that the following characteristics are intended to describe aesthetic responses to the problem, which do entail a political aspect but do not imply an impact on society, as it becomes a very slippery terrain within neoliberal capitalism. With regards to space, the fictive distance covered by the actor in dramatic theatre is underlined as real distance in postdramatic theatre. It is the real distance of the stage and as such it refers to the real space outside the theatre. Moreover, the space of postdramatic theatre does not have a centre where the action takes place, and it happens either in very large or very small spaces, in stark contrast with the dramatic space characterised by a middle size spread around a centre (Lehmann 2006). It is through these very simple but structural changes that postdramatic theatre unveils its space as a continuation of reality, and as such it is used as a dimension of action or even as an artistic strategy. Site-specific performances, which started in the 60s as a result of the increasing integration between theatre and performance art, to reach their peak of diffusion in the 80s, in this sense represent a good example: the point was to cast a new light on the space which becomes, as the other element of the performance, a co-player without having a definite significance in itself or representing something specific: it is made visible as it is. As Lehmann underlines, the space made visible as it is makes performers, spectators and the space all guests of the same place and thus stages a kind of commonality. Not by chance this commonality was usually explored by artists either in old industrial buildings left in the cities in the course of the post-industrialisation process or in public spaces: material and symbolic 'victims' of capitalism on the one hand and the first places of resistance on the other.

More recently, the focus shifted from the dimension of space to that of time. Theorists in the field of performance studies began to talk about the 'end spatiality' (Scheer 2012) and the rise of the 'aesthetic of duration' on the basis of the incredible number of durational performances that seem to privilege time over space as a poetical dimension of resistance. In particular, Lehmann singles out strategies of duration, repetition and acceleration. Practices ascribable to the first one, which points at slowness and deceleration, seem to be particularly conspicuous in the first decade of the current century. To provide an instance, Lee writes: 'it is in slowness and the capacity to parse one's own present that one gets ground on what is coming up next, perhaps restore to the everyday some degree of agency, perhaps some degree of resistance' (Lee 2004: 308).

The idea that slowness could be resistant as such is questionable under different points of view, as are artistic strategies based on acceleration. Still, it is true that like the dimension of space, time is also conceived and produced as dimension of action through stylistic devices that unveil it as it is: continuous with reality. In this sense duration refers to the real time needed to perform an action and acts as distortion of time as acceleration does for example, through the aesthetics of video clips (Lehmann 2006). Duration in this context refers to the time it is actually needed to do things and thus it is used as a factor of time distortion: the passing of time is transformed in a continuous present.

Repetition on the other hand may be more interesting in the spirit of this research, as it interrupts that present that, in the light of what emerged in the previous paragraphs, seems to be continuous enough. Moreover, Lehmann, who does not use the term in a Deleuzian sense, maintains that in theatre there is no such thing as true repetition, since 'the very position in time of the repeated is different from the one of the original' (this is indeed true repetition from a Deleuzian perspective). Thus repetition underscores that impossibility of establishing a relationship with the already known object that is the experience of the New. The echoes of this also emerge in Lehmann: 'repetition is also capable of producing a new attention punctuated by the memory of preceding events, an attending to the little differences' (2006: 157).

Rather than discussing these aesthetics thoroughly, it is here more relevant to focus on the overtaking of time on space. Such a shift is interpretable in at least two perspectives that must be taken into account considering the production of the New. First, it can be read in consistency with Harvey's analysis exposed in the previous chapter. Although both dimensions are connected to the regime of flexible accumulation, it is possible to see them as corresponding to smaller proceedings of capitalism towards an always more immaterial production of value. As the economy was shifting value production from goods to services, space was gaining a central position in theatre both at the level of aesthetics and as an artistic strategy in politics as an answer to the post-industrial condition that produced that shift. In the same way, the poetics and aesthetics of time emerged as an answer to a second shift, namely the one into knowledge or creativity economy, where the most important resource to produce knowledge is time.[46]

Second, the recent predominance of time could be read, as Lehmann does, as a way of going beyond the Aristotelian aesthetics, a step that was due also because of its political implications:[47]

---

46 The importance of time in value production is well-known since Marx with the difference that in those days time resources were embodied in a product, while nowadays it seems to be exclusively represented by the immaterial, such as knowledge and creativity, which in turn can be reduced to time itself.
47 Lehmann refers in particular to the idea that nothing beautiful can come about without a clear overview, the absence of confusion and the reinforcement of logical unity. Drama was based on this, as it brought logic and structure into the confusion of existence. This is also the line that distinguishes theatre (tragedy) from the real world in Aristotle and was then inherited in the modern age.

The Aristotelian traditions are not simply an innocent and nowadays outdated framework but rather an essential part of a powerful tradition against whose normative efficacy the contemporary theatre continually has to assert itself, even if nobody adheres to the norm of the unity of time in any formal sense [...] The basic aesthetic of this tradition can be described as containment of reception, as an attempt to structure the mode of imagination and thought in theatre (ibid., 161).

What is at stake here is exactly that indecidability that gives rise to the doubt endowed with critical judgement: the inheritance of Aristotelian aesthetics entailed an experience of theatre that meant entering a space and a time that belonged to drama itself and thus were something else from reality. The time of drama was in this sense based on a continuity that cannot be interrupted: Lehmann ascribes the same aesthetics to Hollywood movies, and Deleuze carries out a similar reflection in his books on cinema.[48]

With relation to the topics discussed here, the inheritance of Aristotelian aesthetics could be tackled altogether with the innovation discourse, as they both entail the same idea of continuity that prevents interruption in the case of drama, and radical change in the case of innovation discourse. This is why the aesthetic response of postdramatic theatre unfolds primarily by making real time visible as such. Here, the Deleuzian repetition is confirmed once again as a productive movement exactly because it dismisses representation: the time and space of postdramatic theatre are in this sense no longer representation of their fictive versions but are irrupted by the real, integrated to the real dimension of life. As such, it gives rise to that aesthetic of indecidability that could play an important role in the production of the New and provide the theoretical base to look at performance not exclusively as an object of reflection, but also of a subject of reflection, so that its potential in the production of the New could also be fully unleashed in political terms.

Not by chance, Bojana Kunst also refers to the aesthetic of time in her reflection on projective temporality and states that the latter is 'never related to the time out of joint' (2012: 115). The time out of joint–exposed as it is by certain performances–and its inherent potentiality, is exactly what went missing in the overwhelming present:

What we lack is the actual time of the present, because we have sold off the present in return for a project outline. [...] However, the problem is that the future is never truly imagined anew, but remains even more tightly bound to the constellations of power in the present. Only when we are able to simply be "alive" in the present will radical alternatives begin to bloom once again. [...] Art production and creation must therefore rethink the relation between temporality and its production, and new ways in which to push the time "out of joint"; out of the speculative balance between that which is and that which has yet to come (ibid.)

---

48 'Cinema I: the Movement Image' written in 1983 and 'Cinema II: the Time-Image' written in 1986.

4.2 The Institutional Critique yet to Come

Although the dimension of space has seemed to be overtaken by that of time in recent years, it is still very present both in terms of aesthetics and, more interestingly for the purpose of this research, in the form of institutional space. The institutions of postdramatic theatre[49]–already combining the institutional form with the mode of production required by contemporary performance in very different ways–are in a particularly interesting position in terms of production of the New. A very brief and necessarily partial literature review here could serve the purpose to enlighten such a position that, from a first empirical observation, emerges as pivotal and highly critical. If these places seem to be sometimes dismissed by artists who engage in artistic research because they are considered too complicit with capitalism, at the same time they embrace the pleas coming from the artistic community and engage directly with critique and activism independently from the production process that they enact. Recent examples in this sense are the marathon *Truth is Concrete* held at Steirischer Herbst (Graz) in 2012; the day *Performative Utopias* at the Baltic Circle Festival (Helsinki) 2013 and the assembly of assemblies *The Art of Being Many* that took place at Kampnagel (Hamburg) in September 2014.

First, it must be acknowledged that institutions' critical position is not independent from the problem of the compulsoriness of creativity. David Inglis (2010) sees festivals as one of the major social and economic institutions of the 'culture of creativity' (see paragraph 3.3.1) since they connect 'creative' centres or actors at the same time as they present their (often innovative) products to different audiences. In his opinion, such a central position represents a brilliant opportunity for reflecting on how contemporary consumer and economic organisation trends are impacting both the production and consumption of artistic goods; a reflection that cannot be undertaken without a critical approach to the wide diffusion of the Festival format–the 'festivalisation of culture'–that recognises the focus on creativity also in its negative and deeply neoliberal aspect.

Under the condition of what he defines as 'the creativity regime', festivals represent on the one hand the harbour of the perverse process characterising the compulsoriness of creativity, and at the same time, one of the only places where it can be reversed. Festivals are the places where the regime of creativity easily transforms artists into creative employees, reducing their freedom of expression by 'stressing flexibility in the means but

---

[49] In order to give a better idea, here are some examples. Festivals: Kunsten Festival Des Artes, Theater der Welt, Tanz im August, Santarcangelo Festival, Baltic Circle Festival, Wiener Festwochen, Steirischer Herbst, IBT Festival. Theatres: Kampnagel, Kaai Theater, Sophiensaele, HAU, Performance Space 122, Vooruit.

not in the goals' (Inglis 2010). In this sense, compulsory creativity is separating art festivals from the democratic characteristics that are normally associated with them and bringing them nearer to a capitalistic discourse. At the same time, festivals able to resist the creativity imposition are privileged sites of self-consciousness, reflection and (real) creative communication where it is possible 'to imagine a more democratic alternative, to re-orchestrate critical thinking and to engage a defetishisation of the human capacity to create and invent, rescuing it from the control of creativity and innovation' (ibid.). In order to accomplish this noble goal, it is necessary to engage in a rethinking of the political nature and ramifications of the arts festival, showing how they are both complicit in but could in future be reconfigured to elude the creativity fetish (ibid.).

The political nature of festivals and institutions in general is at the core of Chantal Mouffe's (2014) analysis on one of the aspects characterising the position of theatre institutions nowadays, namely their relation to the artists on the one hand and to the system on the other. The premise of her reflection is embraced here as a general premise with regards to researching the production of the New: the refusal of pessimistic views that see artists and art institutions as a necessary engine of capitalist production, and thus too complicit with the system in order to play a critical role within society or to provide a site for artistic practice. If this were true, there would not be any point at all to research the production of the New within the arts.

Chantal Mouffe acknowledges that the post-Fordist stage of capitalism transformed artists into creative workers but at the same time maintains that there are new possibilities of resistance, which may as well entail possibilities of producing the New. These possibilities of resistance are controversial once it is accepted that institutions could play a role within them: 'Should critical artistic practices engage with institutions with the aim of transforming them or should they desert them altogether' (ibid.)? This question, by focusing on the political aspect of the art institution, lies at the core of the role it may play in the production of the New. Mouffe groups artistic practices into 'strategies of exodus' and in 'strategies of engagement'. While the former is based on the pessimistic view above mentioned, the latter is supported by the author who uses Gramsci's theory of hegemony and thus makes space to rethink institutions by virtue of the fact that what is at a given moment accepted as the natural order is always the result of sedimented hegemonic practices. As such, it is always susceptible to being challenged by counter-hegemonic practices that will attempt to disarticulate it so as to establish a different hegemony. Also, Gramsci underlined in his *Prison Notebooks* the pivotal role of artistic practices in this dynamic which could be seen as fundamental today, and according to Mouffe, today the artistic terrain has gained a strategic importance:

Critical artistic practices do not contribute to the counter-hegemonic struggle by deserting the institutional terrain but by engaging with it, with the aim of fostering dissent and creating a multiplicity of agonistic spaces where the dominant consensus is challenged and where new modes of identification are made available (ibid.).

Here it is important to add that artistic practices, contrary to other critical practices, could carry such a challenge by virtue of the aforementioned poetic of indecidability that, besides questioning the present order in its being natural, reminds of the fact that 'reality could always have been otherwise and 'every order is predicated on the exclusion of other possibilities' (ibid.).

In this perspective not only critical practices but also the production of the New could find a fertile territory both inside and outside the institutions. In this sense, Chantal Mouffe (2014) argues that to subvert the neoliberal creativity regime, artistic practices should articulate themselves 'in different modes of interventions in a multiplicity of spaces'. In the context of this research the question regards the role of institutions in the production of the New both at the theoretical level and in their everyday work. More specifically, as it is clear that art institutions need to be reconfigured, the matter regards how far their reconfiguration could result in a fertile context for the production of the New, not only in terms of art works and practices, but also in relation to ways of working.

The imaginative power of art, and more specifically of its institutions, is well explored by Pascal Gielen (2013), who in his analysis of the institutional critique in the art world offers some critical insights on how institutions could act today. Such insights complete and recall the concept of the New as described in Chapter 2, as it will be underlined below.

The premise refers immediately to the role of art institutions in the production of the New: 'Because we can distinguish between the real world and an imagined or fictional "reality", change and innovation are within the realm of human possibilities' (Gielen 2013: 12). According to Gielen, art institutions not only provide the framework to mediate between reality and fiction but also a foundation that may be resistant to market appropriation. In this sense, institutions are in his perspective, 'verticalisation machines'. They not only 'generate an imaginary height but also a historical depth, a foundation to stand on'. Whether this foundation could represent some kind of resistance to co-optation–as opposed to the idea, which emerged in some critiques to creativity derived from performance studies–that sees the ephemerality of performance as a resistant quality in itself, is still an open question. Here it is possible first to notice that such a foundation did not prevent the co-optation of institutional critique itself, which in the first wave, opposed the values of freedom, flexibility and creativity to the rigidity and hierarchy of the institution: 'Paradoxically the ideology of creativity has consistently fought the institution of the museum [...] (neoliberalisation) quickly found ways to profit from the work done by institutional critique by raking over its jargon of 'creativity', 'innovation' and 'flexibility' (ibid., 19-20). When it comes to imagination, this comes as no surprise since, as Gielen himself notices, 'fiction is best combated with fiction' (ibid., 12).

On these premises, the hypothetical third wave of institutional critique should first and foremost reinvent the institution rather than reject it. The reconfiguration should envision an institution able to reaffirm its own values rather than following the logic of the market. In other words, which are not those used by the author, institutions should reconfigure themselves as autonomous subjects of production. This means to sustain an institution able to function according to its own values rather than adopting value regimes specific to other systems. The example provided by Gielen is that of quantitative criteria overtaking qualitative ones in those institutions that used to be based upon them, such as universities, art academies and museums. This provides the illusions of transparency and comparability. Both transparency and comparability are inconsistent with the production of the New.

Transparency is indeed the opposite of that obscurity singled out in Chapter 2 as a fundamental dimension of the recognition of the New, mediated–according to Groys–by the institution of the museum. Moreover, in the contemporary landscape, transparency presents some critical aspects that put it in contrast with the production of the New also in political terms:

By eliminating that which is other or alien, transparency stabilizes and accelerates the system. Such systemic coercion makes transparency society a society of compulsory conformity [...] Compulsory transparency stabilizes the existing system very effectively. In itself, transparency is positive. It does not have the inherent negativity that could radically question the present political-economic system. It is *blind* to what is exterior to the system. It merely confirms and optimizes what already exists, which explains why transparency society and post-politics go hand-in-hand. Only depoliticized space is completely transparent' (Han 2015: 7)

As far as comparability is concerned–besides the fact that the impossibility of establishing a comparison is connected to the recognition of the New–it is, like transparency, reproducing the system by providing the basis for substitutability to unfold, as it already emerged in Chapter 1. When these criteria are applied not only to products but also to institutions, the illusion is produced, according to Gielen, that they 'are related and therefore interchangeable'. These reflections are of fundamental importance in the realm of the arts, since 'social scientists, whether sociologists, economists, etc., can provide us with more or less convincing reasons, and mystifiers can grossly nonplus us, valid literature and art provide us with intelligent and subtle incomprehension' (Toufic 2013).

What is at stake here for art institutions is thus the possibility to contribute to the fulfilment of this function on the one hand and to be a fertile territory for the production of the New on the other. By embracing transparency and comparability as values, art institutions seem to let the market logic define their realm and thus can easily become an engine of the system of absorption, and in doing so, 'they have also reduced the gross global possibilities of imagination' (Gielen 2013: 28).

A second aspect to be taken into account while imagining the hypothetical third wave of institutional critique, as Gielen does, is that of verticality. This is also readable as an argument in favour of the institution to define itself as an independent subject of production, since Gielen talks of verticality in contrast to networks and describes institutions as 'verticalisation machines'. Such verticality, ascribed by Deleuze to true repetition, is used by Gielen to describe the art institution in contrast to networks by virtue of their collective aspect and the foundation they offer in contrast to volatility and ephemerality.[50] Although it would be too superficial to consider networks only as an instrument of the neoliberal logic, it is valuable to recognise that individuals and networks are 'more adaptive than rigid collective structures and that makes them very suitable to the water society' (ibid., 23). What is to be particularly valued here is the idea that the verticality that characterises institutions may make them more resistant to the market logic on the one hand, and on the other may inform a different kind of production of the New based on institutions as collective structures of solidarity, in light of that 'rising up or creating something requires […] a solid cultural ground to stand on' (ibid., 17).

The title Gielen chooses to shelter his reflections is *Institutional Imagination*, and it represents the third meaning ascribable to institutions as autonomous subjects of production. It is this institutional imagination that provides the framework for the aesthetic of indecidability to trigger that doubt between reality and fiction that characterises the poetic of postdramatic theatre. It is in this sense that the institution of the future should first and foremost cultivate its imaginative power against the ideology of realism characterising the neoliberal condition: 'In the free market–which is an institution as well–the exchange between non-fiction and fiction is organised quite differently from the way this is done within the classic art institution. Whereas the latter related fiction to eternal life, or at least to a lasting cultural contribution, the former stresses the importance of surviving in the here and now' (ibid., 26). Here the role of the art institution as described by Groys as the producer of that difference in time and not in form that constitutes the base of the New in art, is enriched by the fact that institutions 'served the purpose of being able to see the world as also always possibly otherwise' (ibid.), in contrast to the postmodern condition where it is not even possible to see the future while drowning in the totalising present.

---

50 Still, Gielen admits that it would be too simplicistic to look at networks as exclusively ideological concepts. Still, he emphasises that networks are increasingly used within the neoliberal agenda.

In this sense, referring to Mark Fisher (2009), Gielen argues that 'by persuading us that there is only one liveable reality possible, neoliberalism slips into the ideology of realism [...] (Where) only that which can be calculated is manageable, and only that which is manageable is realistic and real' (ibid.) Such ideology of realism pairs the aestheticisation of politics and its exemplification in the rhetoric of 'there is no alternative'. What is interesting here is the role of institutions in subverting such an ideology notwithstanding the neoliberal context of production:

> As art institutions increasingly start to behave as corporate organisations, [...] Art still cherishes the idea of that which can always also be otherwise imagined, an idea that it has upheld since the advent of the modern age. Meanwhile this idea has been adapted by advertising, abused by post-Fordism and digested by cognitive capitalism, which is centred on the accumulation of immaterial assets. Art knows however, that this is not about true imagination or an absolute possibility, as it is still breathing this artistic utopia through the cracks and fissures of its institutions. [...] it even, thanks to the existence of the art institution, relatively safeguards the knowledge of the distinction between fiction and non-fiction. And also thanks to the art institution, we are aware that this distinction between reality and imagination is an aspect of all worlds–so also of the world of politics, science and economics (Gielen 2013: 29).

For the sake of completeness, it must be specified that Gielen does not refer to a possibility of keeping neoliberalism or the economy outside the realm of the art institution, and nor does this research. Rather the aim is to underline their roles in relation to it and explore the paths for the reconfiguration of festivals and theatres across the production of the New and the public sphere.

4.3 Open Conclusions on Theory and Practice: Where to Start

All the aspects that have been mentioned in this chapter about the poetics of postdramatic theatre and the role of those institutions, that in the arts focus on production and innovation under the conditions of postmodernity, highlight the centrality of the production of the New within the contemporary landscape. The same could be said of the dimensions of time and space that give form to the productive indecidability within theatre, while within politics their production seems to constitute the basis of power relations and thus the privileged dimensions of resistance to it.

Moreover, artistic practices and the production of the New seem to have a lot to do with resistance, as long as their values, products and flows are not absorbed by the market logic, a dynamic that, exacerbated by capitalism's shift of value into the immaterial, is putting the single and collective subjects that produce the new in an increasingly paradoxical position: how could the production of the New be envisioned in a context of capitalism that has geared towards the exploitation of novelty?

Within the practice of contemporary theatre, the paradoxical position is mirrored by a return of the political dimension of performance, articulated in a range of facts and debates that animate the field, touching on the New but never addressing it thoroughly. Examples in this sense are the debates on performance and labour; the explosion of durational performance; the sudden interest in dance expressed by the visual art system; the return of utopian art; the poetics of spatiality and acceleration; the return of participation practices and the related debate on active spectatorship, and also the rise and fall of *collaboration*. All these could be read in relation to the paradoxical position of the producers of the new in art today, and underline the need to address the question of production, which is an artistic as much as a political question.

In the absence of a real reflection on the New and its production, perhaps the most fruitful attempts in this direction are represented by the theoretical discourse on the dimensions of reality and fiction, that of time and space and that of the collective aspect of production; addressing these topics also means to experiment with them in order to envision new forms of organisations as well as new works of art. A concept that groups all this together is that of 'utopian performatives', elaborated by Jill Dolan (2005), who proposes to envision utopia as 'what if' instead of 'what it should be' so that it would be possible to allow 'performance to experiment with the possibilities of the future in ways that shine back on the present' (Dolan 2005: 13).

It is in this sense that the research conducted here represents a small step towards re-imagining the relationship between the performative and the political, not to do politics at the theatre but to re-enact the category of the possible through performance so that it could also be empowered within politics. The necessary starting point is to engage in the exploration of the New and its production. It is in this sense that this research aims at exploring the dimensions, opportunities, possibilities and downsides of an idea of art production that puts the New and its constitutive aspects at the centre of its discourse.

In this perspective, the notions of New and innovation (or creativity) are put in contrast, not to praise the first and condemn the latter, but rather in the conviction that the conceptual, temporal and value dimension of these two notions must be restated in the context of neoliberal capitalism in order to envision the production of the New, meant as the production of possibility, which can also enrich and enlighten innovation practices.

Putting the production of the New at the centre of the debate may offer interesting insights into the paradoxes that inhabit the world of performance in neoliberal capitalism; it promotes an idea of production that courageously conceives the option of radical change, slipping the paradigms of creation, progress and directionality to revolve around the question 'what if?' rather than focusing on 'what it should be'.

The state of art, in terms of both research and practice, provides fascinating possible paths to follow in order to navigate the complex net described in these first chapters. Still, it calls for an empirical approach based on a productive dialogue with individual and collective subjects in the field, to be put in place in order to complete the research by answering some questions and, hopefully, opening up new ones.

5. Empirical Research on the New: Methodology

The literature review contained in the previous chapters highlighted that the New is a very complex concept, of which many of the aspects it entails could benefit from empirical investigation in the realm of the arts. The empirical ground chosen for this investigation is the field of contemporary theatre, performance and dance, here referred to as postdramatic theatre. The focus of this chapter is on the approach and the methods, which were selected in order to frame and interpret the diverse perspectives composing the illustration of the field provided in the following chapters.

Postdramatic theatre has never been analysed thoroughly under the perspective proposed in this work. In particular, a theorisation of the concept of the New is completely missing and, at the same time, the discussion on related topics is considered relevant and urgent: the field is characterised by different perspectives that call for efforts of analysis and organisation. Moreover artists, curators and theoreticians express insistently the necessity to think on how to act at the collective level given the current conditions of theatre production. In order to take these aspects into consideration, the exploration of the field was based on combining different approaches and methods within qualitative research.

The description of the methods adopted is introduced by a brief summary of the objectives, according to which the research questions were formulated in order to balance theoretical knowledge and perspectives coming from the field. This called for an abductive approach able to combine the logic of deduction with the openness of induction, which is mirrored in the structure of the in-depth interviews. The latter were designed to be conducted with artists, curators and theoreticians grouped according to the principle of theoretical sampling. After this brief description of data collection and sampling, the focus shifts to the analysis, conducted with the help of the software MaxQDA. As explained below, the first two phases of the analysis were aimed at organising the perspectives coming from the field through different coding cycles by mixing coding techniques. The third phase of the analysis collected the most relevant aspects and uses the potentiality of the abductive approach to outline possible answers on what to do next in the field.

5.1 Balancing Theory and Empirical research

At a more abstract level, the objective of the present research is to explore the production of the New in the contemporary performing arts under the conditions of neoliberal capitalism. The explicit focus on the present time called for a qualitative approach that is able, first and foremost, to provide a description of the current circumstances and to collect multiple perspectives on the matter, which in light of its complexity, cannot be tackled in its totality. Still, a description of the current situation represents just the point of departure from which to formulate sensible research questions to address a more concrete objective: linking together the concept of the New and that of production in order to address urgent questions in the field of experimental theatre, and outline possible actions with concrete reference to its practices. In order to address the complexities entailed in this general objective, it is reasonable to choose a qualitative research design, which aims at avoiding simplifications that could have reduced the complexity inherent to the matter, allowing a parallel proceeding between theoretical inputs and empirical findings. The choice of qualitative methods is also driven by the fact that a conspicuous theoretical delimitation was necessary in order to address the research questions, and that the amount of information regarding the empirical area of investigation is limited.

Constituting no exception to other qualitative analyses, the present research aims at striking a sensible balance between theoretical inputs and *a priori* knowledge on the one hand, and the openness required to dealing with the field on the other. Although qualitative research premises acknowledge that a thoroughly genuine reconstruction is not attainable, it is possible to engage in qualitative methods valorising such approximate reconstruction in connection with the categories developed though *a priori* knowledge and literature research. Indeed, combining the two allows the inclusion and control of theoretical references, while also bringing to the surface the genuine meanings and categories offered by field research.

In fact, the research design implemented here merges different methods of qualitative analysis, combining the verification of the aspects highlighted within the theoretical framework with an open approach to the field. As a premise, it should be clarified that the choice of more open methods–in this case the in-depth interviews–is not believed to guarantee the openness in terms of contents. Rather, it is justified by the need to allow the emergence of the dimensions, which could not be anticipated on a purely theoretical ground; in the awareness that the interpretation of the data coming from the field is not only dependent on previous knowledge but the combination of the two, could indeed widen knowledge itself.

In light of this, research questions were developed and distinguished according to the kind and scope of the knowledge already available in the sector of postdramatic theatre. It is in this sense that the research objectives differ not only in content but also in purpose: some unfold in terms of description of the current situation of postdramatic theatre, whereas others are pursued to outline the relevant dimension that can serve as grounds to develop a theory of producing the New in theatre. Given the manifold objectives of the research, the design chosen is the one of comparative analysis with an explicit focus on the present, defined in the field of qualitative methods as 'snapshots'. In contrast to longitudinal studies, snapshots collect through interviews the 'different manifestations of the expertise that exists in a particular field at the time of the research' (Flick 2004: 148). This collection is then used as a basis for comparative analysis so that the single experiences and visions in respect to the production of the New could be compared and contrasted with each other, producing a general overview and allowing for the appreciation of single cases.

In this context, the abductive approach–formulated by Peirce in the late 50s (Levin-Rozalis 2008; Reichertz 2004)–represents a valid framework for data collection and analysis. Abduction is generally described within qualitative research as a means of inference as it is based on logical inference and, at the same time, allows for more profound insights to help widen knowledge (Reichertz 2004). Abductive reasoning proceeds by using theory to interpret the data and the data to build the theory, as it 'derives categories that can form the basis of an understanding of the problem at hand' (Blaikie 2003). The mixture of these characteristics is deeply valuable in the context of this research and consistent with considering theory-based material just as the empirical one. In the particular case of this work, it allowed moving 'back and forth between deduction and induction' (Morgan 2007: 71), and thus to analyse properly the aspects derived from theory as well as those emerging from the field, fulfilling the research objectives in terms of description and interpretation of the current state of the field.

Furthermore, the explicit role assigned to the researcher's interpretation served the difficult goals of identifying the relevant dimensions for future theory formulation and suggesting specific lines of action for the world of postdramatic theatre. Abduction was indeed conceptualised to offer an approach to the interpretation of data leading to the assembling and discovery those combinations of features to which there is no appropriate explanation or rule (Reichertz 2004). As such, it appeared to be the best approach in order to engage with the research objectives aiming at providing an interpretation key to define the ground for future theory development within the fields of contemporary theatre, dance and performance.

5.2 Objectives and Research Questions

The empirical research was designed consistently with the different objectives around specific questions, to be answered in different phases of data analysis. The first objective of the present research is to explore the possibilities of a reconceptualisation of the New so that it could be possible to cast a different light on the paradoxes that inhabit production in the arts on the one hand and, on the other, to explore its possibility outside the framework of innovation and creativity. Such an objective was pursued in the theoretical framework through a multidisciplinary approach, directed at highlighting that the notion of the new is not univocal and that the different, sometimes contrasting, aspects that it presents call for its reconceptualisation. On this basis, this first objective was tackled in the empirical analysis in terms of understanding what the New means to people working in the sector of experimental contemporary theatre.

The empirical investigations of these aspects were not aimed at the quantification and standardisation of ways of conceiving the New, nor the practices of its production; consequently the matter was not reformulated in terms of hypotheses to test.

This does not mean that the presence of theoretical considerations is negated. Rather it is embraced so as to verify their relevance for the actors involved. Still, the openness advocated by the qualitative approach is considered and valued equally so that the specific meanings of the concept of the New could be brought to the fore. Consequently, the research questions were defined in respect of this first objective as follows:

- Is the idea of the new important and present in the field of contemporary theatre?
- How can the New be defined in the field?
- How is a new work recognised as such? What is the reaction in front of it?

An open approach was chosen to test the relevance of the topic for the interviewees, while an explicit reference to theory was kept in order to investigate the definition of the New. More precisely, the relevant theoretical categories were operationalised to trace clear borders between the new and the concepts close to it. Moreover, practical examples of the experience of the New in terms of recognition were collected to test on the one hand the consistency between what was conceptualised and what was experienced in practice and, on the other to let potentially new aspects emerge directly from the field. A clearer idea of this could be evinced by looking at the interview guidelines, better explained in the next paragraph and included completely in Appendix I.

A very similar approach was followed in order to meet the second objective of this research: understanding the dynamics related to the New, its value and its production in postdramatic theatre, with reference to the debate on neoliberal capitalism. Within the theoretical framework this objective was pursued starting from the individuation of the most controversial aspects connected to the concept of New within the arts during the avant-garde period and tracing their conceptual reformulation up to the present day. In particular, the problems connected to the very possibility of the New were analysed in relation to the formation of paradigms. They constitute, together with the compulsoriness of creativity, two of the major sources of the paradoxical position of art production within neoliberal capitalism.

In the context of the empirical analysis, this objective was tackled with a very open approach to the field, trying to set aside the theoretical inputs in order to obtain an understanding of the values that drive the actors and their production practices, in order to appraise how far they are connected to the concept of New. Consequently, the research questions were defined in respect to this second aim to let the personal values of the respondents emerge together in consistency with their everyday practices:

- What are the ethical and aesthetical concerns that animate actors in the realm of postdramatic theatre?
- Could they be traced back to the concept of New or to those of innovation and creativity?
- What are the opinions and feelings of respondents as far as the creativity regime is concerned?
- What are the values involved in the production of the New?
- Under what conditions would the actors stop doing what they do?

The third objective of this research was tackled with a completely different approach because of its very different nature: exploring the concept of production of the New that emerged by connecting theoretical and empirical material within the realm of postdramatic theatre and suggesting lines of action specific for the same field.

Whereas the first two objectives focus on the recognition and production of the New and, accordingly to the available amount of prior knowledge, were tackled in order to provide a description of such dynamics in the field, the third objective is tackled with the spirit of identifying inductively the dimensions that could constitute the ground to develop a theory in further research. More precisely, the information that emerged in connection with the first two objectives was used to define the research questions in order to address the third one. It is in this sense that the hypotheses were developed not so much in order to be tested, but as operational tools in order for the presence of theory and prior knowledge to be embraced while also verifying an approach as open as possible to the meanings and practices coming from the field.

In this sense, research questions were formulated in two phases, first to single out the most important dimensions, and then to understand how they could be interrelated once the data were collected so that the relevant connection could be interpreted and taken into consideration for possible theoretical developments.

First some research questions were formulated in order to understand the relationship between the actors and their environment, and partially also to assess the presence of specific opinions or biases that inform actors' attitudes towards the matter in question in order to give a concrete form to the concepts addressed:

- Is there a debate on the new in the everyday context of production of postdramatic theatre?
- What are the perceptions of the actors regarding the roles and conventions present in the sector?

Successively, other questions were formulated with the aim of understanding how these dynamics are perceived, embraced and contrasted in the system of postdramatic theatre:[51]

- What is the actors' overall perception of the system? How does this inform the practice of the respondents?
- What are the dimensions relevant for the production of the New?
- What comes next?

A provisional exploration of the possible actions and counteractions specific to the theatre system within neoliberal capitalism was carried out at the theoretical level, especially as regards time, space and institutions (see Chapter 4). These theoretical tools were developed as object-related concepts to narrow down the scope of the analysis. However, in the awareness of the very many possibilities that could emerge, the above-mentioned aspects were addressed in the interviews only when directly mentioned by respondents in order to privilege the most meaningful ones. More precisely, the research questions related to this objective were formulated in order to exploit the potential offered from the abductive approach so that theoretical propositions and field observations could not only be balanced and intertwined, but also to enrich each other, to explore future dimensions of action and, in the specific case of this research, the relevant categories for imagining the production of the New in the context of performance within the conditions of neoliberal capitalism.

5.3 Sampling and Data Collection

Given the objectives of the present research and, in particular, the one of finding an order fitting to the matter in question that could also suggest ways

---

51 The word 'system' does not refer here to the concept by Niklas Luhmann; it is used by respondents themselves and thus used as a common reference to the sector.

to act in the present rather than offering a generalisation of results, the method chosen to collect data is the in-depth interview. Once acknowledged that the focus regards theoretical rather than numerical generalisability of the results obtained, the sampling process privileged a small number of individuals with different perspectives and occupations so that a larger theoretical and praxis-based scope could be covered.[52] The inclusion of diverse individuals in the sample, together with the triangulation of diverse methods of analysis, provides fertile territory for possible theoretical generalisation.

Among the diverse possibilities of sampling methods, the respondents were selected according to the principles of theoretical sampling, 'whereby the analyst decides on analytic grounds what data to collect and where to find them' (Strauss 1987: 38). More precisely, the temptation of considering all possible groups and dimensions that could be abstractly connected with a topic as wide as the New and its production must be contained. The theoretical review served this purpose in three different ways. First, it highlighted that the most interesting level to conduct a comparative analysis was the one of the individuals. Second, it provided initial information for the sampling, suggesting the most interesting actors taking part in the phenomenon under analysis. Finally, it underlined the gap between the absence of formal theoretical reflections on the New, and the high informal presence of the topic, embodied in the artworks and public discourse within the field. Out of these reasons, the methodological suggestions provided by grounded theory–whose theoretical sampling is based on openness and flexibility not only with regards to the cases selected but also in respect of the segments chosen to carry on the analysis (ibid., 25-38)–were incorporated in the research design.

Consistently with this, sampling was planned through a 'loose design' (Miles and Huberman 1994 in Flick 2004) that privileged the variety of theoretical approaches and poetic practices of respondents rather than the very strict criteria of selection. This implied that the sampling process lasted until the moment in which the amount and variability of information collected was large enough to cover all the relevant aspects of the research, when further conversations and interviews seemed not to bring any new perspectives to the data set. The saturation level was identified during data collection through coding and memos.

In contrast to other sampling techniques, it allowed a critical appraisal of the data set during its very construction that turned out to be essential in the later phases of research. Theoretical sampling allowed data to be not only collected in relation to the theoretical framework, but also to be shaped since

---

52 Aiming at a numerical generalisation would questionably make sense within this work. This does not mean that some generally applicable conclusions could be taken at the theoretical level.

the beginning by the inputs coming from the field: avoiding a too strict sampling approach provided in this sense the possibility to collect data abductively in the second phase of the research.

The loose design and openness of the sampling process was nevertheless guided by some precise criteria, as it would have equally made no sense to use a random sample. In particular, the prominence of individuals was taken into account, privileging those who–by virtue of their work or their position– could offer a clear vision and influence the discourse in the field. The variety of visions and theoretical approaches of interviewees was one of the most important criteria to guide the sampling process, given the relevance of this dimension in terms of theoretical generalisability. Yet, the possibility to cover really comprehensively the possible visions on the New was limited by the need to portray and analyse the topic within a specific scene, which, although featuring very different perspectives, is still characterised by being leftist and generally contra the system, both in the sense of being anti-capitalism and very critical towards the status quo of contemporary theatre production. This comes as no surprise given the explicit critical endeavour entailed in these artists' practices connected with their high level of experimentation. Still, within this general characteristic, it was possible to include in the sampling different views ranging from classical Marxism to a more postmodern approach.

The diversity of occupations was considered equally important in order to include the main actors of the field who take part in production. The sampling aimed at including artists, curators and theoreticians, which appeared as the most interesting groups to be investigated in the light of the theoretical framework. As a matter of fact, artists could not have been excluded; curators usually work inside institutions and are thus also able to keep that perspective; and theoreticians, besides having a very clear vision and taking part in artistic research processes, are highly influential on the discourse produced in the field. Other criteria were articulated in order to narrow down the temporal and geographical scope of the analysis. Given the fact that the field is very small and highly interconnected, especially within Europe, the sampling focused on this region despite that all interviewees have experience of the sector worldwide, which given the size of the market is not something uncommon.

Data collection was concentrated in international festivals, which facilitated the interview process because respondents were already engaged in theoretical discussion. Moreover, the high attendance and diversity of professionals taking part in these events allowed the spontaneous inclusion of particularly interesting perspectives in the analysis.

The sampling process resulted in a composite group of artists, curators and theoreticians working in the world of contemporary theatre or at its borders. Interestingly, most of the interviewees belong to more than one of these categories, with productive effects on the analysis. The saturation level was reached with seven interviews, of which the content is widely reported and analysed in the following chapters. On the other hand, the biographical information of respondents–being relatively important to the objectives of the research–is not here fully described and the most important details are collected schematically in Appendix II.

The design of the interviews and the time dedicated to them by respondents were fundamental to reach such a large and varied amount of data in such a limited number of cases. Consistently with the objectives of the research, interviews were designed in order to put forward an open kind of prior understanding without rejecting explicit pre-assumptions developed from theory and field observation. This was done through designing semi-structured interviews, where the questions and their order were formulated in advance but could be easily changed to follow the meaningful aspects underlined by respondents. Still, all interviews covered the main points to enable comparison in the phase of data analysis. In this spirit, the scope of themes tackled was constructed according to the results of theoretical research in order to foster interviewees' questioning and building of counter-arguments that could be significant in order to answer the research question. With respect to those aspects characterised by scarce prior knowledge, interviewees were encouraged to provide their point of view through the formulation of very general questions.

As far as the order of questions is concerned, the interviews were organised in three interrelated parts according to the objectives of the research. Part 1 was developed in relation to the first objective of research and focused on the concepts of the New and of innovation, both in terms of recognition and production. Given the amount of information available, the recognition of the New was tackled with direct reference to the significant theoretical inputs. Still, a space for other insights was created through the collection of experiences from interviewees' lives, which could also serve as a way of assessing the consistency between the description of the concept and its actual experience. Tackling the concept of the New in terms of recognition allowed the partial exploration of its production, encouraged by some initial broad-spectrum questions. Part 2 aimed at framing the answers related to Part 1 in the wider vision of interviewees in order to enrich and clarify their meaning. Thus, it investigated the ethical values and the aesthetic horizon to which interviewees refer at the present time, with a very open approach. The main concerns of respondents were explored at the general level first and then, according to the answers, in connection with the concept of the New. The dimension of production was explored thoroughly within the context where theatre production takes place: questions were designed not to address the concept directly, but rather to investigate how respondents make sense of their work and thus to let the meaning and value of production emerge in the field. Finally, Part 3 was structured in order to transfer all the reflections made by interviewees to the concrete level of the system of postdramatic theatre. Here, respondents were questioned in order to pursue the third objective of this research that is twofold: assess the relevance of the central theoretical aspects in practice and explore, through abduction, what concrete lines of action could be undertaken in the light of them. The interview's guideline was built to support the process by which the relevant theoretical dimensions can be partially set aside to seek new and more significant ones at the level of practice.

Initial questions explored the importance and relevance of the topic within the sector and, on the basis of the answers provided, interviews proceeded to investigate how the system of postdramatic theatre is perceived in terms of roles and rules, privileging the direct experiences of work and life within it. These questions served the purpose of highlighting contradictions and unexpected associations that triggered, in the second phase of the analysis, the formulation of a rule appropriate to explain how the different critical aspects relate to each other, and suggest possible lines of action to be undertaken in the very sector that generated them.

5.4 Data Analysis

The data analysis was organised in three phases, with each phase including a preliminary work of data preparation and a proper coding cycle of interview transcripts. As already mentioned, the particular context of this research called for an approach that was able to balance theoretical and empirical information, which implied the combination of different coding techniques at the level of analysis. Such an analysis based on these combinations–namely eclectic coding–is not particularly odd in qualitative analysis, in which 'there are many occasions where qualitative data can be appropriately coded using a repertoire of methods simultaneously [...] The methods should not be random but purposeful to serve the needs of the study and its data analysis' (Saldana 2012: 188).

Using the software MaxQDA, different techniques of coding were triangulated in order to produce a singular method appropriate to the specific analysis, privileging either the inputs of theory (analytical coding) or those coming from the field (theoretical coding). The combination of these techniques made the analysis more complex and required its organisation in the above-mentioned phases, which are summarised schematically in Appendix III. Thanks to this division, the corpus of data could be analysed according to the different principles, which are hardly applicable in a contextual way. The three phases of the analysis are mirrored in the account of the empirical findings contained in the following chapters: it proceeds from the descriptions of results–focusing on how they confirm, enlarge or contradict the theories used–up to the reformulation of the most relevant results into categories of analysis that were then used as material for further reasoning and drawing conclusions.

It must be specified that the coding methods used, notwithstanding the very different premises and ways of proceeding, share some important aspects. For instance, they are based on the interchange between the already available theoretical inputs and what emerges from the data from the very beginning of their collection. In theoretical coding the collection of data, the analysis and the formulation of theory, which results from the previous stages, are closely interrelated and also happen contemporarily up to a certain extent. In analytical coding, the categories at the base of the analysis are also set up in response to the material, and this responsive research-question-driven construction of categories starts at the beginning of the data collection so that theoretical assumptions could also be refined or even excluded during the fieldwork.

The first phase of analysis began actually during data collection, in order to start a progressive reorganisation of data aimed at answering research questions. In this phase the material was read repeatedly and some coding memos were written combining the tools of analytical coding (Schmidt 2004) with those of theoretical coding (Böhm 2004). More precisely, the very open approach suggested by theoretical coding in the preparation phase was mitigated by the analytical inputs that guided the attention to all those aspects that can be related, even though broadly, to the research question. In this phase, segments related to the theory were organised to allow for multiple coding, and the focus was kept on single interviews, leaving the comparison to a later stage. Moreover, notes on spontaneous connections made by respondents were taken, in order to better manage the answers, which in semi-structured interviews could be found independently from the position of the related question, and also to record some unexpected associations to be used in the later phases of research. These operations were conducted in preparation for the first cycle of coding, which was conducted through the mixture of techniques that could offer the best insight into the data.

With respect to the aspects informed by prior theoretical knowledge, the single codes were assembled into analytical categories built thematically around the relevant theoretical dimensions. These categories were corrected and enriched with the information provided by the fieldwork that could not be individuated only by means of theoretical research. For instance, the aspect of obscurity–described in the literature only in relation to the recognition of the New–gained a predominant meaning in connection to production. Next to this, a typical tool of theoretical coding, in-vivo codes, was used for those concepts appearing exclusively through empirical analysis.[53] Coding in-vivo turned out to be a particularly profitable technique at successive stages of the analysis since, by taking the expressions directly from the field, it provides a particularly meaningful description of relevant aspects. This is the case of the code 'new as entirely something', which then appeared as pivotal in the overall analysis. The same technique was applied to particularly valuable descriptions of personal experience regarding the New, well exemplified by the in-vivo code 'overwhelming', which was found in all cases. Although in-vivo codes are usually operated within open coding, in the case of this research they were used to capture significant segments within a rather analytical approach.[54] At this stage, the categories and their relative sub-codes were assembled into a coding index, endowed with a precise description of their content that was then imported into a software for qualitative analysis (MaxQDA). The software has been used during the whole analysis as a tool to facilitate the intellectual effort by allowing the contextual consideration of larger amounts of data rather than as a analysis tool proper.

The first cycle of coding, which aimed to reduce the data to the most relevant segments so that they could also be compared across the different cases, was completed by classifying materials according to the categories previously defined. The comparative analysis was conducted on a separate MaxQDA file in which every segment was given exclusively one code, and in the case of overlapping, the most dominant aspect was chosen as a code. Still, the initial file, containing multiple codes, was kept in order not to miss important relationships to be explored in the following phases of the analysis. The results of the preparation phase and the first cycle of coding were already very satisfactory and marked the following phases. Since a thorough explanation follows in the next chapters, here only some examples are reported that clarify the methodological process and enlighten the premises with which the second phase of the analysis was undertaken.

First, the presence and relevance of unexpected dimensions was brought to the fore and properly registered. For instance, the category 'theory reference' had to be created because of the surprising number of quotations and theoretical allusions provided by respondents. The number of theory references retrieved from the interviews was so conspicuous that a category of analysis was created. Although reference to theory was expected in the sample chosen, its importance was underestimated and thus must be underlined. References range from medieval to contemporary philosophy and include artists' writings as well as literature. Interestingly, the majority of

---

53 In-vivo codes are words or expressions taken directly from the data, which by virtue of their precision or meaning are used as codes and thus can also be applied to other segments in the data set. (Strauss 1987, Böhm 2004, Saldana 2012).

54 Open coding is the first phase of theoretical coding within grounded theory. (Strauss 1987, Böhm, 2004, Saldana 2012).

these references co-occur with the dimensions of production and value while they are not so present as regards the recognition of the New. It seems that interviewees felt the need to fill with theory a space designed for a focus on a practice.

Second, it was possible to reassess the relevance of theoretical aspects, as some of them–once placed in the fieldwork–turned out to have been underestimated (e.g. the dimension 'individual/collective') while others overestimated (e.g. 'representation', 'substitution'). Some fundamental aspects of the theory–such as the abstract concepts of value and production–gained a more concrete relevance. Furthermore, the connection between different dimensions could be reworked in a more meaningful direction for the respondents. Finally, this phase of analysis underlined the internal inconsistencies within single cases and thus suggested directions for further investigation.

The second phase of the analysis began with reconsidering results and redefining categories in order to prepare the transition to the second cycle of coding and thus to select the best method for it. More precisely, this phase focused on conveying the richness of results produced by eclectic coding into a more unified scheme so as to re-organise and re-assemble the data to better focus the direction of research. The technique of code mapping served this purpose and, at the same time, facilitated comparison between the cases. Code mapping consists of different iterations of the codes so as to give 'credibility, trustworthiness and organization to the observation and analysis' by first listing the codes, then analysing the relationships between them, successively building categories and finally abstracting these categories to the level of concepts (Saldana 2012: 188). This transitional phase was deeply intertwined with the second cycle of coding, which exactly aimed to differentiate the codes present in the data and categorise them through the technique of axial coding, which is a process very similar to that of code mapping. Both techniques can be used to organise concepts into categories on the basis of the relationships between them. Whereas code mapping provides an overview of all codes and relationships between them, axial coding focuses on the relationships around a single concept. Within grounded theory, axial coding could be seen as the operation following open coding, although a very precise separation does not mirror the practice of analysis (Böhm 2004). Strauss describes axial coding as 'an essential aspect of open coding. It consists of intense analysis done around a category at the time [...] By doing this, the analyst begins to build up a dense texture of relationships around the "axis" of the category being focused upon' (Strauss 1987: 32-64).

This technique of categorisation primarily regards aspects found exclusively through fieldwork and thus is very different from the theory-based one used in the first cycle of coding. Axial coding results in the construction of axial categories. Such categories are not only thematically constructed but also contain information about the phenomenon, such as the temporal and spatial relationship it has with different aspects as well as other conditions under which the phenomenon occurs (Böhm 2004). In the case of this research, it was sensible to formulate axial categories around concepts rather than phenomena, which increased the complexity but provided a fertile terrain for the last phase of analysis.

Focusing on concepts and relationships among them, it was possible to get a better understanding of the dynamics at work in the field. For instance, some contradictions rendered as central by the first cycle of coding (e.g. 'creation' as opposed to 'transformation') turned out to be only moderately important once connected to the category (in this case 'directionality and purpose'). Moreover, it was also possible to find links that could not appear in the first cycle of coding: for example, the two strategies of production, self-betrayal and suspension, could be re-considered as complementary up to a certain extent once related to the axial category 'individual/collective'. Another instance is represented by the dimensions of space and time, of which different sub-codes could be restructured according to other categories such as 'conflict' and 'autonomy' that appeared as very relevant, and also re-organised according to the diverse theoretical approaches of respondents. Furthermore, some new categories were built in order to collect into one abstract concept the part of the data to which there was no prior theoretical knowledge. This is the case of very important axial categories, such as 'conflict', 'non-organisation', 'coexistence of differences', 'responsibility'. This is why this phase of the analysis was highly connected with the second and third objectives of this research: the axial categories produced not only highlighted the central aspects of the New and its production, but also placed them in a network of relationships able to convey information on the political and cultural environment where these dynamics take place. The most important outcome of this process was the identification of all relevant dimensions at the core of the New and its production, including the significant data coming from the field, which could be categorised and made more abstract, becoming thus suitable for the third and final phase of analysis.

In the third phase a last cycle of coding was carried out: segments belonging to axial categories were arranged following the technique of selective coding, which postulate a very active role for 'the researcher as author' (Böhm 2004), and it is thus perfectly suited to the abductive approach chosen for the last objective of the research. More precisely, within a grounded theory context, selective coding 'pertains to coding systematically and concertedly for the core category. The other codes become subservient to the key code under focus [...] the analyst delimits coding to only those codes that related to core codes in sufficiently significant ways' (Strauss 1987: 33). In other words, selective coding is aimed at singling out the core-category able to explain the phenomenon under investigation. This core-category, according to Böhm (2004), should be already present in the research question and could either be included in one of the axial categories or represented by a concept to which more than one axial category relates. In the specific case of this research, selective coding was aimed at identifying a concept able to provide an interpretation key for the dynamics connected to the New within neoliberal capitalism, rather than an explanation of the phenomenon. The concept of production–in its conceptual and concrete meaning–appeared to be the most suited for this purpose in the third phase of analysis. Consistently to methodological suggestions, it was indeed already present in the formulation of the research questions and its central position could be assumed but not really demonstrated exclusively within theoretical research.

Axial coding was indispensable for the emergence of Production, both as a core concept and as a concrete practice. It also allowed capturing it in all its essential aspects by virtue of the number and quality of relationships it presented, with all the axial categories. Selective coding permitted a better exploration of such relationships and thus to set the results of the analysis into the specific context of postdramatic theatre. On this basis, it was possible to investigate abductively the possible answers to the question 'what to do next?' and at the same time, to provide an interpretation able to explain the most relevant dynamics in the sector.

Consequently, while the abductive approach was embraced in the whole research process, it is possible to say that it was used particularly in the last phase of analysis, when the most meaningful aspects were already available. This presented interesting and unexpected interrelations that could not be explained unless by constructing a specific rule, a situation that represents the initial condition for the abductive approach to be fully applied.

In this respect, results–contained in Chapter 7–are remarkable and exciting. They suggest reinterpreting the unexpected connections that emerged in the data on the basis of the concept 'production of possibility' or more generally 'production of production'. This first outcome was obtained by reconsidering abductively all pivotal categories, of which the relationships provided the terrain to re-conceptualise production as 'production of production'. Here, the abductive approach provided the theoretical ground for basing such hermeneutical efforts not only on logical rules but also on associations and intuitions. This approach helps in building an interpretation based on an intellectual process grounded in logical rules up to a certain extent and preserves the space for unexpected connections or intuitions to be explored. In this way, it guides the research process towards the formulation of a new rule that emerges from and at the same time describes the cases in question (Reichertz 2004).

Successively, this concept or rule could be applied once again to the very same categories in order to single out concrete propositions of action that are consistent with it. These proposals represent the second important result of abduction: they can be concretely put into practice in the realm of postdramatic theatre and are particularly meaningful for this field. In this respect, different reflections on how to put the production of possibility in place are imagined on different levels that range from artists' strategies aiming to shift the borders of the possible, to collective operations aiming to dis-organise the whole system, starting from the very same categories rendered as central.

It must be specified that, consistently with the premises of abduction, the suggested interpretation rule is neither complete nor fixed: it is undertaken provisionally, to reconstruct the data so that they could be used in the practice of postdramatic theatre. The impossibility to formulate the 'production of possibility' as a general law presents different advantages. For instance, the combination of categories emerging from this analysis is valid to suggest future actions in close relation to the current situation and its perception in the field, rather than offering a rational reconstruction to inform such actions.

At the same time, the continuous interchange between the abstract rule (production of possibilities) and its material manifestations ('problem-creating', 'work in regress') provided the opportunity to confront the theoretical propositions with empirical data. On the one hand, this comparison highlights the limits of the research by acknowledging the specificity of socio-cultural conditions. On the other, it allowed to reach a certain degree of theoretical generalisability through the formulation of the rule "production of production" that, although specific and provisional, comprehends an array of interrelated theoretical tools that could be easily applied or at least investigated in other realms. In this sense, it offers the space to imagine opportunities for further research on the New between performance and politics and the potential to develop a theory of producing the New in the future.

6. The Concept of the New in the Theatre of the Present

This chapter focuses on the main findings of the empirical research conducted in the field of postdramatic theatre. The results are presented in connection to the theoretical framework built in the previous chapters and a lot of space is dedicated to perspectives coming from the field.

First, the relevance of the topic in the field is assessed and described following the account provided by the interviewees. Second, the dimensions of the recognition of the New specific to the field are presented, highlighting their relationship to the theoretical framework and especially the aspects in which theory was enriched. On this basis, the most interesting aspects of the production of the New and the way it is envisioned in the field are listed and analysed. Finally, the reflections of respondents on the value of its production are examined in relation to the perception of the role of art today.

In order to give a precise account of the field of postdramatic theatre, the empirical findings are presented with the aid of interview extracts, which are reported here exclusively with the initials of the interviewee. Further information, such as personal and professional details, is available in Appendix II.

6.1 The Concept of the New in Practice

Before entering the core of the analysis, it is important to underline that the topic of the new emerged as central and urgent in the fieldwork, consistently with what is expected in light of the theoretical framework presented in the first chapters of this work.

All interviewees either recognise the importance of engaging with the concept at the aesthetic, political and personal level or refuse the notion expressly in order to make a political statement. The concept of the new that emerges from the interviews is always controversial; it entails at once positive and negative aspects and results in a problematic notion. Interestingly, all interviewees spontaneously connect the concept of new to their 'occupation in life': the paradoxical position characterising the production of the New in the present appears immediately and strongly in the field, showing that the new is indeed present as a topic, and that it has become especially urgent nowadays. The paradoxes connected to it are expressed more or less consciously not only by artists but also by theoreticians, curators and programmers:

I reflect on the notion of the new every day, all the time, the new is one of the few things I think a lot about ... considering what I've taken to do as a job, I think of it rather as occupation in life [...] I also think that the new is the only thing I can be concerned with (MS).

It is something for sure I've thought about; I've also used but I think it's quite perverse actually to use it [...] I do think about it, I tend actually to fight against it also because in a way, I think in the performing arts world we want to have too much new in a way (MG).

These extracts are taken as example of the two extremes that highlight the urgency of the topic at the personal level, where no indifference was recorded. All negative opinions (MG, GP, ML) relate to the compulsoriness and the commercial use of the concept as label. This aspect also represents the main trigger of interviewees' reflections on the topic in the past:

Something I noticed recently is the use of the term 'turn' that has a lot to do with the new... "the affective turn"; "the curatorial turn"[...] In this sense I thought about it suspiciously because it is always used as label. I was disturbed by the overuse of the word 'turn' because it ascribes to the new the idea of the turn at the expense of the one of a complete re-foundation. It gives to the new a referentiality, which does not belong to it (GP).

With regard to the presence of the topic in the sector of postdramatic theatre, all interviewees acknowledge a lack of a serious discussion on the New that most of the time is tackled exclusively in terms of creative policy or used as a label. Innovation and creativity are so much present in the field that triggered a refusal to discuss the new for some interviewees. At the same time, its reconceptualisation is felt as so important at a personal level that some wish to re-establish a more collective discourse on it, since the debate 'was partially addressed although lately this was done also in connection with a misunderstanding on the role of the artist' (DBG).

Interviewees who give a chance to the New outside of the frame of innovation notice that 'there is a "cloud" of thought on the new that is appearing now as an atmosphere inside which some places and festivals are conceived and programmed; with reference to which some artists think about their work...but there is not yet–neither in artistic production nor in its operational modalities–an effectiveness that creates something evident with which one must come to terms with' (SB).

In the perspective of these interviewees, the search for the New is accepted and should not be condemned as such. Rather it becomes a matter of encouraging the discourse around it by taking individual and collective responsibility for the way art production is organised–as will be deepened later in this chapter–and the narrative that is built around it:

I think that the new is always something calling us. We don't need to limit the new in itself, we should rather question the direction of this new...it would be reductive to see it exclusively as a step forward (DBG).

Notwithstanding the fact that the matter is problematic, every interviewee acknowledged a strategic importance in it, which may be best summed up by this extract: 'I think it is fundamental that we insist on it... that we insist on, that we, at least, that we don't stop thinking about it' (MS).

This research was initially motivated by a similar concern; insisting on the New means first to get a thorough understanding of its meaning, no matter how controversial. In this paragraph the results obtained are presented in relation to the first objective of this research: exploring the possibility of the reconceptualisation of the New, starting from its meaning, circumscribing it to the field chosen for the analysis.

The extracts reported above already contain important aspects of the New, which emerged through conversations entailing both practical examples taken out of interviewees' lives and interaction with the arts as well as an abstract reasoning on what the New could be and how we could recognise it. These are presented here according to the main categories that emerged in the data analysis. Generally speaking, it is possible to state that the perspectives of the interviewees are consistent with the theoretical framework presented and that they delimit some borders while exceeding others: theoretical concepts and accounts from their practices together constitute the building blocks of the New within postdramatic theatre and interweave possible paths for its production.

6.1.1 The Difference of the New

First and foremost there emerges a need for a clearer distinction between what is New and what is innovative or creative. Such a distinction is indeed also fundamental in political terms: '...this word can take you in two directions. In a very positive way and in a very conservative religious way, so in this sense I'm saying problematic' (RM). The concept of the New is indeed problematic and all interviewees express the need of a clearer definition:

If I think about the new within the performing arts, I think about it in this double facet...not as innovation, meaning not as transformational process (SB).

We usually consider it as alternative to what exists but this perspective is strictly temporal...The new, in a conceptual perspective could be opposite to the complete (DBG).

Innovation as I conceive it, has a different temporal dimension... it's the logic of the project, innovation first of all, innovates something that already exists, in other words triggers change with reference to a given status... contrary to the category of new, innovation is a proposal (GP).

These attempts at giving an account of the New share the tendency to define it in relation to something that it is not and contain at the same time the seeds to formulate a working definition of the concept around the ideas of transformation, change and completeness; such words in the analysis are highly related to the category of difference.

The concept of difference and the related possibility or impossibility of establishing a relationship is confirmed by the interviews as main categories in terms of recognition of the New:

There are two different kinds of new if we speak abstractly: on one side there is the new that is dependent on, or is traceable...or that you can find... and then there is another kind of new, which is the one that interests me more: the new to which there are no relations, to which there are no grounds, to which there is no backdrop (MS).

The extract above exemplifies the level of theoretical knowledge possessed by the sample and in this particular case exposes the Deleuzian perspective informing the opinion of the interviewee. Still, the impossibility of establishing a relationship to it is a common defining parameter of the New, regardless of the interviewee's theoretical background.

It is important here to underline the significance of the acknowledgement of this impossibility: 'the new is the unimaginable, when you recognise it as such' (GP), says another interviewee, whose theoretical background is grounded in Marxist tradition, also referring as an example to a dance piece in which as a spectator, she noticed that 'there was no recognition...really no recognition of the trajectory' (GP).

The presence of a trajectory allows recognition to take place while in its absence a possible experience of the New seems to arise, where there is no discovery of the unknown or clarification of the obscure: 'something is operating on to my system but I cannot say I need to eat or I need to...whatever now I feel...there is no solution to this question or to this demand of the body, I don't know what to do: the difference again between being scared and being in fear... is basically the same, right? So scared, I am scared of horses, I feel fear for things that I don't have any name for' (MS).

The urge of getting rid of the unknown, highlighted by Horkheimer and Adorno (2002) as one the most problematic inheritances of Enlightenment, and the possibility of a New that does not work as a clarification of the obscure in Groys' insights, re-emerge in the field. Accordingly, it is with reference to the obscure that the fieldwork enriched the theoretical framework in another very important aspect: obscurity, a constitutive aspect of the new work of art according to Groys, and the pivotal facet of contemporariness in the opinion of Agamben. This recurred in the interviews, in the attempt to better define the New, and also as practice for its production. RM, describing his work as an artist, says: 'a new work is an invitation not to understand: when there is clarity, when you're able to see very well, then you've to make things more obscure [...] It is about "uncomprehending intelligently" (RM).

This perspective coming from an artist is paired with that coming from a curator, according to whom curating is about preserving the obscurity that a work of art brings. The work *I topi lasciano la nave* by the group Zapruder is, to SB, an instance of both the recognition and the production of the New by virtue of its obscurity:

> That was a load of mystery - in the sense that looking at it, you're not able to define its genre, between dance contest, concert, live performance, film... The burden of obscurity that the work maintains, it has a lot of pleats and a plurality of levels of existence that open to something that has to do with the production of the new. [...] I think I felt that we created a terrain, a space to work that implied that I had to leave to them my curatorial space and allow them to do a work that is based on obscurity. That was the power of that work (SB).

The impossibility to establish a relationship with the New, the need to escape a clear trajectory and the centrality of the dimension of obscurity both in terms of recognition and production of the New lead back to the possibility of the truly new, traced by Benjamin within the old and by Kierkegaard and then Groys within the ordinary. Fieldwork analysis provided a better understanding of this aspect: the ordinary belongs to the experience of the New as long as it is characterised by being overwhelming (MS, DBG, GP, SB, RM).

Drawing a parallel with the submarine of *Twenty Thousand Leagues under the Sea*, MS brings this aspect to the fore: 'Under no circumstances he can comprehend this monster, it's an absolute wonder. He can recognise it when it is there but he could never produce it. He could just make himself available to it. Monsters of post-structuralism are surprising and conventional, this one is ordinary and overwhelming'.

It is exactly the overwhelming aspect of the ordinary that is able to produce that sense of obscurity, which develops around the experience of the New distinguishing it from that of innovation. More precisely, it is the co-presence of the ordinary aspect and the overwhelming one that produces the impossibility of establishing a relationship to the idea, or object, presenting these two characteristics together. This also emerges clearly in the example provided by another interviewee, who tells his experience of the New in art at the personal exhibition of Andreas Fisher at the Cologne Museum. The interviewee refers to the artist's rudimental assemblages of waste materials that have nothing in common with proper forms of human physiognomy but still are characterised by small movements that recall some kind of life, which seem not at all mechanical but indeed human. The interviewee refers to the impossibility of establishing a relationship to these objects that in their ordinariness are indeed overwhelming, and singles out this aspect in order to give a more theoretical definition of the New:

> The new is a search for a similarity that is not based on aesthetic categories like recognition or visual empathy, but on belonging. The acknowledgement of belonging to something you cannot define, being a structure open to infinite possibilities; it's overwhelming (DBG)

The ordinary and the overwhelming co-exist as difference and no matter how radical the difference, the experience they produce is that of belonging, in opposition to comprehension through comparison and relationship. It is in this sense that the New might look like the ordinary but it is not: being experienced as an incomprehensible form of belonging, it does not regard a difference in form (Groys 2008) or the uncritical attachment to positive values happening in a transparent world. It is an obscure form of belonging based on disguise and intuition that, in the form of an artwork, overwhelms the spectator with a doubt on reality. This very important aspect must also be kept in mind in relation to the possible political value of the New, an intuition of which also emerges in the example provided by another interviewee: 'Something overwhelmed me, because I was confronted with something for me unimaginable and this could be reflected in my opinion from the aesthetic to the political category' (GP).

The category of difference whose margins have been traced through data analysis is thus a difference in kind, whose acknowledgement escapes comprehension and comparison to revolve around belonging and obscurity. In other words, it's not a difference between different entities but a difference constituted by different entities.

6.1.2 The New as Incomplete

The central characteristic of the category of difference within the field regards its being constituted by the coexistence of radically different entities. In light of this, it is not surprising that all interviewees share the conviction that something–in order to be New–has to be 'entirely something', 'altogether different', 'whole': partiality does not belong to the New. Theory highlighted recombinant novelty as a characteristic of innovation, and creativity and was also found in the interviews, as 'innovation, if compared to the new, is characterised by a certain partiality' (GP). Recombinant novelty also echoed postmodern thought, which was indirectly criticised in the fieldwork (MS, GP) exactly because 'continuity and divisibility' (MS) are not compatible with the production of the New. All statements in relation to this aspect refer to the fact that one should not be able to recognise the parts in the whole, as that would imply the establishment of a relationship. It is in this sense that the critique of the term 'turn' could be read: 'the word "turn" implies a linear trajectory of partial elements that as such cannot be new' (GP). Contrariwise, the New is something 'to which one could not say "it's a little bit like this" or "a little bit different like that" but something that is altogether different' (MS).

The New conceived as entire entails very important implications in terms of production and value, as well as in terms of politics. These themes will be deepened in the course of the analysis. Here it suffices to notice that the impossibility to deconstruct the parts of a whole produces a difficulty for the system to react to the otherness that entered it: 'what can we do? Where is the broom? Where are the weapons? How can we divide it? So that, what he sees there, in front of him is an absolute oneness, right? An absolute oneness that is foreign to the environment that it is in,' says MS again with reference to the example of *Twenty Thousand Leagues under the Sea*. Here it is very important to specify the following: in no sense can the New, conceived as entire, mean 'closed' or 'complete.' Contrariwise, the New is to be found in the objects and ideas that are 'open' (SB, DBG) and 'allow misunderstanding' (RM):

> It will make it like, what word would we use? 'Present'? So it's about the re-reading of things; about the interpretations and sometimes about misunderstandings, I think misunderstanding is very important. The text that is open for interpretation is very important to make things alive and, like, go on with time and not death (RB).

In order to be New, something must be entire but at the same time open, not only to interpretation but also to misunderstanding and this represents another very important aspect emerging from the fieldwork. Boris Groys (2008) also associates to new artworks the characteristic of 'being alive' in comparison to those that have been part of the museum's collection for longer time. Here different interviewees refer, although not explicitly, to Benjamin, as such a vision is also based on the possibility to experience the New in what is historically old, as long as it is not closed or complete: 'It would be like acknowledging a hole in history that reveals itself as new, as unexplored or not systematised' (DBG).

This New is conceptualised by DBG in relation to 'the possible', where the latter is not opposite to the real but rather to the complete: 'it is not something unreal but rather something that is "not yet" and has the opportunity to partially stay in this unshaped state'. Similarly, by looking at the New as alternative to the 'definite' rather than to what exists, it is possible to open the concept to possibilities, 'inviting you to construct them, without offering an alternative: an invitation to enter a space where the world may be thought neither as it is nor as its alternative, but as an incredible sum of possible moments concentrated in few instants' (DBG).

The New as entire and incomplete paves the way for different reflections, which will be carried out in this section following the guidelines offered by the data analysis. Theorising the New as incomplete might help containing the aspects of postmodern thinking that find in partiality an ally to endless reproduction and the narrative around it; at the same time, it might allow to think in terms of production, avoiding modernism's excessive aspects by preserving a space of potentiality that contains multiple trajectories or even the possibility of misunderstanding–and thinking outside of–a trajectory altogether. In this sense, an incomplete work or concept might entail precious political value within capitalism's transparency and realism (see Han 2015 and Fisher 2009): it could shelter obscurity, trigger reflection on reality and yet, by being entirely something incomplete rather than open, it might offer a possibility of resistance to the market's co-optation and substitution mechanism. This latter possibility will be explored in paragraph 6.3.

6.1.3 Eternity and Ephemerality

The above-mentioned aspects were at least partially contained in the theoretical framework provided, but the fieldwork underlined other characteristics that enrich theory in the conceptual definition of the New and suggest directions for further exploring its temporal dimension. Field analysis suggests that the category of time is closely related to the production of the New, while it seems to be not so relevant when it comes to its recognition. A similar differentiation emerged with reference to the category collective/individual: the recognition of the New is perceived and described always on the individual level; its production appears impossible without a collective subject.

The theoretical framework engaged with questions and perspectives regarding how long the New might last and highlighted two different positions: according to Deleuze, the new is eternal, as it constitutes its own category, characterised by the 'power of beginning and beginning again' (Deleuze 1994: 172) while according to Groys, the new artwork, although being such on the basis of a difference in time, is ephemeral. The exploration of this question in the field was represented by the code 'duration', which comprised two sub-codes referring respectively to ephemerality and eternity. The former appears as the most relevant in terms of recognition of the New, while the latter–together with other codes belonging to the category of time, such as 'synchrony'–present a stronger relation with the production and the value of the New and thus will be tackled in the following paragraphs.

As regards the recognition of the New, it is the acknowledgement of the impossibility of establishing a relationship to it that influences the duration of the New, which is perceived as such up to the moment in which a relationship with it is established. The New stops being such in the moment in which it is defined as such (MS, GP). This aspect, although elaborated through very different, sometimes opposite, perspectives, is acknowledged by all interviewees, as also mentioned above with reference to the possibility of conceptualising the New as opposite to the definite.

The duration of the New is thus a fruitful perspective to distinguish the former both from innovation and creativity, as the moment in which you give a name to the New may represent the beginning of innovation:

In an abstract sense, a thought of difference in kind will necessarily be a new thought and when it has been thought, it needs to be connected, it cannot be here, disconnected from everything, but then all of a sudden, whoops! Blame! We have to give it a name and then it is already inscribed in difference in degree (MS).

Now I can better focus the difference between the new and innovation. Innovation is something that can be passed: at that moment I reached a state...a form that is an acquired form that can be passed to you... it can become something that is recognizable (GP).

The aspect of ephemerality brings for all interviewees a sense of melancholy in recognising the New, 'because whenever the new comes, it's immediately old' (RM) and 'then the rest of our carrier is all about hunting that moment that is absolutely incomprehensible, absolute being' (MS).

In this context, the individual dimension connected with the recognition of the New becomes almost loneliness: 'there is a terrible melancholy when you recognise the new as such precisely because in the moment in which you recognise it, you know it won't last. I believe that innovation has a component of happiness that doesn't belong to the new...there is the happiness of having achieved something (GP).

The code 'contemporary' was also connected to the recognition of the New and that of 'ephemerality'. This represents another instance of the interviewees' theoretical background as all of them were familiar with Agamben's text on the contemporary and spontaneously link this idea with the ephemerality of the New as a way to heal this melancholy, but only if conceived within the definition of Agamben, which indeed allows some agency.[55] It is once again the concept of relation to be used to put the contemporary and the New on the same level, although they are two things that 'as categories almost never correspond' (GP). Still, they share the aspect of ephemerality, as acknowledged by all interviewees and well expressed by MS: 'the moment when the contemporary comes out of somebody's mouth, "contemporary", then it's over, right, then it's only in time and it's already in language and then it's already terrifically perfect and then it becomes a matter of what we do with it'.

The action of giving a name either to the contemporary or the New represents their end, and neutralises the fertile obscurity that characterises the experience of the New and the darkness that Agamben calls for in order to establish a different relationship to time to nurture agency. This is why the category of difference and the related possibility of establishing a relationship remains the central one as regards the recognition of the New: it presents strong relations with all the main aspects that emerged in the first phase of the analysis, from obscurity to incompleteness, and leads back to incomprehensible belonging, which paves the way for establishing a different form of relationship with the world: 'I'm not convinced that the new and the

---

55 What is the Contemporary (Agamben 2009) See Chapter 2.

contemporary go together but now I'm thinking that the new belongs to the contemporary in the relationship we have with it' (DBG).

The aspect of ephemerality and the possibility of establishing a relationship greatly influence the way interviewees envision production. As explained below, the conceptualisation of production also works through the search of ways to work on ephemerality, sometimes to extend it, sometimes to envision production as eternal. The latter aspect cannot be considered separately from the collective dimension and the possibility and responsibility to change things in the theatre system, which is felt by all interviewees and deepened in paragraph 6.4.

6.2 From the Concept of the New to its Production

The results presented in the previous paragraph with reference to the recognition of the New were obtained through a deductive approach, discussing the matter with interviewees with specific reference to the theoretical framework. The production of the New was investigated in the field with an inductive and abductive approach, and aimed at exploring the possible reconceptualisation of production itself with reference to the New as described by interviewees themselves. As mentioned above, interviewees tackled the matter including spontaneously diverse theoretical references that they found useful in order to engage in the envisioning of production.

Before offering a description of these lines of thought, it is important to make a step back to consider the meaning of production itself, in which urgency was expressed very clearly by all interviewees. More precisely the interviewees' opinions differ on whether the New 'just happens' or is actively produced as well, as the matter concerns the creation of something anew or transforming that which already exists. Generally speaking, the majority of the retrieved segments refer to the New using the word 'production' rather than 'happening'.

Moreover, it must be taken into consideration that interviewees that see the New as simply happening specify that 'you've to make yourself available to it' (MS) or that you 'stumble on the new' (RM) if you put yourself in certain conditions, underlining a possibility of agency in the processes connected to the New. Likewise, interviewees that prefer the term 'production' to that of 'happening' make it clear that such a production also happens in ways that are not easily describable (SB, MG, ML) and often out of control (GP, DBG, SB).

Given that the New surely cannot be produced in the common sense of the word, the problem of transformation and creation emerges, and the account of the field in this respect is just as complex as the one coming from the theory. The first cycle of coding highlighted numerous contradictions within the single interviews and suggested, at the general level, the tendency to connect the production of the New with the idea of creation rather than with the one of transformation. Still, the second cycle of coding highlighted that this distinction does not play such an important role once connected with the dimensions of directionality and purpose. This connection, which emerged strongly in the analysis, highlights that these words can acquire meanings that shift the focus on their implications:

Creation could be transformation but not a pre-given transformation, not easily predictable but rather something able to open doors through which it would be possible to go off the rails, to escape a directionality (SB).

The new is the unimaginable within a system that does not give you a direction towards transformation, where even transformation itself could be imagined as re-foundation (GP).

The role ascribed to creation by the sample does not mirror the presence of a romantic conception of the artist in the field. This appears in the wording chosen to tackle this issue and was also confirmed during the analysis of all aspects regarding the possibility of the production of the New, where the focus shifts clearly from the individual to the collective perspective.

The above extracts well exemplify that when it comes to the production of the New within the arts, the dimensions of purpose and direction can overcome the dichotomy between creation and transformation to assume a more important role. Still, it must be specified that the matter remains complex and the echoes of this complexity unfold with regards to the relationship between the production of the New, the responsibility involved in it and politics. In this sense, while some interviewees have no problem with the word 'creation' and see themselves as possible creators or agents of transformation of what exists, others refuse the term because of its religious implication:

I don't like in an artwork that they use the word create, especially in French for example, *création*, they use it for artists and theatre makers etcetera... like as if this happens, like you create it, like there is rupture with history and also I don't believe in this because I believe you do something based on what has happened. So you're based on history, on your past, on other peoples' past, on civilization, there is this accumulation and we always come from there and it has no meaning. And then there is also this problematic about beginnings and going back to point zero, as if you can... a new start, a new beginning. I am against this logic, like if the new means rupture with the past or the new means that now history starts, it's a very religious discourse but also very fascist, very dictatorship: history now starts, before there is nothing and after us there is nothing, actually there is only us (RM).

The critique here looked to the concept of origin, of 'new beginning', from which a linear trajectory develops. On the other hand, the capability of beginning as conceptualised by Hanna Arendt and mentioned by one of the interviewees (see GP above), suggests that the New could be produced as 'the setting up of a space of action that was not there before' (GP). and thus does not imply any development of a linear trajectory. The different opinions on this matter of course influence the perception of interviewees on their role within society as regards the possibility of change, but the concept of trajectory and continuity seem indeed to cut across all the different opinions collected. With reference to Fassbinder, an interviewee says:

> What does it mean to change something? Movement is indeed no synonym of change. We would never think about the solar system as something capable of changing, but it is still in continuous movement. However it moves on prescribed orbits through which we can foresee that they will move according to the same pre-given trajectory. Change would happen if and when the planet deviates from its trajectory. This is why I believe that also within performing arts the new could result from the creation of something that is not exclusively innovative but rather able to suspend for a moment what was expected, what it should have been (DBG).

As it will be explained, the perspectives on the possibility of production in the New develop in ways that interact with the concept of linearity either by betraying it or by suspending it, as mentioned in this last extract. It also serves as a reminder for what makes the live arts alive, and thus opens the possibility of the New not as movement, but rather as the incompleteness of the trajectory in its possibility to be escaped.

6.2.1 A Coexistence of Differences

Before focusing on how the production of this New could be envisioned, it is important to specify that the category of difference emerged spontaneously in the fieldwork as regards the production of the New. This could be expected given the theoretical background of the sample and, if at the abstract level it is mainly consistent with the theoretical framework, the sub-codes related to it constitute the main aspects underlying the production of the New on a more concrete level. This category has been at the centre of the abductive analysis and thus will be described thoroughly in Chapter 7, while reported here are some of the most important aspects that emerged in the course of the interview, which influenced the first and second stage of the analysis and, of course, the ways interviewees envisioned production. The analysis produced five different codes that could be grouped as sub-codes of 'difference'. Some of them were already mentioned in the previous paragraph, given their relevance in term of the recognition of the New (e.g. 'no relation new', 'altogether different'). Others are, on the other hand, relevant in terms of production, such as 'memory', 'coexistence of difference' and 'autonomy'.

As far as the notion of memory is concerned, interviewees connected it to the recognition of the New (in the sense of the impossibility of establishing a relationship to it). Yet, this subcategory of difference–considered both as individual and collective memory–constitutes one of the bases of production, something that is not possible to set aside and can become a tool for the production of the New. This double function of remembering mirrors the difference, explored in Chapter 2, between remembering as conceptualised by Kierkegaard–according to whom no difference could ever be new because if it were we would notice it through remembering and thus make a comparison–and remembrance, as conceptualised by Benjamin, which being characterised by creative destruction, could serve the production of the New. Remembrance shelters the possibility of forgetting and it is this characteristic that is most valued in the field:

> I am working a lot on the category of forgetting ... whether it could be something that opens up to the possible or the new in this case, whether it could be the moment in which something raises. In an historical sense I believe that forgetting is an occasion that allows you to make something resurge... in which you allow yourself the possibility not of discovering what it has been but rather of imagining what it could have been (DBG)

Benjamin's thoughts with regard to making incomplete what was before complete, allowed for the argument in the theoretical framework that the concept of creative destruction could be re-thought in terms of producing the New and not exclusively as the movement underlying the production of innovation. The possibility of following such a direction and conceptualising the production of the New as a step towards the incomplete received good feedback in the fieldwork, regardless of the different theoretical background of interviewees, as shown by the two following extracts:

> I don't think that the production of the new must go through the destruction of reality, which, if developed programmatically wouldn't result in something different from another closed reality (DBG).

> What will happen to you is that you will be in absolute excessive fear. Out of nowhere, you will produce a relationship. We have to talk about how this production happens: you will produce something but this production is not made because of who you are but is rather because of who you aren't, because at the moment when you do this, you aren't (MS).

The first extract underlines that the production of the New cannot unfold as only creation and neither as only destruction. Rather, it might live between the two, leaving a space of potentiality devoid of creation. The second, coming from a different theoretical background, also resonates with such potentiality and seems to call again for incompleteness.

The fieldwork underlined how something, in order to be New, must be entire: to go beyond difference and be altogether different by remaining at the same time incomplete, as mentioned in the previous paragraph. Tackling in the field the production of the New, this result could be better formulated specifying the difference between the indeterminate and the incomplete.

At the conceptual level, the former might be an entity in a flow, with no specific borders and could prevent being given a name. The latter might be an obscure entity whose borders are clearer and yet porous: it might escape naming in a different way, still allowing an interruption of directionality. The two concepts have very different implications in terms of value, as it will be explained in the next paragraph. As the indeterminate appears as sheer potentiality, there is the inherent risk of being named in all possible ways, to become determinate and thus an object of all possible uses. Another risk, in light of what has been discussed in the theoretical framework, might be for the indeterminate to remain a full potentiality that reproduces full potentiality, and thus the same, without ever becoming something.

The incomplete, on the other hand, seems to shelter the potentiality of becoming something different and produce differences by virtue of its borders that make it entire and yet open. What the incomplete nurtures is, in another words, coexistence of differences. The category of coexistence of differences developed in close relation to that of autonomy in the fieldwork and emerged as a pivotal category for the production of the New, which could be produced by nurturing the simultaneous presence of radical differences. A possibility in this sense seems to be traced by interviewees exactly in those spaces where differences can coexist without being synthesised in a solution (DBG, SB, MG, RM), but rather share a time and a space as autonomous subjects (MS, GP). In more concrete terms:

What I try to do as a curator–what I am interested in trying to do because I think it is important also for a festival–is, rather than reasoning in terms of positioning on a specific discourse or scene, to ask how to make diversity exist inside one singular, given context, differences that are also irreconcilable, disorientating (SB).

6.2.2 Suspension and Self-betrayal

On the basis of the analysis, it is possible to group the different ideas on production that emerged in the interviews in two categories consistent with a different conceptualisation of the New. On the one hand, by privileging the aspect of obscurity and complexity, interviewees envisioned a production based on self-corruption practices and betrayal (GP, MS, RM). On the other, by highlighting the temporal dimension in terms of both duration and asynchrony, with reference to a 'nebula' that seems to be more matt than obscure–although the two concepts seem to work in the same way– interviewees envisioned an idea of production based on suspension and indeterminacy. The result of the first is a painful process, which may result in the determination of being only New and forever New (GP). The second looks at collaboration and conflict (DBG, SB, MG), as a way to work on the ephemeral aspect of the New to include it systematically in the concept of production. As it will be explained, the qualitative analysis highlighted that the two approaches, notwithstanding radical differences, could be considered complementary up to a certain extent. With reference to the first group, indeed the New may be produced 'because of who you are not,' and this leads directly to self-betrayal, one of the most interesting results of the field of analysis. Accepting and exploring the high potential of obscurity entailed in the New, the need emerges to rethink production in order to embrace this obscurity: 'We need a protocol to fool ourselves out of language and set up a two-fold practice, which is self-corrupted and makes ourselves available for the possibility of the new' (MS). In order to do this, it is possible to directly engage in betrayal:

> The new is maybe when you betray yourself, your beliefs and your thoughts and then the new comes, but it comes only for yourself [...] When I feel in danger, when I fear, I know I'm on the right track because I'm touching some obscure spots in myself, that's not so easy to find and talk about them, so when I'm afraid or sceptical I force myself to go on (RM).

> What I know is that every now and then, like a sort of snake, I change my skin and my writing becomes something else. In these moments there is a very painful gestation... painful because I don't know what it is becoming and I am powerless, I can just let it happen. In that moment it is impossible for me to do the work I'm capable of doing because there is something new–here I can use a word to describe something that cannot be described differently–really something new that is happening and that I can't recognise... it is in this sense that I betray myself (GP).

Self-betrayal also emerges as a practice of repetition and, consistently with theory, seems to look at the New as eternal: the Deleuzian new that begins and begins again is marked, according to these interviewees who do not ascribe to a Deleuzian perspective, by self-betrayal.

As already mentioned, all interviewees recognise the New as ephemeral, but the fieldwork highlighted a shift as regards temporality in going from the recognition of the New to its production, where the melancholic feeling of ephemerality is either matching the feeling of an overwhelming present, or is turned into a Deleuzian eternality, or is stretched out of itself through a trust in collective agency. This shift appeared first in the difference between the two groups regarding how they consider ephemerality. In this sense, one interviewee, reasoning on Avant-garde (a concept that of course was recurrent in the data), notices: 'If I think about personalities that left a mark, something like a constellation of the new in the 20th Century, like Artaud or Bataille–yes, let's take them–they were both expulsed but that is not exclusively a social thing of being expelled from the surrealist movement...it is exactly...in both cases I see a very painful gestation of the new that prevents you to be in the group, that somehow condemns you to be only new'

(GP). In this sense, art production emerges as continuous work that could become eternal:

> This means that you need to and in this sense, it's like there is no any goal, because each one is creating or founding another one. So in this sense it's a continuous work, it's a non-stop project, you have to go on; when you stop you're in a way dead. So it's either suicide or you go on this way, which is like our destiny. And this is how I understand art; it's something that should go on. So it's an endless voyage but it's like a mental voyage, in one sense is very poetic and in another sense is very hectic 'cause you just have to go on and you know that when you reach a point it's already dead, you have to go on (RM).

The extract above entails the paradox of an ephemeral New matched by the impression of a present time that is hard to grasp and produces the feeling of reproduction, underlining the modern dynamics exacerbated by neoliberal capitalism and discussed in Chapter 3.

Yet, the overwhelming present entails a possibility of production that stretches the ephemeral into a Deleuzian eternal: 'Martin Kippenberger did everything in his life and did it by betraying himself continuously: it is impossible to recognise a *fil rouge* in his work. However, this was absolutely anti-humanist, he wasn't Leonardo who did everything and did it perfectly...he did everything compulsively. Now will start a phase of critical appraisal of his work, also thanks to this exhibition, but at the time he received no recognition, also because there was no recognition of his trajectory' (GP). This example brought up by the interviewee comprises the double aspect of the present time as exposed in Chapter 3 by describing an overwhelming present bound to reproduce the same labelling of the New that still, on the ontological level, constitutes the only time where it is possible to open up a space of action and potentiality.

The double meaning of the present time shelters the shift from the recognition to the production of the New in terms of temporality. In the first cycle of coding, the following codes presented a strong numerical presence: 'indeterminacy'; 'possibility'; 'cloud/nebula'; 'suspension'; 'making a hole'; 'problem-creating'. These were then reduced to one single category in the second cycle of coding, which looks at production in terms of 'possibility':

> It is important here that is not the production of... but it is always a production of the possibility, 'cause they cannot produce it, they cannot tell us what the new should be. What they do is they set up concepts whose force, whose intensity is the production of the possibility of the new (MS).

The reference to Deleuze in the extract above is clear, but the category of possibility seems to go across specific literature references of the individuals to encompass diverse perspectives and is affirmed once again in opposition to the idea of a linear trajectory. This perspective is also embraced in practice, in a specific approach to the production of theatre:

This is to us fundamental on the theatrical perspective: we always worked by researching a space of indeterminacy to be given to the spectator. The creation of a form that shouldn't be comprehended but could open up many cracks where each one could find not a solution but rather a perception of the fact that the world could be thought in every moment neither as what it is, nor as its alternative, but rather as a sum of possible moments concentrated in few instants: that is what theatrical experience is for us (DBG).

Such an approach to production presented a strong co-occurrence with the concept of reality in the retrieved segments, which in turn recalls the potential, already emerged in the theoretical framework, of working on this dimension. Since this emerged in the analysis as one of the major dimensions, it will be deepened in the next chapter. Here it suffices to say that the production of the New does not go through a negation of reality, nor does it go through its destruction. It entails a close relationship with what exists, but such a relationship unfolds in the acknowledgement that reality is not necessary but rather contingent. The production of the New in art thus appears in this perspective as 'making a hole into reality', so that it can suddenly appear as not necessary and contingent, and therefore subject to be transformed. This 'hole' taken as in-vivo code from one interview–and resonating with Benjamin's making incomplete what was complete–widely overlaps with that of 'suspension', a word mentioned by all interviewees either with reference to the concept of trajectory or to that (the one) of reality, and is nonetheless implied in the description of the practice of self-betrayal.

Still, while self-betrayal practices seem to spring in concurrence to those perspectives on the New that privilege its obscure dimension, the practices of suspension emerge in relation to the image of the cloud, which well embodies this 'idea of possibility as pure contingency…awareness of an indeterminacy that can also remain such for an instant, that mustn't always be solved in a route to direct to somewhere' (DBG).

The image of the cloud appeared already to describe ways to think about the New (see 5.1) by virtue of being atmospheric rather than concrete; such atmosphere could emerge as a very fertile territory to engage in practices of suspension that are applicable not exclusively by artists, but also by institutions:

> One of the themes of *Shared Space* is Weather: there is the need to engage with something that is beyond our control. Weather is something on which we've no control, in which we're immersed. As humans, we impact on it but still it is not something completely other from ourselves because we're inside it, it determines you also in a sense of belonging […] In this sense, looking at the overall conception of a festival, the production of the new represents an interesting space in terms of curatorial work. What a festival can produce within its frame next to more specific questions and works of course, is that of being atmospheric, rarefied, that characterises the new… that in comparison to them is not characterised by such a clear direction (SB).

To look at production as a 'cloud' turned out to entail important implications in the analysis, with regards to the dimensions of space and time and their interconnections. As it is also clear also from the extract above, the image of the cloud represents first and foremost an image of space, a dimension that is addressed in the interviews from different perspectives. Among those, institutional space plays a fundamental role, as it will be explained in the next chapter. Independently from this, interviewees that envision production as suspension, as 'making a hole' in reality, ascribe to space an important role as a dimension of action: 'there are spaces that represent this cloud, this possibility not exclusively in temporal terms but also in spatial ones...there are for sure various contexts in which the category of space plays an important role (DBG).

Although all interviewees look at space and time as dimensions that cannot be considered separately, the analysis shows that those who look at the production of the New through practices of self-betrayal refer more to time, while those who engage with suspension seem to privilege space. This aspect is indeed consistent with the important role played by the category of reality over that of politics in the case of this second group. For instance, this second group conceives the dimension of asynchrony, which, consistently with theory, is important both in temporal and spatial terms, mainly in the latter ones: the practice of suspension overlaps with segments referring to asynchrony as 'a step aside', rather than a change in speed.

Such spatial conception of asynchrony seems to lead to a very different way to tackle the ephemerality of the New that also highlights the fundamental role of the collective aspect in terms of production, completing the shift in temporality from the ephemeral to its extensions. Contrary to self-betrayal, which is generally described as an individual, indeed as private, activity, the image of the cloud that sums up the practice of suspension becomes powerful by virtue of its plural functioning:

There is a beautiful image that I use a lot to describe this idea of the possible that is not always projected into the future. Giordano Bruno in his Clavis Magna talks about the materiality of the world before its creation. He describes it as a cloud of matter that is capable to assume whatever shape and is pushed by winds in every direction. Because of the impulses coming from every direction it keeps on changing and the incredible thing is that it is exactly this multiplicity of impulses that prevent it to assume a single shape. And, I believe that this multiplicity contributes a lot to indeterminacy and suspension. This multiplicity of directionalities makes it substantially alive, suspended, indefinable, indefinite (DBG).

Offered here is a completely different perspective through which the ephemerality characterising the New could be tackled: how long the New lasts depends not so much on repetition of difference as within practices of self-betrayal, but rather on the multiplication of differences. The conflicting impulses inhabiting the same space at the same time has an impact on the duration of the New, or at least on the experience of it, depending on how long the suspension lasts. Intuitively, such a suspension can be produced exclusively by a plural subject. It is in this sense that the above-mentioned category 'coexistence of difference' unfolds its full potential and that the two visions on production could be combined: as it will be shown, this co-presence also plays a role in terms of time in connection with the category of asynchrony. In this paragraph it is instead worth underlining that all interviews highlighted the importance of reasoning on a dimension that was named 'individual/collective', under which a conspicuous number of segments was coded. As mentioned in the previous paragraph the analysis showed a concurrence of the individual dimension as regards the recognition of the New, the same could be said for the collective one when it comes to production: 'it is thrilling to acknowledge that something happens or is produced in a way that it would have been impossible without the co-presence of two...when you run risks together there is the production of a common space' (SB).

Moreover, by following the conceptualisation of production that is emerging here as informed by the reconceptualisation of the New, it is possible to look at the relationship between the individual and the collective under a particular perspective, here expressed with reference to the question of identity: 'you're also producing the condition for the new, you produce the condition anew for what an individual can be. And, the moment of individuation...well, identitarian production is always individual and general, individuation is always singular and at the same time universal' (MS).

The collective dimension is made up by different sub-codes that also allow its analysis in terms of dimensions of action, which were retrieved according to the interviews: sharing, exchange, network, and collaboration. It is very interesting to notice in this sense that all sub-codes of this category co-occur or occur in the same paragraph with the code 'conflict', which also emerged as a fundamental category of analysis, putting together these concepts with those of space, time and difference. As it will be widely explored in Chapter 7, the idea of collaboration, in particular, recurs in all interviews with an interesting connotation, according to which conflict represents a fundamental dimension of the production of the New: 'as a possibility of coexistence of those who are different in a space of conflict that could be active and working without interrupting the productive activity of these subjects within it' (SB).

6.3 The Theatre System and its Value(s)

The way the production of the New is envisioned by interviewees cannot be considered separately from the conditions in which such production happens and the dimension of value. Diverse statements in the interviews highlight the paradoxical situation in which art production happens under the conditions of neoliberal capitalism, and they present a strong co-occurrence with the dimension of value, interweaving with the ways interviewees perceive the system where they work and envision strategies for change. In order to give the best possible description that the fieldwork provided with relation to these dynamics, this section addresses the main findings related to the understanding held by the interviewees the New and the value of its production within the system of contemporary theatre, introducing their views on the role of art within knowledge-capitalism that are addressed in the next paragraph.

The analysis highlighted that the majority of theoretical references were brought up by the interviewees in relation to the topic of value, and accordingly, all interviewees are very aware of the dynamics connected to the production of the New within neoliberal capitalism:

We struggle with the idea that the production of the new is also what neoliberalism wants [...] we have to be careful if we don't want to end up being well-meaning capitalists (MS).

Looking for the new is a very capitalistic strategy; I try to fight it a lot [...] it's also economically stupid: we produce a good product and without giving it time, we want something new (MG).

These statements highlight the perception that the concept of New itself has been ated by neoliberal capitalism as the starting point of interviewees' reflections, which revolved around two main issues: the shift of value production into the immaterial and the problem of co-optation. The analysis highlighted the presence of open questions in the field as regards the possibility of producing 'worthless art' as opposed to the narrative of purposeful art that developed concurrently, or engaging with the politics of use as regards the value produced. It questioned again the potentiality and downsides of the indeterminate, together with the need for funding so as to legitimise their work within the conditions of neoliberal capitalism. The production of value through the immaterial constitutes one of the main shifts of the neoliberal turn and is perceived by all interviewees as the core paradox underlying their role as producers: 'it's all a matter of us consuming images and wanting to consume them, in a way that makes us want to consume them more and this production is made through capitalist thought, ah-ha, so basically it becomes all about the capitalist circulation of meaning' (MS).

In the theoretical framework, the theories by Benjamin and Harvey were used in order to underline how capitalism's structural conditions not only affect the materiality of cultural and artistic production—the commodification of the image supposed not only the production of the image itself but also an increased production of immateriality and volatility that integrated artists fully into the logic of capitalism—but also the need to build a narrative around this mode of production and transform it 'into some kind of successful spectacle' (Harvey 1989: 347). It is in this double mechanism that the production of immaterial value increased in the overall value production ratio of capitalism, and the new as a label became dominant.

The most recent effect of this process was traced in the data as a preoccupation for the future of the system of contemporary theatre in relation to that of the visual arts, as well as its relationship to performance and the immaterial value it may contain. Performance by virtue of its immateriality and volatility represents a perfect example of how the shift of value into the immaterial was translated into art production: 'The Venice Biennale and last year the Documenta were pretty fresh. And, after 1960, the fresh has become more and more economically... valuable' (MS). The 'fresh' emerges in the interviews as a common way to describe innovation and usually implies the idea of co-optation in some cases and that of commercial value in all of them: performance in itself seems to represent the fresh for the visual art system, which 'can today be used as a model for the worst thinkable of business opportunities, it's a very interesting territory' (MS).

As many interviewees (MS, GP, SB, MG, ML) noticed, dance has been popularised extremely in the museum system over the past few years, and this could be interpreted as an example of appropriation in a system that does not rely on objects anymore for the production of value. In this sense, the presence of dance inside the museum is defined as 'strategic' (MS):

> The society that we have today is knowledge, movement, globality... the choreographer is the new architect. And the dancer is much more the model, than the visual artist. [...] What I want to say with this is that the reason why dance is in the museum is not because somebody likes dance but because it cannot not be there. Right now it is exactly what the society wants, the time of the object is kaput... and, what the museum wants to do is to expand the market. According to them, what the artist and these people should do is also produce knowledge or expand knowledge so that other sectors can harvest (MS).

Here again is the return of the question of immateriality, the object of a lot of attention within performance studies in the 70s, showing the interviewees' theoretical background and perspectives, who generally dismiss the possibility to look at performance as something resistant to market logic in itself. With reference to that, GP says that those theories were: 'a very naïve attempt to locate performance, by virtue of its ephemerality, outside the possibility of commodification. That's completely wrong, especially today because ephemeral products are exactly what neoliberal capitalism is looking for. I think the best example of this is the performance artist Tehching Hsieh. His work is emblematic of the potential of subtraction from market logic...how could that be a strategy of resistance? To think this of ephemeral works *tout court* makes no sense, especially because we're talking about art and we're talking in particular about performance, where production and consumption co-exist'.[56]

Yet, if the theories that argued the contrary are generally considered dated or naïve within the field, the level of the debate on the question of value and the attention paid to the indeterminate show that the questions on immaterial value production are still open and burning in the field, informing different positions among the interviewees on the problem of co-optation and the possibility of escaping it.

At the general level, the problem of co-optation is described either as dynamic inherent to the system–resonating with Luhman's system theory and the philosophical question of the paradigm–or as an explicit form of exploitation, relying on Marx's use of the term. The former perspective sees co-optation as an answer of the system to the existence of a strange element within it: 'we cannot have this inside, in order for us–for this organism–to survive, we have to accommodate it, we have to assimilate it' (MS). The latter underlines how this dynamic is present and exacerbated in today's art system:

> Exploitation is still...if we think about it with reference to the appropriation of one idea, that is work and thus a product, we find the possibility to discuss the condition within which such an exploitation happens...this is why it is to me inconceivable that the Occupy movement was placed inside an art gallery naively and with good intentions and was then appropriated: that was an agreement. In the standard definition of exploitation by Marx, there is a tacit agreement between the two parts and there is a reason for it (GP).

When it comes to what and how gets appropriated by the system, the shift of capitalism's production of value into the immaterial indeed seems to change the rules of the game: 'it is very different...we're not talking about people but about practices, signs that become appropriated and here the territory becomes definitely slippery' (GP).

The fieldwork showed different directions where the attempts undertaken on this slippery territory could unfold. At a more abstract level, the interviews point at the possibility to work outside of value altogether or, in contrast, to the politics of use connected with value production:

> It's becoming problematic to think about art that takes upon itself to sort out some asymmetries in society and at the same time, considering itself to be contemporary because–this is my argument and it can probably be contested and it is from time to time– my proposal would be that, if you want to do contemporary art, with any respect a little of

---

56 Here GP refers to the performance in which the artist decided to disappear from the art world, to become invisible for 13 years. The performance was announced by a statement of the artist: 'I, Tehching Hsieh, have a 13 years plan. I will make art during this time. I will not show it publicly. This plan will begin on my 36th birthday on Decemner 31, 1986 and continue until my 49th birthday, December 31, 1999'. And ended with another statement, declaring: 'I kept my self alive. I passed the December 31, 1999' dated on January 1st, 2000. The statements and further information can be found at www.tehchinghsieh.com.

a bigger C, then you have to make sure that your art is utterly and extensively worthless. And I mean not that you're making bad or lousy art but I mean that it cannot have value or worth in an economic or in any symbolic sense. So this cannot be an art that makes life better for those people in the suburbs here or there. This cannot be an art that is good for people that push heroin or something like this, no, what we have to do is an art that is... that doesn't give a flying fuck, about these consolidations (MS).

A statement like the one above calls for art production whose result is devoid from any form of value. The premise seems to resonate with Adorno's analysis, according to which attaching art to a purpose results in the loss of its autonomy. However, the conclusion seems to point at a refusal of value altogether, which is very different from what has been highlighted in the theoretical framework as a possible dimension of resistance, the possibility of conceiving art and the New as *pure means* that, detached from a specific purpose do not disappear in what they make visible, and thus are able to trigger critical thinking. The majority of interviewees did not perceive the production of value as critical in itself, rather they thought that perverse dynamics arise when the production of value is instrumental to something else:

Reasoning on camp, some critiques said that it was nothing more than reinvesting the derelict of an exchange value. I don't agree with this. According to my point of view there isn't something outside exchange value, consequently when it is reinvested, the critical point regards the politics of use to which this exchange takes part...so I don't believe that using the new as productive strategy is necessarily to be condemned (GP).

If the fieldwork confirms the importance to think about the production of the New and to reconceptualise it, rather than to dismiss it because it is subject to appropriation, the same is valid for innovation and creativity:

Creativity and innovation policies...why not? They're more than welcomed. Still, I would like to think about the possibility that they are not directed to something else. This is the point, the important aspect of this. If you think about it, today you hear everywhere people talking about creativity, failure and even suspension; the problem is that you hear of them exclusively as fundamental steps on the path of growth. That's similar to creativity [...] when it is exclusively a means for something, it loses its uncertain character on the next step...the uncertainty of not having one direction, where its genuine value may lie [...] I have a positive opinion on creative policy, but now it is more about using than valorising (DBG).

Taking the production of value as non-problematic in itself, the question regards the politics of use of the value produced, which are mentioned by all interviewees in relation to the system's mechanism of production and cultural politics. Before exploring the major dimension of counter-action that emerged from the analysis, it is important to state that how the system, and the individuals composing it, use the value they produce presents a strong connection with the category of trajectory, of which the extract above constitutes a good example.

The centrality of the abstract concept of trajectory and its being recognisable emerged clearly in relation to the recognition of the New, and here as regards the problem of co-optation: appropriation happens the moment in which the new work of art gains a recognisable form (MS, DBG) and it can be passed on (GP). If all interviewees agree on this and the analysis locates in the category of trajectory–and the related one of purposefulness– the core of the problem, the field also represents how much this issue remains unsolved at the level of the production of discourse and, in particular, how it focuses again on indeterminacy and ephemerality, two aspects obviously connected to immaterial value production. Notwithstanding what has already been explained with reference to the specific characteristics of performance and the way they determine production in the system (see 5.3.2), the potential of ephemerality is not completely dismissed in the data. Rather, the number of segments retrieved under this code allowed dividing the data into two groups according to the perspective on the possible strategies against appropriation and reproduction. One links production to a 'foundation' and the other links it to 'indeterminacy', two words that emerged as in-vivo codes in the course of the analysis. The former sees a possibility of resistance to co-optation in establishing a solid foundation for production. Examples of such a foundation are the institutions, history as well as ethics and politics. The latter co-occurs as expected with the vision of production based on suspension, and presents a high correlation with the need of escaping the linear trajectory of production.

This second group does not naively privilege an indeterminate form that by virtue of not being recognisable is also not appropriable, but does not dismiss it completely, believing in its potentiality given certain conditions. Although the analysis did not produce a clear answer to the question regarding how the production of value should work in order to escape appropriation, the analysis of these two opposed visions highlighted some critical aspects that constitute an important result. The most relevant aspects are collected here below, as the question also underlying these two opposite visions–whether production should be informed by privileging indeterminacy or its contrary, a solid foundation–presented interesting connections with the dimension of autonomy, the problem of the trajectory and more abstractly, with the conceptions regarding the role of art.

Besides the critique shared by all interviewees to the idea that performance can be produced outside market logic, the biggest problem presented by the perspective advocating indeterminacy is indeed the one regarding production in its abstract form. The problem was already presented in the theoretical framework with relation to the conceptualisation of novelty as an infinite recombination of pre-existing elements, highlighting how this conception is closer to innovation than the New and posed, in political terms, a paradigm so flexible that accommodating incremental change prevents radical change, i.e. revolution, to happen. The same emerged in the analysis and was addressed by tracing the difference between what is indeterminate and completely free of borders, and what is on the other hand incomplete. Embracing indeterminacy as a strategy of resistance within the conception of production as suspension shifts the focus to a more concrete question that goes to the core of the possible political role of art within society: 'the difficulty of this question regards how it could be possible to live in the present while keeping open a space of the possible' (DBG), that is, how to regain in the present the possibility to interrupt, make visible and work on the narratives regarding the future as a category of action. As a matter of fact, the interviewees do not underestimate the problem of production:

> Talking about indeterminacy, talking about the absence of a form... of a moment in which the form is subtracted from its clarity is important, but once that is done, the question becomes: and now? Where does indeterminacy bring us? If we are talking about potentiality, the question would be, is there an action that follows? Does the potential become something (DBG)?

Although all interviewees perceive the necessity of subtraction from an established path, it could be argued that, if this subtracting remains about suspension there is the risk that no production phase follows (GP, DBG, SB). It is in this sense that interviewees advocating suspension are far from unfamiliar with the debate around value and the critical aspects of postmodern discourse: they acknowledge that this aspect creates confusion with regards to the role of the artist and art organisations, and underlined how their work seems forced, somehow, to be useful, that is, to produce an easily recognisable impact. The rise of socially engaged art was analysed in this light by Claire Bishop (2004) in her critique of relational aesthetics; the need to limit indeterminacy to found the artistic work into something also becomes a matter of legitimation in the field analysis. The interviewees reflect on the need of grounding their work in something that cannot be exclusively put down to political engagement, which under the condition of neoliberal capitalism becomes problematic, as it implies the subjugation of art to a value system other than its own, namely that of neoliberal capitalism, which insists on attaching art to a purpose, lately defined as the social impact of art, exactly in order to appropriate and defuse its transformative potential. This critique could be considered not only in relation to the dimension of autonomy that emerged in the data, but also to that of verticality provided by Gielen's reflection on institutional critique (2013) in the theory, as the extract below well expresses:

> I'm suspicious on this idea of 'foundation' because it forces me to think about some kind of legitimation, like if... in a hypothetical abstract competition of things that matter, in which politics and neurosciences are winning and thus their place is recognised, art should aim at gaining the same place according to schemes that are arbitrary (GP).

Moreover, this idea of foundation could also represent an obstacle to production and even pave the way to reproduction: 'Foundation could also represent the same basis from which you don't depart, and this has nothing to do with the concept of resistance. It has to do with origin [...] we need to distinguish that from the concept of foundation as a new beginning and in this sense it has to do with the new and with production' (GP).

It is in this sense that it is possible to add a further critical aspect to the problem. A conceptualisation such as foundation is absolutely irreconcilable with production envisioned as self-betrayal, a concept that provided a much more fertile perspective in order to analyse the dynamics here in question, and builds interesting resonances with the Deleuzian repetition of differences. For the sake of completeness and complexity, this aspect of the debate was worth being mentioned, especially because it powerfully influences the interviewees' visions on the role of art within society and on the personal and collective responsibility of the theatre system: there is the need to elaborate a meaning of political engagement grounded in art's specific values, and rethinking the New and its production constitute a possible starting point in this endeavour, as it will be explored in the next paragraph.

6.3.1 System Reproduction and Disorganisation

The interviewees' accounts of the system within which they operate is not free of the criticism they expressed to the visual art system, and besides acknowledging the problems connected to immaterial value, they also address other aspects. The reasons behind this seem to be related to characteristics that are specific of performance and its production. On the one hand, 'museums, city theatres and factories belong to the same kind of economy' (MS). On the other, there are some characteristics specific to the postdramatic theatre system that should not be underestimated:

> the museum is a much more contemporary dispositive for experiences, the audience is much more susceptible, there's much more money involved, there are different kinds of money.... the dance system is always funded by the state... that is also one thing that is a problem and that theatre festivals will survive best next year as long as nothing changes... And what is also peculiar with dance and theatre production is that it's slow and heavy-footed (MS).

In this sense, the dynamics of the visual art system around the problem of appropriation of immaterial value are described as what the theatre system may expect, if a counter-action is not put in place (MS, DBG, GP, MG).

All interviewees perceive the general risks connected to capitalism that is infiltrating theatre's system of production and values: the focus on dance in museums is interpreted as the latest move of the system into immaterial economy, where the new as value and as label plays a fundamental role in terms of value production. Although all interviewees acknowledge that the theatre system is part of the same immaterial economy, possibilities of counter action are envisioned with reference to the recognition of the New as obscure and its production as the coexistence of differences. Moreover, a personal responsibility is felt by all interviewees who express the need for a change and the conviction that this change has to start from the actors involved in the field:

> Sometimes it seems that the artistic, the cultural, the views on the artistic sector or the artistic sector thinks about itself is that well, it's weird now, but soon we're going to be back in a society that looks like 1967. But this is certainly not going to happen. I think what we're looking forward to is a very abrupt and radical change of what, what art is to look like. And if the museum is also... and city theatre, and also Kampnagel, they are institutions that are... or frames that are strongly connected to an economy that is also over (MS).

Once acknowledged that the responsibility for change is shared by all those who take part in the production, the perspective on what needs to be changed differs from interviewee to interviewee. Still, the analysis of the segments highlighted that the rhythms of production, together with its general organisation represent the most relevant ones and that the categories of 'asynchrony' and 'non-organisation' shelter the possibility of changing things concretely regardless of interviewees' different perspectives. The other important aspect highlighted by the analysis is the shift from the individual focus that characterised the recognition of the New to the collective dimension as regards its production and the responsibilities connected to it.

The first cycle of coding produced the following codes: 'immaterial value'; 'co-optation'; 'asyncrony'; 'act inside/outside'; 'acceleration'; 'slowing down'; 'clarity'; 'non-organisation'. The analysis led to their grouping in two main categories connected with counteraction: asynchrony and non-organisation, which belong respectively to the dimension of time and that of obscurity.

Asynchrony and non-organisation are of course related as their meaning partially overlaps, entailing an aspect disjunction and resistance, and the analysis showed that the different rhythms of production–either faster or slower in comparison to those perceived as the system's–and the concept of non-organisation could be included in a wide conception of asynchrony, entailing both a temporal and a spatial dimension. Moreover, they both emerged as possible directions to explore while envisioning change in the system as a result of economic conditions that sets the rule of production within the system, provoking its acceleration and investing in its transparency.

As regards non-organisation, the field of experimental performing arts is described as too organised and clear by some interviewee. It is interesting to notice how the word clarity recurs (SB, MG, ML, MS, DBG) to describe the problem of production and of course it must be considered keeping in mind the relevance of obscurity that the analysis showed, with regards to both the recognition and the production of the New; and the description of transparency, provided in the theoretical framework on the bases of Han's analysis (2015), who finds in it one of the major characteristics by which capitalism reproduces itself. Capitalism, if it is perceived to be incredibly fast and so clear as to be transparent (SB, MS, MG), causing a sense of suffering, the idea of non-organisation assumes in the opinions of interviewees a particular role in terms of counteraction:

I think everything is possible, a lot of new things are possible. But we are in a system that is very much organised. If you change the system from the start and artists are completely funded in another way, presented in another way... then in the end people will start to create new kinds of work to present in this context, now the system is just so...well organised in a way. [...] We won't get any new work because the frame is too, is too set up in a way. The only way to create something new in the way that you mean is to be completely out of system (MG).

As the statements above show, the dimension of time and that of (non)organisation represent for some interviewees a possibility to think of the production of the New beyond the problem of appropriation. The idea of making unorganised what was before organised could be the concrete version of Benjamin's making incomplete what was before complete in its application to the field of postdramatic theatre.

As far as the rhythms of production as concerned, the system of postdramatic theatre is perceived as too fast and such acceleration is to be blamed on capitalism: 'There is a lot of bad work but most of the time is because the artist didn't have enough time to work on it, or it was the first idea that he had...so, in a way I think we let the new happen too quickly' (MG). The problem of acceleration appears to be particularly felt at the personal level, as the following segments highlight:

We're trapped...we would have to rethink the entire time process (ML).

My work never exists as such, it exists only as spatial-temporal concretion of the time rhythms I've been given, or of my aspirations and this is fatal in my opinion (GP).

On this basis, it comes as no surprise that all interviewees addressed the dimension of time by reflecting on how it could be possible to free production from the dynamic of appropriation. Although the majority of the interviewees acknowledge that an acceleration in terms of production processes happened (DBG, MS, GP, MG, ML) and generally think that the system of postdramatic theatre makes no exception, only two of them express the need to go slower. In slowing down the rhythm, they see a possibility for a production of the New, whose value could be indeed enriched by this mode of production and thus escape co-optation; such a theory, which is easily and rightfully subject to criticism, was already found in the literature review. If these two interviewees refuse the idea of acceleration, one instead states that acceleration represents the only possible way outside co-optation within the frame of neoliberal capitalism, expressing his familiarity with the accelerationist theories that recently entered the discourse:

> Neoliberalism is altogether interested in the production of the new. The way that we need to make ourselves, the way that we can produce the possibility for the new is by being a completely... a mystical organization: same as the new kind of company. And, for two reasons, on the one side to be able to expand, to be very, very dynamic, to be hyper-mobile, but also to not be visible, because the moment that you're visible you get copied and co-opted (MS).

From a more thorough analysis it emerged that neither acceleration nor slowing down represented such an important dimension as the notion of asynchrony, that what they embody is only a reductive part of the story. Moreover, as GP notices, they tend to be appropriated as such:

> There is the historically valued idea that there was a progressive acceleration that today reached its peak and thus velocity represents a value of capitalism. This is undoubtedly true from an historical point of view... as far as the acceleration of production processes is considered... still, I think that such an idea lacks critical considerations on some phenomenon happening in the past 20 years that have to do with the valorisation of slowness (GP).

This critique is accepted here: as long as there is no change in the mode of production, these strategies run the risk of remaining sterile and it will also be further developed with specific reference to aesthetic strategies based on time in theatre in the next chapter. In this respect, the analysis leads to the notion of asynchrony that, consistent with theory, is perceived in the field as fundamental in order to reconceptualise production. Asynchrony conjugates the idea of producing according to a different rhythm on the one hand, and results not in synchrony, non-fitting the organisation of the system on the other. The notion of non-organisation that emerged from the field seems to suggest an organisation that is not in synchrony with the system as a way out of its reproduction. As the theoretical inputs already indicated, a very clear, organised and synchronised production seems to lead to reproduction. The question of the paradigm is also implicitly addressed here together with the idea of working outside of it, although it must be specified, this view is considered very suspiciously in the data (MS, GP, SB, DBG).

Moreover, the interviewee that advocates the production of the New out of the system indeed refers to it. This clearly emerges in the practical examples he provides, specifically the festivals *Pazz* (Germany) and *In Between Time* (United Kingdom), which represent a very interesting experience with reference to the possibility of resistance to acceleration and asynchrony, but cannot be defined as working completely outside the system. Both festivals work and produce on a time scale that is indeed very slow in comparison to the sector and by virtue of this also produce and present some of the most interesting works. Still, their rhythm of production is developed in relation to that of the system and thus they do not constitute an instance of working outside the current paradigm. In this sense, the analysis of the interviews shows, as expected, the impossibility of producing completely outside of a paradigm. Still, it is important to specify that this does not result in a disillusioned and remissive approach. Contrariwise, all interviewees understand the production of the New as endowed with some revolutionary potential as long as the market does not absorb it.

The analysis shows that this possibility lies, in the opinion of the interviewees, in a particular notion of asynchrony comprising both a temporal and spatial dimension. With regards to the dimension of time, it is indeed the notion of asynchrony that presents the strongest relation with the code 'co-optation', also summarising the notions of acceleration and duration, which although controversial, are still present in the field in terms of discourse also because of their prominence in terms of artistic strategies. Moreover, asynchrony includes–as already stated in the theoretical framework with reference to Agamben's notion of contemporary–a strong spatial meaning, by which asynchrony emerges in relation to the possibility of escaping temporal linearity, to which the fieldwork added the fundamental notion of non-organisation.

With regards to the problem of appropriation, asynchrony emerges as important in relation to a production of the New that cannot be co-opted as long as it is conceived in a rather spatial perspective:

Asynchrony to me is always part of that 'step aside' in relation to the present that represents the opening of a crack in it. Thus it is a tool that forces the borders of the present and allows the other to appear as epiphany. Consequently I wouldn't exclude acceleration as a strategy, I don't' think it's antithetical, it is just that it doesn't represent the only option, and neither does slowing down. The point is: in which direction are we going faster or slower? If you're going faster towards building another paradigm you fall back into progress and innovation (DBG).

The production of the New outside co-optation, if possible, must thus embrace asynchrony in its spatial dimension, in order to allow the existence of an element strange to the system inside the system itself that might put it in question. This element might be nurtured, not so much as an indeterminate form, but rather as the cultivation of something incomplete, which is kept as such through strategies of non-organisation in the theatre system, cultivating obscurity in its poetics.

This asynchrony must be radical in order to unfold its potential and as such it shares, on the conceptual level, important characteristics with the New itself: 'it cannot be just a wrong gear that is still in the gear box. So, whereas the radically contemporary or the contemporary with the big C is this ending up on the side, it is ending up anachronistic, it is ending up paradoxical, it can also not be produced' (MS).

It is also in this light that it is fundamental to keep in mind, as the interviewees do, the relevance of the paradigm that the system represents: asynchrony becomes a dimension of action in the opinion of the interviewees just as long as this action takes place inside the system, notwithstanding personal ethics and some structural doubts:

> I never trusted it but if you go there, you go there to...you have to be like in a war strategy, you have to be, you have to enter the other camp to know what's inside, so you have to be ready for that (ML).

> I believe, where they say, ah-ha, you know it's not about being in the margins, that's easy...it's super easy to be you know, experimental film-maker in Finland, and backslap each other, we're 8 people, everybody is gonna love each other. The difficult thing is to be in the middle and change speed. No revolution is made by being on the outside, neither, right? So we have to be totally in the middle, but I think...but it is also a question where the middle is, right (MS)?

In these extracts, it emerges again how the interviewees tend to consider time and space as too deeply interconnected in order to be discussed as separate possibilities of counteraction and the potentiality of asynchrony lies in this interconnection. As it will explained in the next chapter, it is highly related to the dimension of autonomy and to that of collective production.

6.4 Art and Politics: Values and Roles

The dynamics involved in the production of the New after capitalism's immaterial turn are very complex: the previous paragraph showed the level of awareness and theoretical reflection in the field of postdramatic theatre. The investigation of these dynamics, which are motivated by capitalism's absorption not only of artists' work but also their values, would not be complete without the exploration of the perception of interviewees on the role of art within society and as regards the perception of their responsibilities. Although the current state of art could lead to a refusal of production and a dismissal of the system or to a spread sense of cynicism and powerlessness, implying a particular evaluation of the role of art today, the account of the field shows the willingness of thinking together about art's role and addressing individual and collective responsibilities in the conviction that art practices have consequences on reality.

On the other hand, the endeavour of changing things is neither perceived as an individual mission nor as characteristic of the art sectors: all interviewees can imagine the possibility of stopping doing what they do, and one interviewee actually did it exactly because of the dynamics described above. All the others have no doubt about the abstract possibility of doing something else, although they are not able to provide a concrete example.

Still, as it emerges clearly from the extracts collected in this chapter, the visions of interviewees do not point at a refusal of value in itself, nor of production, and reflect the urgency of changing the system: this depends on the important role they ascribe to art within the context of neoliberal capitalism, which emerges also as the main trigger to the willingness to reconceptualise production in itself: 'frankly I'm not for attacking the idea of production. Still it should be a free and liberated production... in this sense I do believe in the necessity of a foundation' (GP).

On the other side, it is very difficult to envision such a production under these conditions and one interviewee even doubts its possibility: '...and activist art, and then socially engaged art, all that stuff, that is not for me and is not for you. And, art is never particularly liberal, liberated, it's always... is never very independent but is always hooked up with the state' (MS).

As these last extracts highlight, the question around the role of art is deeply intertwined with the concept of purposefulness: fieldwork highlighted the importance of ethics in addressing not so much the contents but the modalities of art production, and the politics of use that the system sets for the value produced, which can be influenced through a collective effort. On the basis of the field's account, art has a political engagement which has little to do with politically engaged art, as it appears according to the narrative of neoliberal capitalism. This emerged in the analysis through a particular distinction between two ways of thinking art's role, in relation to 'society' and in relation to 'reality'. The word 'society' was used in the field in relation to what is generally described as social practices, or socially engaged art, and showed a point of view highly critical of all those art practices:

> But in art I can't be an activist for example; because when you're an activist you have answers, you know what you want. And you're fighting for it. Or maybe you don't know what you want but you're fighting for what you don't want, but you know' (RB).

This perspective can be read as a response to the pressure on artists and art organisations to be useful, and is criticised as far as they find their value only in relation to society's needs and thus ground their practice in relation to it, privileging heteronomic values over autonomous ones. In this sense, it is linked to the necessity of re-thinking the notion of political engagement under the conditions of neoliberal capitalism: interviewees ascribe a very important function to art, that–in order to be fulfilled–must be detached from any clear social purpose, underlining how Adorno's reflections are still very valuable today.

The role of art in the society of purpose and clarity then unfolds in its capacity to ask questions and enable the discussion that these questions trigger:

What I am proposing in art is that you really have a question you don't know. So you can't really be an activist for something that you're still doubting, still questioning, when you're betraying yourself. And really I don't want to change anything in this sense, with art. I don't believe that art should change anything so it's not about changing... It's about creating a conversation and dialogue. So it's the after performance which is the issue... we're giving them on the hope that we go on for a next step together in the future (RB).

As this extract suggests, there is a profound difference between art and politics with respect to dimension and possibility of change. Neglecting such difference by attaching a clear purpose to artistic production would imply defusing the political power of art, which is recognised by all interviewees in the dimension of obscurity as opposed to the clarity that characterises politics and political activism. The potential of art, contrary to that of politics, does not unfold in making a strong proposal of change, nor in offering a clear solution, but rather in the opposite direction: it is not about proposing an alternative but rather in letting people acknowledge the existence of many different possibilities.

It is very important to underline that this perspective has nothing to do with a step back from the current issues, and regards the necessity to defend art's values and autonomy, not negating its potential for change but actually cultivating it despite the mechanism of capitalist absorption. It is in this sense that interviewees feel a personal responsibility: if the production of the New does not unfold in making a strong proposal, it might be grounded in a strong statement.

One of the interviewees (GP) defined innovation as a proposal on what exists that has an impact on it appearing mostly through incremental changes. In light of the exploration of the field's value, it can be argued that the production of the New could be oppositely defined as a statement. It is in this sense that thinking the role of art with reference to reality rather than to society provides interesting insights. According to all interviewees, art production entails a potential in terms of change, although it cannot be conceived and evaluated according to the criteria of purposefulness and effectiveness of politics (DBG, SB, MS, RB). The potential and value of art lie in rethinking its engagement with what exists at large, by reducing the purposeful engagement that capitalism promotes not only with reference to society, but also in relation to what exists:

I don't think that engagement isn't interesting... it is absolutely interesting to harvest the existing but, when you do something–no matter whether as artist, curator or researcher–and you feel you created the possibility of being suspended for an instant, of seeing reality without having offered a solution but having given rise to a doubt... then that's wonderful (DBG).

The role of art is described in the interviews as that of 'instilling the virus of the doubt' (RB) and thus implies not only a focus on questions rather than answers, but also the detachment of artworks from the category of information.

This result could be read again as a facet of the need to defend art by remarking the differences from creativity and, at a broader level, to distinguish the New from its alias: the compulsoriness of creativity, discussed in the theoretical framework, contributed to a narrowing of its meaning into problem-solving. It is also in this light that Gielen (2013) underlined the historical role of the artist as problem creators. More precisely, the role of art is conceived in the interviews as that of 'widening the texture of reality' (DBG), so that its redundancy could emerge. Here the need to respect the difference between art and politics is clearly expressed by all interviewees who connect the role of giving precise information and to propose alternatives to the latter, while wishing to re-affirm the opposite function to the former.

The analysis showed that this conception of art does not imply any playful or romantic description of the artist as someone that refuses to assume the responsibility on the consequence of his or her production. More precisely, this sense of responsibility unfolds in acknowledging the potentialities and limits of art production, filling them with meaning on the one hand, and on acknowledging, on the other, that such a fragile production may entail serious consequences:

Many do have this responsibility, but without being pretentious, I believe that the sense of what we do as researchers, artists, curators...lies in shifting, in moving even a few millimetres, the texture of reality to let it appear in its being non necessary [...] In a political perspective, such questions are explosive: the society in which we live is natural or is it just one of the diverse possibilities that we could have chosen? These questions are dangerous, destabilizing...they could undermine any system (DBG).

In this sense, the production of the New in art gains a political dimension on the individual level: not necessarily in engaging with social and political issues directly at the content level through modalities that have been set in other spheres, but rather in the methodological widening of the texture of reality.

Accordingly, it is possible to speak of concrete change just by tackling and changing the mode of production, and here the individual responsibility must be matched, according to the interviewees, by a collective effort. Going back to the category of the trajectory and the necessity of escaping it, and the difference between the indeterminate and the incomplete, the field locates the possibility of concrete change in the moment of interruption; the presence of a clear trajectory that can be undermined through specific indeterminate forms, made again incomplete, and suspending it for a moment. This moment of interruption is characterised by not knowing where collectivity is directed, and in terms of concrete change, everything depends on what the collectivity builds in that moment of suspension: we cannot be sure that the concept of experimentation will not be re-absorbed in the system and yet, sometimes, according to the field, it might be good not to know. This is what the field describes as real collective artistic experimenting, while regarding the question whether it is possible to escape the linear trajectory and change things radically, that calls for a political answer that is a collective one.

The fieldwork showed the centrality of the collective aspect. Yet, the account it provides does not regard a notion of collaboration devoid of critical aspects, which has occupied the discourses and practices in the field in recent times. As it will be deepened in the next chapter, it is a collaboration developing in the coexistence of differences, which through conflicts and non-organisation is enabled to act on the dimension of time. The latter also recurs in relation to art's role within neoliberal capitalism in so far as the present time must be opened up, enabling the community to take part in the time that is yet to come, and thus in the possibility of changing things concretely.

7. The Production of the New in the Theatre of the Present

The notion of the New suggested in this work differs from the one common in innovation research in its conceptual, temporal and value aspects and is characterised by the impossibility of establishing a relationship to it. This impossibility depends on the coexistence of radically different concepts (the eternal and ephemeral, ordinary and overwhelming) in a whole object or idea that yet remains open. Its production is characterised by the absence of directionality and of purpose. Purposelessness and the absence of a linear trajectory allow the New to express its full value and function, at the individual, collective and political level.

This working definition resulted from the analytical combinations of theoretical and empirical research and singled out the dimensions to be considered when tackling the concept of the New within neoliberal capitalism and within the specific field of postdramatic theatre, offering at the same time theoretical tools that could be applied in other fields. In particular, the field analysis highlighted the possibilities of addressing the problem through the dimensions of time and space, the cultivation of differences, the possibilities of escaping the linear trajectory of production and its narrative, and the importance of the political aspect across individuals and communities. Moreover, the fieldwork allowed for other dimensions to emerge, such as conflicting collaboration, autonomy and non-organisation, which complete the account of the field and help to address its specific needs and discourses in order to envision possible directions of action.

In this chapter, the most relevant dimensions are tackled again with an abductive approach, aimed at highlighting the synergy emerging from their interconnection. Researching their unexpected connections allow for investigations into how they can be put into practice in the field of postdramatic theatre.

7.1 Art Institutions as Frames

The concept of paradigm–related to that of trajectory, which recurred in all aspects of the analysis–is particularly relevant as it emerged from the very beginning of the fieldwork: the New is defined as something to which it is impossible to establish a relationship and it lasts as long as this relationship is not defined, as long as its trajectory remains illegible: 'in no way the new can become a canon…the moment in which it becomes a paradigm, that's the constitutive moment of innovation' (GP). In this sense it is also possible to look at the Avant-garde that represents the moment in which the question of the paradigm in arts came to the fore. At this standpoint of the research it is possible to look back at the modern discussion on the new becoming tradition and state that it seemed to regard the process of innovation more than that of the production of the New. The following extract expresses this aspect directly:

Avant-garde, from an etymological perspective, is a military term, they are outposts; they are ahead exactly because the others will then follow. I didn't think about it in this sense up to now, but maybe there is a deeper connection between innovation and avant-garde rather than new and avant-garde with reference to this (GP).

If the modern debate on the new becoming tradition remains relevant today, it was taken as a starting point to elaborate on the New and its production within the contemporary context and to explore the concrete translation of this problem into the sector. In this regard the analysis showed two particularly relevant connections: the question of who defines what is New within the field and the debate on institutions that focus their production on innovation.

With reference to the first, the voices collected in the field are unanimous: innovation–or what in the field is described as 'the fresh'–is always defined in the sector of postdramatic theatre by somebody, who could be 'people in power who also force it' (RB) or less cynically, 'much more connected to non-individual forms' (DBG), which include artists, curators and above all, the audience (DBG; ML; MG; SB; RM). On the other hand, nobody can decide what the New is; it defines itself as such and here results were equally converging. The appearing of the New in the field does not depend on any external recognition and could also happen in the form of a proclamation:

Then, maybe one can think that there's new with a big N and instead of saying new with a small 'n' we re-baptise it 'the fresh' for the moment. So the new, nobody defines. The new with the big N defines itself and it is always a network, but it is through complexities that are extra-human in some other mystical fucking way... these things, they usually don't end up in the big museums. What ends up in the big museum and what museums define together with collectors and people sitting in the collectors' board and people sitting in the board of the collectors and blablabla, which are the same folks, they define 'the fresh' (MS).

Interestingly, the majority of interviewees in order to describe this difference refer to politics, and two of them bring up the example of revolution (DBG, GP):

This second moment that sets up the form is the moment of innovation that builds a paradigm on what's left from before. But the first moment, that of uprising...it is very difficult to say who decides that. It's a question exploded in a certain moment and in the moment in which it is born, it explodes as pure potency and then it transforms and legitimately looks for the new paradigm, the new form, the next step... and it is just then that you can say who decides, people who are more or less influential in political terms decide (DBG).

This aspect is of course highly related to another axial category that emerged in the study, that of autonomy: the New, defined by the impossibility to establish a relation to it, is deeply autonomous in its self-definition: such New does not result from an external recognition but is rather a 'proclamation' (GP). When this external recognition is given, a relationship is defined and that is done of course in relation to the current paradigm or in the case of more radical change, by creating another one that will result as new in comparison to the precedent one, being this the process of innovation.

The second connection that emerged from the abductive analysis in relation to the paradigm is that of institutions, with a specific reference to innovative theatre and festivals operating within the field. Investigating this relationship highlights that acknowledging the New as something that defines itself apparently outside of a given paradigm–more precisely, in the interruption of a given trajectory–does not imply that interviewees believe that the New could be produced out of nothing. The relationship between the code paradigm and that of the institution underlines the opposite: a frame is necessary to the production of the New and art institutions often provide it. Moreover, in the analysis, institutions represent a starting point to reflect upon reproduction and change not exclusively in reference to the theatre system, which is a concrete example of a more abstract discourse.

Institutions are generally perceived as one 'naturally conservative' force within a system that tends to reproduction and this applies to theatre festivals and institutions. The conservative soul of institutions obviously has to do with the survival of the system. Consequently the production of the New inside them is generally very difficult, as it would imply the existence of an element extraneous to the system within it and this regards the production of both new works and new work practices, which impact on the possibility of rethinking the theatre system anew.

In this sense, 'a young artist would go for–like most people–a work that is original, maybe not new, to fit in the frame and make a living out of the practice and not say, 'ok, I'll go completely against the system and create something that...' (MG). Although this sentence did not come to end, it is true that most of the people indeed, independently from their occupation in life, are 'alone in front of the alternative between not producing and producing in a rush because of the conditions you're given... also to remain inside an institution' (GP). To 'fit in the frame' (MG) is then also a matter of survival for individuals whose production inside the frame seems to lose any potential of resistance. With reference to activist art practices inside institutions, GP says: 'you cannot present such a work as a strategy of resistance, unless you tell me, "I'm acting as Torquato Tasso did, I live at the court and there I produce masterpieces"–I would respect you more'.

All these segments could be traced back to the political awareness of the interviewees who all acknowledge the dynamics of appropriation and reproduction as innate to the system, it being capitalism or postdramatic theatre, where institutions themselves have to fit in the frame at the cost of their survival: 'it is difficult that a system puts itself in the conditions of letting live inside itself something that is so different that can't be recognised...I mean, I find it normal that there is a normalising tendency' (SB).

Notwithstanding this awareness that is shared by all interviewees, institutions emerge as the necessary frame for the production of the New; this also represents an important result with reference to what has been said in the theoretical framework regarding the debate on engaging with or deserting art institutions in the quest of changing the current situation of production and work conditions. To use the language of the interviewees, conceiving institutions as frames may allow an interesting dialectic between their conservative force and the production of the New:

On one side they're not going in the direction of the new, on the other they're always in the context where the new is formed. I don't think that the new will come by destroying institutions. The new is always a 'crack' inside an existing architecture: eliminating the architecture would eliminate the possibility to see the possible beyond it (DBG).

This extract shows the importance of the frame as such to envision the production of the New and could be read consistently with the role ascribed to institutional space, and especially institutional imagination within the theory: Groys (2008), Lehmann (2006) and Gielen (2013), although from very different perspectives and within different arguments, stress the importance of the museum or the art institution in allowing visitors to see the difference beyond the difference, the possible beyond what exists and also question the latter by virtue of being in a privileged space of observation. It is also in this sense that the category of autonomy–stressed by Gielen as regards the institutions' role to defend the art sphere's autonomy in defining its own values–must be considered in relation to institutions as single theatres and festivals:

I'm convinced that the political aspect specific of artistic production lies in the mode of production itself and this is also the terrain on to which institutions can then forge their relationship with other spheres [...] Autonomy has always to do with the production of the new...because it is something unimaginable (GP).

Theatre institutions are also under pressure to fit in the frame which, as already mentioned in the previous chapter, is 'too set-up to get any new work' (MG): in the case of institutions this regards not only the risk they undertake to sustain the production of new artworks but also how they set up the production itself in terms of modalities and work practices. The frame constituted by the institution of the market is set so that all elements could indeed fit in it without undermining it. In this context, institutions of postdramatic theatre could be envisioned as:

> one dialectical space, or rather a 'space of conflict' between the conservative movement that is ingrained in them and an element of rupture that I believe could be brought inside their dynamics of production (SB).

Consequently, art organisations and festivals may represent the necessary frame of the production of the New, as long as they are able to put themselves in the condition of letting the unrecognisable, the difference beyond the difference exist inside them. Suggestions in this direction emerge in connection to the diverse aspects that constitute the main results of the field analysis, addressed through an abductive approach. In particular, institutions could be sites of cultivation of difference, as it will be considered in the next paragraph, where the collective dimension, both in terms of collaboration and conflict, represents an axial category of analysis.

7.2 The Collective Cultivation of Difference

If the experience of the New arises when two radically different attributes coexist–the ordinary and the overwhelming, the entire and the open, the old and the contemporary–its production must be envisioned in order to cultivate such differences and of course their coexistence.

Here, the dimension of autonomy should not be forgotten, as it represents the basis to talk about coexistence in the first place. Autonomy in this context also informs a possible reconceptualisation of the dimension of collaboration, which recurs in all interviews with interesting connotations, according to which, conflict represents a fundamental dimension of the production of the New, 'as a possibility of coexistence of those who are different in a space of conflict that could be active and working without interrupting the productive activity of these subjects within it' (SB).

In this sense, the most interesting way to tackle the abstract category of autonomy into the field of postdramatic theatre is to consider it in connection with the category of collaboration, in its sub-category of 'conflict.' Moreover, the analysis clearly shows that conflict and collaboration must not be perceived as opposite in this context. Collaboration based on conflict is affirmed as a fundamental dimension of the production of the New:

> I mean, if you fix two logics together, if you choose–because it is just a matter of choosing in my opinion–if you choose to work together in a togetherness that doesn't imply to look for mediation but rather that is about creating a space in which each logic, each modality,

could unfold fully, becoming stronger by clashing with the other... it is rare to find the right conditions but I believe that there is an incredible revolutionary potency in it (SB).

The potentiality of collaboration has also been addressed by Bojana Kunst (2010), according to whom, collaboration cannot be considered aside from the temporal dimension and in close connection with potentiality: 'through collaboration, we condition our future lives together, which of course means that, in order to open up the time, we have to take time out of the obsession with presence and participate in the time what has yet to happen. Working together is a time constellation, which opens a spatial potentiality for proximity, something which appears as a neighbouring space, a space that is added' (Kunst 2010: 28). Collaboration based on conflicts represents a valid tool both at the individual and the collective level. Curators and artists perceive in their mutual collaboration–to be enlarged to include also organisers and in some case the audience–a possible dimension of action to produce the New: 'I believe a lot in conflict...especially between artists and curators, looking at them as machines, in the sense of building blocks of an engine, deeply autonomous one from the other, characterised by thoroughly different functioning that are also profoundly conflicting' (SB). It is interesting to notice that conflict here emerges almost as a *conditio sine qua non* with regards to the curatorial work that is perceived, contrary to the artistic one, as love-driven, spontaneously conservative and horizontal rather than vertical (SB, ML, RB). The production of the New, in order to be called such in postdramatic theatre cannot happen without the coexistence and cultivation of differences like the one described above.

The account the field gives of conflicting collaboration does not emerge as a dialectical process between two different subjects aimed at reaching a synthesis. Rather, it recalls what Sennet described as a dialogical exchange–a word he borrows from Bakhtin–whose process is opposite to the converging dynamics of dialectics, used 'to name a discussion which does not resolve itself by finding common ground' (Sennet 2012: 19). A dialogic exchange does not aim at overcoming differences; rather it engages the cultivation of their coexistence and nurtures the temporality it requires. The term coexistence implies a spatial dimension as well as a temporal one, since this conflicting exchange must be hosted somewhere and kept open without solving it in one precise, entire, complete identity, at least for a while. Here, institutions are the privileged actors in terms of space as is the community in terms of time.

Institutions in this sense represent the possibility to provide the unshaped differences and conflicts with the entireness, the frame that emerged as fundamental for the recognition and the production of the New in the field. At the same time, the collective dimension may act on how long this exchange in suspension could last, influencing directly its time dimension in terms of duration and thus also offering a way to work on the ephemerality of the New:

The duration of the new has to do partially with the idea of community. It's difficult to make this suspension last when you reason as single, as 'curator-subject'. It is probably the sum of the impulses that makes it impossible for the new to assume a single form and be defined as such, to keep open a non-determined that escapes the establishment of a paradigm (DBG).

As it appears in the extract above, the idea of community allows a reconsideration of the paradigm question because it addresses in concrete terms one of the major critical aspects of the postdramatic theatre system within neoliberal capitalism, that of being too organised and clear. The coexistence of differences in fact suggests an idea of production able to slip out of clarity and organisation to focus on betrayal and suspension, which, as a matter of fact: 'springs out non-coordination' as 'it's the conflicting impulses that make this space still alive' (DBG). In this perspective, the institution is affirmed once again as central, on the one hand because it represents one collective subject capable of producing non-coordination and on the other because of the spatial dimension that the concept of institution entails: 'it is the institution that as space can allow the existence of a complexity and the coexistence of radically different identities' (SB).

7.3 Curating Obscurity

The non-coordination of multiple, conflicting impulses gives a more specific form to the urges that came forth in relation to production, already described by interviewees either through the terms obscurity, indeterminacy and cloud. In the spirit of thinking together with the interviewees' perspectives on the concrete implications of these concepts, the connections between them and the dimensions of non-organisation, and of the individual and collective effort, have been investigated. If self-betrayal and obscurity are conceived and connected to the individual aspect of production, the idea of the nebula and indeterminacy hardly seems to be able to become tangible without a collective subject behind it.

The reflections collected in the data on putting these ideas into practice seem to converge in particular on festivals–a format of production interviewees are very familiar with–that were considered as particularly interesting subjects in the light of the reflection carried out in relationship to these concepts. In the field, festivals, with due differentiations regarding their size and scope, are fully considered art institutions. Yet, given their particular mode of production–the spatio-temporal intensity that characterises their appearance as a moment of interruption of normal rhythm and the temporary community they create–the same characteristics also turned them into a very fertile format for neoliberal mechanisms; they are considered a particular kind of institution. They are described as able to conjugate the individual and collective instances by offering a curatorial approach based on obscurity and transforming the festival itself into something obscure that could in this sense resemble a cloud and thus flourish on the diverse impulses that animate it. The opportunity to conjugate the individual with the collective in these particular terms, allows further reflections on the aspects of clarity, transparency and organisation within festivals:

> I'm deeply interested in the debate on more or less thematic festivals, more or less 'traceable' festivals in terms of curatorial and organisational strategies. When such strategies are very clear, their focus or modality is very legible...when it comes to curating, easily readable strategies may defuse the revolutionary potential of many works. What interests me is to create a bewildering horizon of diversity where different visions could pop up (SB).

A curatorial approach based on a clear theme is then perceived as an unviable strategy because of its deep inconsistency with the relevance of obscurity–a vital characteristic of both the New and art at large–emerged in the field analysis. Contrariwise, a festival able to value obscurity could also produce that 'nebula'–characteristic of production as suspension–that makes one available for the possibility of the New. More precisely, festivals organised around a topic became more and more a showcase devoid of critical thinking, subjected to the neoliberal tendency to privilege exhibition over production. The curatorial approach here described can also be thematic but must be grounded in a research question that creates the conditions for production both as regards the concrete support for the material production of performances and in terms of critical thinking.

Festivals in this sense represent an interesting place where the collective dimension embodied in the 'nebula' is fuelled by singular practices based on obscurity and self-betrayal, operated by artists and curators that, in the context of a festival, may become universal.

If the festival could be a place for bewildering, the single works must be an invitation to enter such bewilderment. In this sense, the idea of production could be reconceptualised within festivals following the satisfaction of the incomplete, through valorising questions over answers and bewilderment over information.

> On the idea that artists should propose a strong idea... I believe that an artist's proposal is strong exactly in the moment in which it is fragile, I mean when it is an invitation, when it doesn't pile the spectator with information but rather invites him or her to enter the bewildering, this cloud of the work, the performance (DBG).

More precisely, interviewees envision here festivals as time-space units where it is possible to use in infinite ways, to have a program that could be misunderstood (RM, SB) and thus turn into a place of production.

Such a production is described as 'singular and universal' (MS) at the same time and develops by virtue of producing first and foremost a doubt, 'which is not a private, existential doubt but rather a universal doubt on the present as we know it. It is not a mean to reach a goal, to find an answer, but a mean without a goal–let's say, quoting Agamben–that's the core of the question' (DBG). Following this direction, the festival format, already a paradigm of neoliberal appropriation could still entail a resistant element, and produce a space of non-organisation, a space in between the works, where the audience, the artists and the temporary community of the festival could think together and take part to the creation of the overall experience not so much in terms of sterile participation; rather taking part in building the politics of use of this particular format and its particular contents.

7.4 Roles and Rules: Impossible Possibilia

The results presented in the previous paragraphs emerged out of a distinction operative in the field, sometimes more explicitly, sometimes less, between the role of the artists and that of curators, and another between individual and collective subjects. These distinctions are quite relevant and thus deserve a deeper reflection as regards their connections with other important aspects. In particular the abstract category of 'possibility' showed the highest number of co-occurrences in the analysis with diverse codes regarding the conventions, the rules and the roles of the actors, as perceived by the interviewees that take part in production, including the audience. More specifically, the production of the New based on the category of possibility–a production that goes through the process of making incomplete what was before complete–is described indirectly by ascribing to the artist the role of problem creating, underlining again the need to distinguish the production of the New in art from the general idea of creativity and resist the pressure of other spheres on art's values. In relation to this, the role of the curators–and the rule for the institutions in which they work–is that of giving up control.

It is interesting here to reason on how the suggestion of giving up control could be combined with responsibility, especially as regards the responsibility of the producers for the audience, whose role emerges in a particular balance between active and passive. On the one hand, the audience's role is essential for production: fieldwork highlighted many times that the lack of consumption of a work would put in question the very concept of production when it comes to performance. On the other, the role of the audience seems to be informed by particular rules and conventions that set it partially outside of production: 'The role of the audience I guess is...well of the artist first, is to come to the audience to share his questions and doubts' (RM).

Here, it is interesting to notice how the dimension of collaboration is equally relevant to the audience, as it was to artists and curators, but when it comes to the former, conflict is completely out of the picture; in its place, collaboration takes the meaning of sharing which, in turn, is completely absent between curators and artists or at least in the account that interviewees give of it. This does not imply any kind of inequality, as 'an artwork is not like an expert on stage, doing something and then non-expert watching it and... it's another kind of relationship' (MG). As above-mentioned, the audience cannot be underestimated in the production of the New because when it comes to performance it makes no sense to talk about production without consumption. Moreover the fieldwork highlighted that 'for something to be validated as new, it also needs an audience' (MG), and its role is recognised as pivotal by all interviewees, not only in terms of validation but also in terms of production, here well described: '(as audience) you produce it and this production is your production, it is not the performance that tells you what to produce, but it is telling you that you cannot avoid production; either you look away or you have to step in, so to say' (MS).

Yet, the very nature of the works constituting the field appears, especially for the audience approaching them for the first time, as deeply self-referential, in particular when artistic research is tackling the New. If this relationship is not about an expert on stage and a non-expert watching it, it might be that described by Rancière on the basis of his reflections on the ignorant schoolmaster, who does not know the 'stupefying distance, distance transformed into a radical gulf that can only be bridged by an expert' (Rancière 2014: 10), and thus engages in an emancipatory practice with his pupils. The very nature of the New–and generally the nature of experimental art forms–creates a distance with the general public, which could be the object of critique as regards the democratisation of the arts. Yet, according to Rancière, the distance is entailed in the performance itself, conceived as an autonomous thing between an artist's idea and the spectators' comprehension. As such, it is necessary:

> In the logic of emancipation, between the ignorant schoolmaster and the emancipated novice there is always a third thing–a book or some other piece of writing–alien to both and to which they can refer to verify in common what the pupil has seen, what she says about it and what she thinks of it. The same applies to performance. It is not the transmission of the artist's knowledge or inspiration to the spectator. It is the third thing that is owned by no one, whose meaning is owned by no one, but which subsists between them excluding any uniform transmission any identity of cause and effect (ibid., 14-15).

Envisioning the relationship with the audience in these terms could be part of rethinking the political engagement of art and doing it according to art's autonomous values, leaving traditional education to the sphere it belongs and interweaving different paths of knowledge production across different groups.

The fieldwork highlights that the roles and rules informing the productive activity of artists and institutions are not set aside from the audience. Still, in order to concretely embrace production as possibility, the perception of the interviewees unfolds in a particular relation to them, highlighting once again the role of conflict and non-organisation which, as already stated, needs a collective subject, provided by the audience. More specifically, artists could put the production of possibility in practice by more or less deliberately creating problems, and institutions could embrace artists' contributions in order to actively engage in the non-organisation provided by these problems.

In this scenario, the curatorial approach must loosen or even give up control. SB provides the example of an artist who noticed how everything in the festival was functioning perfectly: such organisation resulted in inflexibility, with a pressure that defused the questions he had, and undermined the contribution–in the form of problems–he was bringing to the festival. The reason for this collision can be found in the perception that artists have of their role in the first place: 'what we do, we don't bring truths, that's the job of the scientist, but what the artist can do is mystical, is mystic truths, not mystical but mystic truths, in the sense that it is definitely the truth but we don't know how' (MS). It is in this sense that the role of the curator emerges by loosening or giving up control and maybe also in taking part in the creation of problems: 'I would like to have the possibility to say to an artist: 'ok, then I will take responsibility for it...as far as I am concerned, you come here to bring us some problems [...] I think that institutions could somehow welcome these problems, I mean as a curator inside an institution I could try to propose this, to pull some tricks, to create problems to people... I think it would be also the right thing to do' (SB). As the accounts of experiences of production based on problem creating and giving up control are numerous in the data, questions rise on what the consequence could be of embracing such an approach on a broader level, for instance on applying this to a whole festival:

If this happens on the project level, I ask myself what would happen if someone decides that the whole festival is a field of experimentation in this sense...what if as a curator you could say: 'ok, I leave the festival open, I let it be used in a way different from how I conceived it; I let artists' processes to go off the rails and go where we haven't thought (SB).

Still, although curators (SB, MG, ML) express the desire that artists as well as audiences could feel free to use the festival they envisioned in different ways, and thus give up control, they all acknowledge that this is very difficult to put into practice. Such a difficulty does not exclusively depend on the roles and rules of the game–which are entrenched in the system and naturally work for its reproduction–but also on the strong sense of responsibility, that seem hardly compatible with the idea of giving up control. As already mentioned in the previous chapter, this sense of responsibility is highly felt also by the artists interviewed, notwithstanding the value ascribed to the possibility of creating problems: 'But there are rules. Like ok, I already prepared and the audience is coming… they are very generously coming without, sometimes without expectation or with generosity' (RB).

'What if?' thus emerges as the guiding question not only for artists but also for institutions, and in the interviews, this 'what if' represents the concrete tool to explore and envision production as possibility, and more interestingly to go beyond the roles and rules of the game.

It is in this sense that the data offers the chance to think the question 'what if' also in terms of political value. If rules demarcate the borders between what is possible and what is impossible, envisioning a production based on the 'what if'–in its double facet of problem creating and giving up control–could indeed shake such borders. It must be specified that such reflections regard the political aspect within the field of performance and thus within art: it is the artistic context, with all its limits, that allows playing with the possible and the impossible. Still, as had already emerged in the previous chapter, this does not imply the absence of consequences: on the one hand, the doubt on reality as we know it has the potential to destabilise any system; on the other, framing this as only art could force potentially powerful artworks in the category of the exception that confirms the norm as the strange element re-absorbed by the system.

Moreover, it is important to remember that such approaches are thought in the spirit of rethinking production, and this implies that some kind of production must take place. In this sense one of the most interesting questions emerging from the field regards what could be able to 'keep all this together' (MG, SB, DBG). If the New is produced in a structure that must be entirely something but at the same time 'incomplete' or 'open', a dimension that guarantees this being entire must be singled out. Also keeping in mind the potentialities and downsides of art's consequences on reality, the following paragraph addresses this problem from within a larger perspective.

7.5 Works in Progress and Failure

It is possible to state that the concept of linear trajectory arose in the theoretical framework as one of the most useful to trace the line between the

New, innovation and creativity, and the field analysis confirmed this dimension as fundamental. However, once crossed with visions on concrete dimensions of action in the realm of postdramatic theatre, it is what characterises the linear trajectory that offers the most interesting insights and in particular its aspects of continuity and divisibility.

In particular, the idea that the New could be recognised only as 'altogether different' alongside the need to subtract oneself from a linear trajectory emerged concretely in the field as a refusal of partiality. In relation to this, innovative works were distinguished from new works by the fact that the former are described as projects and the latter as events (GP, SB, ML). Moreover, the complexities related to the system relying on projects were brought to the fore in the theoretical framework, underlining the specific temporality they entail that unfolds exactly in the divisibility of a linear trajectory. This puts the artists in the paradoxical position of having to propose future scenarios, being trapped at the same time in a present that seems to repeat itself and escapes the possibility to be inhabited for actually benefiting the potentiality of thinking the future.

Thinking how to connect these abstract categories with today's theatre system, the fieldwork highlighted that 'the new can happen only in terms of product' (SB). Still, there is the need to readdress the matter in the field, where 'what happens very often is that you tend to have finished works that actually are work in progress…you see work which is called a production but actually is still very much in research…I cannot find every year more than 30-40 shows, we see quite a lot …that can be presented, the process is never finished but at least it reached a point that is strong enough to share…a lot of work we see is just a work in progress that is called a work' (MG).

Here, it is noticeable that although all interviewees stress the importance of production and thus of product over processes, the vision of production provided entails indeed a process quality, as also SB notices: 'if we think in terms of "what if", that is thoroughly a process. Still the new can happen only in a finished product. We all know that'.

It is in this sense that the institution, could offer the space and the structure where these processes maintain the openness they require and still gain the status of products, since the New that is envisioned here emerges as a whole product that yet remains incomplete. A possible path to follow that developed in this direction is represented by failure. In the light of what emerged up to now, this is not a surprising result given the attention dedicated to works in progress and errors in the field at large. As logic maintains, errors are linked to process while failure is linked to product. Consistently with other aspects that characterise contemporary production, failure:

was first rejected and then reintegrated as a productive moment of a given trajectory. This is fully acceptable and doesn't present any problem in itself. The problem arises when failure is seen exclusively as positive. This idea is well expressed by the English way of saying 'falling ahead' which means that even when you fall you make a step forward on a trajectory. Well, there are situation where you fall exactly where you are and those should be accepted as possible and valid as such independently from the path in which they're inscribed... I see here some affinity with the discourse on creativity (DBG).

Indeed, as creativity seems to have substituted the concept of the New, charging it with diverse positive characteristics that bestow certain lightness to the concept, errors seem to have substituted failure:

> Contrary to failure, errors are something that belong more to our contemporary times, to its uncertainties and contrary to failure I see it as perspective, as a wide vision: errors are not a terminal point of a process, they can be repeated in different forms. They present an aspect of multiplicity in space and in time (SB)

Here, it is necessary to underline that errors could be a powerful trigger of the production of the New just as long as they do not substitute the possibility of failure, as such substitution would imply the smoothing of the potentiality of errors into a neoliberal narrative. Works in progress exemplify the risks of such substitution. By negating the option of failure, errors may be seen exclusively as steps forward on a linear trajectory, which is inconsistent with the idea of production here developed. It is in this sense that SB states: 'We need to shift the focus again on product and failure, out of which we collectively run away to refuge in a conceptual comfort zone'.

A second very concrete possibility is represented by a critical approach to works in progress, as it was already possible to evince from the segments collected above. Also from the point of view of an institution that produces and programmes works, the importance to be one open structure in order to nurture the New triggers reflection on the practice of producing, programming and presenting works in progress.

Although some aspect of openness and indeterminacy characterising works in progress may be seen as consistent with the idea of the New presented here, it is important to underline that the New could be such just as whole, outside partiality and process. In this sense, festivals encouraging too much work in progress do not represent a good context for the production of the New. It could also be argued that they are not even producing at all (GP). As a matter of fact, works in progress are inconsistent with the idea of product, or more precisely, constitute a way of fixing a process in an easily recognisable form able to work within what Kunst (2012) defined as the project horizon:

> When you propose it to the audience, you give a name to it, you fix it: that is the crystallisation of your product and you are responsible for it. Somehow you run a risk but you have to... it is inconceivable that you put that thing within brackets as partial element of something... the logic of work in progress should be eliminated by institutions. Works in progress are almost always strategies that we use to fix in the form of product what we're

doing...so that we can finance the continuation of our work...this represents to me the death of the new (GP).

Moreover, stressing the openness that never reaches the status of a product, it is inconsistent with self-betrayal, which indeed needs something specific to betray: contrary to innovations that take the form of the proposal, betrayal and suspension require the form of a statement.

7.6 Theatre Production in the Meantime

All the aspects that appeared as pivotal with reference to the New lead to the possibility to reconceptualise production within postdramatic theatre. Among them, the time dimension–with its relevant spatial aspect, as exemplified by the importance of asynchrony as the coexistence of differences and the 'step aside' from the linear trajectory–is the one presenting the majority of connections with the other important aspects defined in the study. Consequently, actions within it also represent the trigger for the reconceptualisation of production.

More specifically, it is time that at a more abstract level conjugates the ideas of obscurity, coexistence, conflict, progress, collaboration, self-betrayal and suspension to trace the borders of production within postdramatic theatre and thus leads to the reconfiguration of production as a production of the incomplete, a production of production.

Time seems to me particularly interesting right now within artistic production...maybe because among all this elements it is the most obscure one. For instance, if you think about the relationship with the audience, working on time is more interesting than space because of the conditions of perception that you can create for spectators. Space turns the lights on what you're doing, very clear, bright lights. On the other side, time is smoother, is a question where maybe something unexpected could happen, where things are less clear, less on the surface (SB).

Moreover, the dimension of time appears as particularly interesting on the borders between coexistence and conflict, both with regards to the recognition of the New and in reference to its production in terms of asynchrony:

I believe that it is possible to discover the new also in something that is not specifically contemporary, because of the recognition of the co-presence of different presents and also of the past-that would be equally the new (DBG).

It is the coexistence of the present time with a time in non-synchrony to it, isn't it? In this perspective of the conflict, the focus is exactly on the coexistence of such different times (SB).

In this sense, the coexistence of different times offers another way to 'widen the texture of reality' (DBG), exposing the linear trajectory both at the level of the mode of production and narrative construction; as such, it also allows important reflections on politics: 'Why is natality a central category of political thought? Because it allows interruptions. That is a key point to me: the possibility to start again, the possibility that an action exists that wasn't yet imagined; that wasn't done and maybe imagined but, while redoing it, I do it differently, I do it newly' (GP).

Moreover, it is the dimension of time that offers the best way to combine the practices of production based on self-betrayal with those based on suspension and indeterminacy. As the analysis showed, the two approaches are only partially inconsistent. More precisely, the different premises on which they are based do not prevent them from being considered together and this juxtaposition offers insights on how to put the engine for the production of production to work. The opportunity to betray one's self is not compatible with many aspects characterising production in contemporary theatre today. First of all the one of time: betrayal is hardly a gesture to be performed overnight. Practices based on suspension on the other hand present a strong temporal dimension: the possibility of opening a space characterised by infinite possibilities and no directionality seems to stretch the duration, thanks to the collective aspect of production on to which it is based and its inherent potential for non-organisation.

In this sense, it is very important to state that time is indeed a fundamental dimension of action and cannot be set aside while envisioning production. At the same time, it is even more important to make a distinction between the temporal aspect of production and the aesthetics and poetics that use time as a stylistic device in the conviction of acting on production and politics:

> In this respect, the distinction between acceleration and duration is to me absolutely irrelevant ... such a distinction is even dangerous. I mean that it risks to ... well, I mean that is hypocritical. It substitutes a structural problem–how production takes place, how are we working–with a stylistic problem (GP).

This insight allows a further reflection on works in progress, whose logic appears to go exactly in the direction of confusing a structural problem with a stylistic one.

The focus on work in progress has to do with acceleration and does not appear here as a way of changing the structural mode of production but rather as a way to shift the focus away from the real problem: 'you're not transforming the way in which you're working. You're transforming work itself into something that can be divided...because you need to go faster, you can't wait. The extreme consequences of this dynamic are that I don't have a context, I don't have an institution, I don't have a public sphere where my work exists' (GP). This aspect is even more important once considered that the production–when it could be defined as such–and distribution of work in progress represent the work modality of the majority of those festivals and institutions whose mission focuses on artistic research and whose funds depend on the very capacity of innovation. Works in progress emerge as an *escamotage* to create a space of experimentation–which is advocated by some interviewees–but cannot, in the light of what emerged, constitute a root for the production of the New. This space for experimentation is often created in order to meet the requirements set by public policy for financial support in the category of artistic research and innovation and is very different from the actual risk-taking advocated for artistic experimentation based on the creation of problems and giving up control.

Contrariwise, combining the dimensions that appeared as fundamental in the field, it is possible to envision a situation–an institution–where it is not the New to be produced but it is the production of the New itself to be produced. This can only happen in a context where there is no equilibrium inside the institution, no percentage, no marginal space in which failure is accepted and another amount that is protected from it. This produces a dialectic aimed at finding the common ground, the proposal on what exists and can bring about innovation but never the New.

This is why a reconceptualisation of the New able to inform production emerges only if the New is conceived exclusively as the engine of production of other New that is different from itself and produced autonomously. Embracing these ideas, production needs to be reconsidered in terms of an incomplete production, which by virtue of its incompleteness, can become 'production of production', and its temporal dimension must also be reconsidered in light of the notion of autonomy:

'In the meantime' could be the time of the new. That's because we don't live alone. Your time is always a 'meantime'. In this meantime, the possibilities for the recognition of the new are two: the dimension of autonomy and the dimension of the unimaginable–that we may call future. The new is the unimaginable. Its only political potential lies in its becoming an engine for the production of other new that is other from itself (GP).

This extract is fundamental to highlight that the possibilities for the concept of New to entail a political value could not be set aside from its time and more specifically, from the category of the future.

It is in this sense that the meantime could be the time of the New. The meantime regards the coexistence of differences, starting from its privileged, contradictory feature of being not considered really time at our disposal, and yet being the only time we have: our time is always a meantime as we live within a collectivity and its modes of production. It comprises two meanings: 'the intervening time' until something happens and 'at the same time' of something else happening. Within neoliberal capitalism, the meantime might easily become the moment still usable to contribute to the system's production and reproduction. In spite of this, or maybe exactly because of this, the meantime is the time we need to address, rethink and re-appropriate as we envision resistance. As the coexistence of different times, inhabiting conflicting spheres and discourses, it might be the asynchronous time able to interrupt the neoliberal narrative so that a present could be opened up again within the overwhelming present characterising the condition of postmodernity. Being the time separating us from the future might constitute the working concept to envision a liberated art production and an exercise in re-establishing the future as a category of action. The New as engine of production of a different new–a production based indeed on a Deleuzian repetition–unfolds its potential against the desertification of the future as perspective that characterised the postmodern condition, shifting the efforts away from production to focus only on reproduction that is the production of the same. As a Deleuzian repetition, the meantime could be envisioned as a suspension in disguise within the normal temporality of production; open to interruptions and (im)possibilities; passionate about the utility of the useless, where it can unfold as a pure means.

In the Meantime: Performance Remains, writes Rebecca Schneider (2011). As capitalism's value-production shifts to the ephemeral, the meantime hosts performance's materiality and gains political potential through between 'possibly errant acts and possibly errant forms' that could be activated anytime. Rebecca Schneider refers to Gertrude Stein's description of theatre's syncopated time–being one thing and the other at the same time–to ground her argumentation: 'a syncopated doubleness which (re)occurs; travel and returns' (ibid., 94). In this repetition, performance unfolds its potential in being incomplete. Being situated in a meantime while creating it, it points to a suspension in disguise. The meantime emerges as an ongoing tangle, between reality and fiction, materiality and speculation: it cannot be approached through strict dichotomies and might help to escape the dichotomies that force art into the category of the exception that confirms the norm, or the new destined to become tradition.

In this reconceptualisation of the New and production, the notion of the possible plays a fundamental role, enriching the political value of indeterminacy: to put in place the production of possibility means, according to one interviewee, to engage in the philosophical exercise of imagining oneself for an instant without that future. Interestingly, what seems a contradiction in terms arises as a way to reconstitute the future as perspective. Such a gesture cannot be realised immediately, and here lies the potential and the limits of all the reasoning on the production of possibility: its presence contrasts the category of the present in which it lives.

The potential and role of art in the production of possibility is now clear, but since art is first and foremost constituted by people that engage in its production and consumption, the approach of individuals should not be underestimated:

I believe that we live in a paradigm in which we're used to think of the possible with the attitude of masters of our own possibilities, a dominant approach on our future. There is indeed a very strong category of action on the possible that should be contrasted with a passion about the possible (DBG).

The re-establishment of the future as category has to go through the production of the New where the latter is the New that differs from itself. This is indeed a production of possibilities emerging from the incomplete
, where a singular approach to the future, once re-conceptualised as a passion about the possible rather than as control of it, can become universal.

Conclusions

The research presented in these pages arose from the need to discard some fashionable debates around the concepts of innovation and creativity–overbearingly channelled in research and practice in the sector of performance–to focus on the essential aspects characterising the New and its production in the contemporary landscape. On these bases, the drawing up of the research objectives and design, proceeded by the idea of paradoxes at the core of art production in neoliberal capitalism, could be approached by reconceptualising the New and that such an effort could enrich practices in performance and theatre while fostering the reflection about its political potentialities. Rather than offering another critique of creativity and innovation, this work aimed at shifting perspectives on them through an idea of production that, by embracing the New, admits radical change and recognises the role art practices play in it, notwithstanding neoliberal capitalism. This effort was undertaken by investigating how the production of the New could develop around the question 'what if' rather than be driven by 'what it should be' (Dolan 2005). Envisioning such production in the realm of postdramatic theatre constituted the most concrete goal of this work which, understanding the paradoxical position of the arts in the context of a capitalism premised on the exploitation of novelty, stresses their potential: arts still cherish the idea of a world that can be always otherwise imagined (Gielen 2013). This realm opens up the possibility to take a step aside from a trajectory of production set by capitalism and the narrative around it that constructs it as the only possible reality. Performance, like the all the arts, allows for approaching production at large with a passion of the possible rather than a control on the future and, being passionate about the utility of the useless, it can contribute to think of and act on reality as always subject to change.

This work, conjugating theoretical and empirical research, investigated how the New could be redefined in the context of postdramatic theatre, and how its production could be rethought and put in place across the many dimensions of action and counteraction that–though specific to the field–could be applied at a wider level. Moreover, it explored how the reconceptualisation of the New and its production could inform practices within theatre and dance on a more concrete level, so that it could become and remain a place of change rather than a cogwheel of neoliberal capitalism, while also rethinking the current theatre system in this direction.

The results obtained composed a very fertile framework able to offer interesting insights both in terms of theory and practice and to suggest further directions of future research. First, it was assessed that a reconceptualisation of the New outside the framework of innovation is not only possible but also desirable. The space for such reconceptualisation and its limits were defined through a schematic juxtaposition of the aspects characterising the notion of the new and that of innovation in social sciences and humanities in the theoretical framework, which was then refined in the empirical research. In social sciences, the new is equated with the unknown, and the possibility for its recognition lies in acknowledging its difference to what already exists. The opportunity of the progressive clarification of the unknown, the possibility of recognising the new by establishing a relationship to it through the comparison with the existing, and the positive values that naturally spring out of this possibility characterise the recognition of novelty in the social sciences, whose discourse converges on the notion of innovation and excludes other possible meanings. Contrariwise, in the humanities the new is defined by the very impossibility of establishing a relationship to it, its recognition seems to escape the category of representation to revolve around that of belonging. The concept of difference here is equally fundamental but rather than omitting meanings it multiplies them, admitting the possibility of the New also in what is historically old or ordinary: such difference cannot be acknowledged through comparison and emerges by virtue of this impossibility.

The systematic exclusion of other connotations in the idea of novelty entailed in the concept of innovation results in the general acceptance of novelty as recombination of existing elements and of its production as a transformation happening on a linear trajectory, a narrative closely related to the mechanisms of neoliberal capitalism. Creative destruction represents innovation's movement of production and deprives the New of its peculiar temporality–that is either ephemeral or eternal–by binding it to a given life expectancy and irrevocably links the concept of innovation to the one of substitutability and purposefulness.

The concept of innovation suggests an idea of production in which, holding a clear view on the existing, it is possible to embrace the new as a step forward on the linear path of progress that characterises a vision of the world, which is partially reinforced by the idea of innovation itself. Innovation is thus an instrument produced in order to reach other purposes, which have to do more with the reproduction of capitalism than with general progress. It is in this sense that the innovation mechanism exploits the semblance with the New, profiting the immaterial value of the label to disguise its conservative force at the system level. Still, theoretical research signalled a margin to reconceptualise production itself outside of substitutability and purposefulness: the truly new, to be found in what seems the same, might be disguised as the ordinary and undermine the current mode of production bringing actual change. In this sense, the literature review provided the directions to engage with further theoretical research on a concept of the New that escapes continuous renewal, which might prevent radical change from happening.

The traces of this paradox were followed back to modernity and the Avant-garde to explore the inherited changes in the mode of production and the debates around the New left in terms of conceiving the possibility of the New and its implications in terms of value. The modernist new, which was becoming compulsory, consistent with capitalism's developments at the time, evolved in the compulsoriness of creativity that characterises *The Condition of Postmodernity* (Harvey 1989). Moreover, the modernist new, bound to become tradition, seemed to correspond in the condition of postmodernity to a dismissal of the New at large, emerging as the impossibility to conceive a different future. If the time-space compression characterising neoliberal capitalism produces an overwhelming present, it is only in the present that the collectivity could regain its ability to imagine the future. Art constitutes one of the privileged sectors for conceiving radical change and re-establishing the future as category of action. Today, the reconceptualisation of the New entails a political value, notwithstanding the implications entailed in terms of value and appropriation exacerbated in neoliberal capitalism, and the arts still constitute the ground to nurture it.

The most interesting outcomes resulted from combining the theoretical research with an empirical investigation, which not only verified and reinforced the theory but also contributed to its widening. First, it was possible to suggest a notion of the New–a theoretical tool rather than absolute definition of the concept–that differs from the one common in innovation research and general understanding in its conceptual, temporal and value aspects that at the same time informs the concept of production.

The New is the unimaginable recognised as such. It is characterised by the impossibility of establishing a relationship to it and as such depends on the coexistence of radically different concepts in a whole object or idea that yet remains open and takes the form of an incomplete structure.

The New is ordinary and overwhelming at the same time, producing an atmosphere of obscurity that shelters its recognition and fosters its production: opposing comparison-based categorisations, it nurtures an in-between space whose acknowledgement escapes comprehension and there is no difference in form between entities but a difference constituting itself as the coexistence of different entities.

It is contextually ephemeral and eternal, and its temporality, characterised by the blurring of trajectory and the absence of a clear purpose, dismisses partiality to emphasise wholeness. Its function emerges in the experience of the altogether different–hardly likable but undoubtedly lovable–and thrives in the cultivation of differences. At the same time, the New as entire and incomplete nurtures a coexistence of differences as a space of indeterminacy marked by precise borders made porous by its content. As such it gains a privileged position of resistance within the contemporary stress on exhibition and reproduction–fostered by the postmodern narrative– and in the hypermodern focus on the linear trajectory of progress, its ideology of realism and transparency, characterising the condition of postmodernity.

Such cultivation of differences regards the abstract conceptualisation of the New as much as the practices to experiment in its concrete production: self-betrayal and suspension. The production of the New emerges across these two strategies as a production of possibility grounded in and nurtured by the co-presence of radical differences that do not proceed dialectically in the search of a common ground but rather dialogically, coexisting and interweaving an exchange without being synthetised in a solution; this produces an in-between where autonomous subjects of production can share a space and a time. If self-betrayal emerges as a mechanism of differences in repetition, suspension cultivates the multiplication of differences relying on the collective subject, extending the former and appearing in the opportunity to look the world as contingent and to re-imagine it continuously.

These ideas opened up the possibility to rethink production around the notion of the New suggested here and, together with the other dimensions that emerged in the analysis, to single out the directions for rethinking the theatre system so that it could shelter a concept of the New able to express its full value and function at the individual, collective and political level while resisting the imposition of heteronomic values and mechanisms of production. This is the reason why the most relevant and thought-provoking outcomes were obtained by considering the concepts of the New and of production together through an abductive approach, linking systematically the aspects related to the two concepts and interpreting their connections.

This hermeneutical analysis produced first a rule able to put in relation the unexpected connections of all relevant aspects and then explained the cases on to which it was built, suggesting directions for the field of postdramatic theatre, answering the question of what to do next and addressing urgent matters, starting from the problem of appropriation up to the discussion regarding politically engaged art practices.

The rule provided to explain such art production encourages its own breaking in the specific cases it explains, emerging as a ground of interpretation and action of the current situation, whose margins can always be exceeded and questioned by practices and discourses.

It is consistent with a concept of the New that unfolds by shifting the borders between the possible and the impossible and exploring the space in between, and with its production unfolding in the time in between. At its most abstract level, the New suggested here is deeply informed by the concept of production: it is an engine for the production of a new that is different from itself. At the same time, the concept of production–here intended as an abstract category and as concrete theatre production–is highly informed by the reconceptualisation of the New: this is expressed as the production of the possibilities to produce the New, and can be conceptualised as an undoing, as *a step towards the incomplete*. Such possibilities emerge in the space between the conflicting features that constitute the New as altogether different. Its temporal dimension unfolds autonomously *in the meantime*, fulfilling an important political function: within capitalist production rhythms, the production of the New contrasts at the level of discourse the category of the present where it unfolds, questioning both the capitalist mode of production and its ideology of realism. As a category in contrast, it emerges as freed of the exceptional character proper of innovation and unfolds in between the copresence of different times in a spatial asynchrony of times. In between reality and fiction, it produces that sense of indecidability that presents the rules we live by as contingent rather than structural. As such, this production might free the New from being bound to become tradition and actually affect our present and future.

Within the theatre system, the New as altogether different opens its contents and modalities to interpretation and misunderstanding, underlining the centrality of thinking in terms of a politics of use when it comes to works, organisations and festivals. More concretely, this interpretation suggests possible counteractions within the sector of postdramatic theatre, whose current functioning is not compatible with the production of the New: being very organised, clear and constantly accelerating, it resembles the capitalist system through its adoption of neoliberal values and mechanisms at the cost of its autonomy. Still, it is in the theatre system itself where some unfortunate dynamics could be reversed by envisioning a production able to slip out of clarity and organisation. The risk would be, in this perspective, to encourage a vision of production where interruptions and self-betrayal are possible and fostered by a forms of undoing and non-organising, not so much to oppose neoliberal growth with a sterile rhetoric of de-growth, which would simply follow the linear trajectory in the opposite direction; rather in making the trajectory incomplete and open to a production of differences able to question the trajectory itself. Taking these reflections as the point of departure, its concrete implications in terms of future actions within the theatre system were collected and are listed below.

First, collaboration is a remarkable tool for the production of the New as long as it focuses on conflict, the role of which must not be underestimated, and aims at a dialogical exchange (Sennet 2012). Collaboration based on conflict can be cultivated by artists through practices of problem-creating, and by curators and institutions by giving up control; across the dimensions of the individual and the collective–the artist and the audience, the festival and its community–it must be addressed as a time constellation opening up a space of potentiality (Kunst 2010).

Second, this space of potentiality could be created through a practice of non-organisation which regards theatre production and could be implemented at the institutional level, in particular within festivals that emerge as the privileged sites of the cultivation of difference. If the museum walls allow the visitor to perceive the difference in time disguised in the semblance of the ordinary (Groys 2008), and art institutions provide the ground to imagine reality in terms of an always possible otherwise (Gielen 2013), theatre institutions constitute a territory for and an object of counteraction. On the one hand, they provide the necessary space to be inhabited by radically different individuals and their concerns, putting production based on non-organisation and obscurity in place. In a frame that is too rigid, a curatorial approach that embraces obscurity could produce the 'nebula' that inhabits the moment of suspension in which the possibility of the New appears. Yet, a singular subject could hardly trigger the production of the New, and festivals represent the institutions where the multiplication of differences could be put into motion at best through sustaining a practice of non-coordination that opens up a space 'in between' that, through multiple inputs, could stay alive. Within the festivalisation characterising neoliberal cultural production, festivals can re-appropriate the spatio-temporal intensity that makes them an interruption of the normal mode of production. In order words, festivals could be thought and produced as pure means (Agamben 2000), instruments without a goal, whose function resolves in opening a reflection on the practices with which we engage, on the politics and ethics we address, on the value that we produce, both in terms of material production within theatre and knowledge production within a theatre system hosted in our particular present.

In this sense, festivals cannot rely on their ephemerality and indeterminacy in order to escape co-optation; they have to cultivate their autonomy and politics of use. A festival can be given to the audience as a space that can be used in infinite ways, as a program that could be misunderstood and yet grounded in its autonomy: only insofar as the festival is able to build solid ties with its territory, audience, community it can be used in infinite ways without being exploited in infinite ways and places. By defending its autonomous values, whose politics unfold in the *how* as much as in the *what*, a festival can turn into a place of liberated production–unimaginable in its autonomy–to oppose neoliberal participation and postmodern reproduction. It can turn into a place of production of the New that, instead of becoming tradition, becomes the engine of production of other forms of new different from itself.

Third, production would not be such without taking into consideration the audience. If artists and curators engage in self-betrayal and in a form of collaboration that has to do more with conflict than with a common goal, only the audience can fulfil production. On the one hand, the specific characteristics of performance imply the simultaneity of production and consumption, placing the audience at the centre of any conceptualisation of production regarding this field. On the other, in the spirit of rethinking production on the basis of the New, when it comes to the audience collaboration takes the form of sharing, where what is shared is an uncertainty rather than a conviction. Notwithstanding the complexity at the heart of experimental art forms, placing the audience at the centre of production does not imply bridging the distance, necessary to performance itself, renouncing autonomy in the sphere of art to take up roles in other spheres: as a mean without end, artworks, just like art organisations, might– and do–contribute to widening an audience's knowledge and perspective without being attached to this specific purpose. Rather, in the spirit of setting up a liberated production, the emancipation of the audience must be grounded in that necessary distance, in that asynchronous space, emerging as an autonomous entity between the performer and the spectators (Rancière 2014).

Fourth, the New happens only in terms of product. Escaping any possibility of comprehension through comparison, the indeterminacy and processes described here must constitute a whole, a single structure that yet remains incomplete and allows misunderstanding. In this sense, institutions that present too much work-in-progress do not represent a good context for the production of the New, if they are producing at all. Works in progress are at the same time the result and the corroborating force of a project's temporality, which binds art production to the accelerated rhythms of neoliberal capitalism and subjugates its contents to the impossibility of inhabiting the potentiality of the present to envision possible futures. Works in progress are inconsistent with the idea of a product and yet are a form in which neoliberal mechanisms profit from their semblance with the product: their function is to fix a process in the form of a product so that the immaterial value can be capitalised upon faster and, at the same time, they punctuate an infinite process deprived of interruptions where the trajectory can be questioned and overcome. In this sense, they are risky *escamotages* that create a space of experimentation to attract the financial support related to it that ends up forcing the same experimentation in the confirmation of the current paradigm, and where no actual risk is taken: works in progress are instruments with a clear purpose, that of producing innovation.

Coherently, the production of the New must accept and embrace the possibility of failure. If the notion of the New, deprived from its constitutive characteristics, becomes exclusively innovation and the notion of failure is reworked solely in the idea of error, the possibilities to engage in the production of the New are none: the production of the New can only happen in artworks, practices or organisations where there is no protected percentage dedicated to safe experimenting but a thorough risk-taking where, it is possible to engage in the cultivation of differences.

The production of the New proposed here re-addresses the political engagement of art by calling for the consideration of performance and politics as two radically different subjects of reflection on reality. Only if their radical differences are respected and cultivated can performance reveal its political value. An approach aimed at combining the two might, on the contrary, defuse its potential: art is political as an invitation not to understand that triggers a reflection on reality; its instruments, contents and modalities differ radically from those useful in the sphere of political activism–or scientific research–which illuminate the inequalities of the contemporary world by producing information and fostering critique. The former produces and thrives in an obscure atmosphere that undermines the latter. More importantly, the political dimension of art lies in its mode of production and has little to do with its contents; it regards how production processes are set up on the concrete level and takes the form of methodological experimentation on the level of poetics.

In this sense, in order for the New to unfold its political potential, its temporal dimension must be reconsidered to be *in the meantime* of the general rhythms and modes of production. The meantime emerges as the time of the New in its contradictory meanings, as the time simultaneous to something and the time intervening before something happens: all our time is a meantime. It releases the temporality of the coexistence of differences and as such, acts as a suspension in disguise: it interrupts the current modes of production, interfering with the present characterised by the production of the 'ever always the same' and opens up a time for rethinking the future as a category of action. In this moment of interruption, a real risk could also be taken at the collective level in order to re-imagine theatre production and its political engagement.

Further Research

As it emerges clearly from the short collection of results provided above, the approach and methods selected allowed not only to answer the research questions, but also to formulate new ones. In the spirit of pursuing a good research practice through the formulation of good questions, the aspects that, although relevant, could not be addressed, are here still considered as important as the answers provided. These elements constitute a new starting point to reflect on the production of the New within neoliberal capitalism as a solid and at the same time very fertile ground for future engagement.

In the spirit of avoiding a short-sighted opposition between the New and innovation at the conceptual level, further theoretical research must address the concept of the New within innovation studies as well as the one of innovation within humanities. This investigation was partially carried out in the present work, privileging the need of tracing a clear line between the two concepts in order to demarcate their essential aspects and explore the narratives and implications the two concepts entail. Still, theoretical research underlined that binary oppositions between the humanities and the social sciences or the New and innovation limit the nuances and complexity of the matter: some discourse produced on the New within humanities falls back into that of innovation and, at the same time, some research on innovation attempts to escape the problems of linearity and substitutability that locked the concept in the reproduction of capitalism.

Next to this, the empirical findings highlighted a strong influence of theory on the visions collected. Still, it was only partly assessed how it influences everyday practice and discourse production. Moreover, the sample was built to bring different perspectives to the fore and, although this objective was widely met, these different perspectives can be all ascribed to a progressive, leftist position which resulted in an account of the contemporary theatre and dance fields as radically anti-capitalist. On the one hand, it could be argued that the perspectives covered are too homogenous, while on the other they also represent a faithful description of the fields: like the majority of experimental art, they are characterised by a contra-position, and the different perspectives collected within this contra-position are what animate the debate in the field and punctuate its production. In this sense, they represent the most interesting territory of analysis given the objectives and scope of this research.

Considering these two aspects together, further research could enlarge the perspective and investigate how the words and vocabulary used in the field could be de-fetishised, starting from the question on the need for a new vocabulary. Not by chance, language is one of the broadest institutions and its rules–like those of theatre institutions or capitalist institutions–might bend, break or be more commonly misunderstood. Exploring the potential of misunderstanding within the arts means rethinking the politics of use, opening unexpected connections in terms of the relationship with the audience and posing an interesting juxtaposition with the need of creating a new vocabulary. Re-appropriation of institutions or words allows freeing the form from its content, inventing a new one; making it incomplete to create the conditions for the production of the New. Directions for further research could start by addressing the necessity of a new vocabulary and new institutions that emerged in the field, by lingering on the potentialities of misunderstanding the forms that we already possess and their politics of use.

In this spirit, further research could address two main interrelated topics: the first regards theatre institutions and the people constituting them, addressing the modalities of production they put in place and the theatre-system they can (un)do starting from their practice. The second regards the relationship between performance and politics and the possibility to articulate it in the current context, from the broader level of the capitalist mode of production and postmodern narratives to work practice and discourse production within theatre.

As regards the first, art institutions emerged as a necessary frame for the production of the New. They offer the space for the cultivation of difference and in the best case the foundation that keeps the conflicting aspects together. Yet, they fulfil this role as long as they are able to put themselves in the condition of letting the unrecognisable, the unimaginable, exist inside them and it is difficult to conceive of an institution able to sustain the nurturing of a completely different element without either absorbing or rejecting it. The questions around the problem of co-optation remained open in the fieldwork and a provisional answer was found in the dimension of asynchrony. Yet, the most interesting direction for further research regards a concept that, although recurring both in the theoretical and empirical research, remained slightly in the background: the incomplete.

The notion of the incomplete represents an interesting key to explore art production within institutions and concrete practices. The first step in this direction would be to further develop the conceptual difference between the indeterminate and the incomplete, addressing it as another chance of overcoming the dichotomies that facilitate the absorption of what is other into the system and prevents the production of the New. Contrary to forms of absolute indeterminacy, the incomplete might nurture an indeterminacy protected from the risk of exploitation by virtue of its borders that offer a foundation that is yet porous, thus nurturing a space of potentiality where the New could unfold as the engine of production of other new that differs from itself.

On these bases, a possible direction would be to explore institutions as sites of cultivation of differences not only at the abstract but also at the operational level. In order to do this, the roles and formats that have been more bent to the rules of the capitalist theatre system–such as the artist, the curator or the festival–could be rethought according to art's own terms. Collecting the suggestion of the field, festivals could be conceived as thinking entities that–by virtue of their particular spatial and temporal dimension–could nurture radical differences and, at the same time, address their politics of use, subverting the neoliberal dynamics of festivalisation.

The curator might be the person caring for and taking responsibility of what is incomplete and non-fitting, not in order to complete it but to keep it as such. How can we envision curatorship as the practice of taking care of the incomplete? It might be grounded in welcoming and nurturing the questions and uncertainties raised by the artworks in order to create a festival able to find a production drive in what is obscure, letting the audience build their own adventure in the space emerging in between works and discourses; within an art sphere that cultivates and shares a doubt, which can raise in the most ordinary, unexceptional objects suddenly mantled by an indecidability compelling us to reflect on whether we are dealing with reality or fiction, with performance or with politics. This model of curatorship happens and needs to happen within the context of art institutions and festivals, so that taking responsibility for art's own value could be grounded in a collective structure: in a theatre sector that is increasingly organised and clear, art institutions act as producers and guardians of the rules underlying the system, whose change is thinkable only at the collective level. This regards the collectivity at large: the coexistence of difference suggests an idea of production able to slip out of clarity and organisation to focus on suspension, an interruption of the linear trajectory, whose duration, and thus potentiality of change, depends on multiple impulses.

In the light of this aspect that emerged as fundamental in the fieldwork, the relationship with the audience in the context of the production of the New must be further addressed. If the emancipation of the spectator regards the preservation of a distance where a third space in which the work–or the program of a festival at large–emerges between the performer and the audience, what form of togetherness could represent a ground for political resistance at large? If politics is about transparency and the search for a common ground, art might engage in resistance through obscurity and non-coordination. But, on a concrete level, how could we imagine a form of togetherness not based on a blind trust in rational comprehension? Following Sennet (2012), empathy supports dialogic exchanges, allowing the possibility of attending to the other on one's own terms without striving to overcome differences through logic. How could the curator, the institution and the collective engage in such a joint adventure of the cultivation of differences?

There is another aspect highly related to theatre's functioning and discourse production that, at the theoretical level, deserves further exploration: the opposition between processes and products. The need of freeing theatre from a capitalist form of continuous and constant production led to an over-focus on processes, embodied on the material level in works in progress, and present at the discourse level in the field, for instance with regards to collaboration or the potentiality of indeterminacy. At the same time, the research showed the centrality of wholeness and thus of products. This counter reflection could be also interpreted as a reaction to the ubiquity of processes, projects and works in progress especially today, as the idea of processes being un-commodifiable proved to be inapplicable in the context of neoliberal capitalism: 'the desire for stepping out of the necessity of constant production risks totalizing production itself' (Manchev 2014), as exemplified by the blurred boundaries between work and leisure, production and rest, which disguise the neoliberal equation between living and producing.

Fieldwork advocated production driven by a 'what if?', highlighting interesting inputs for the practice of the future as much as doubts regarding the applicability of a conceptual distinction between products and processes. Today both of them might constitute the oil lubricating capitalism's mechanisms and a potential territory of re-appropriation of existing forms. What we are dealing with does not seem to be process replacing products or vice versa, rather a blurring of the two aimed at corroborating capitalist value production, where value loss is no longer admitted. As works in progress and the mediation of processes fix the indeterminacy of the former into a complete, readily marketable product, the distinction between the two seems weaker: as Manchev (2014) notices, every mediated process is fixed in the form of a product and 'the ontomedialisation of the social world tends at establishing a sphere of total mediation, in which the substance of the product is reduced to fake substance, while process itself, the form of human doing, becomes paradoxically impossible'. It is in this sense that further research could engage with questioning the actuality of such a distinction and exploring an incomplete form of production aimed at re-appropriating product and processes as forms whose content could be always re-imagined.

This research built the basis to address questions regarding the relationship between the performative and the political, which constitute the second main ground from where to engage in further research. It highlighted the necessity and the urgency of widening the horizon of the political in art, going beyond the short-sighted strategies that end up defusing art's potential. Such effort could start from the idea of the production of the New presented; once again from the cultivation of difference: if the performative and the political are tackled as intertwining concepts, what are the potentials of approaching them as two radically different entities? Respecting the performative and the political as two radically different entities without looking for mediation between the two means to explore the potential that derives from their cohabiting society. The above-mentioned paradox of the rule–setting rules as 'the collective and individual conception of the dyadic possibility and impossibility of possibilities'–cuts to the core of the political potential of art, where the dimension of reality and fiction offers a fertile territory to produce new questions.

This is particularly true today, where the question on art's role within society fuels two opposite approaches to theory and practice: a plea to underline again the political value of an art detached from reality, and a strong claim for the urgency of an activist art with a clear impact on society. Both these perspectives reflect and corroborate the borders between the fictional and the real and, by doing so, might defuse the transformative potential of art. The idea of art production they entail produces works and narratives that only apparently disrupt the status quo and end up corroborating it, by reducing imagination to a space of entertainment or escapism, provided in a world that is perceived as impossible to change.

The ground built in this research calls for an effort to rethink the relationship between performance and politics, starting by putting in question these dichotomies: thinking of the New in the context of neoliberal capitalism and its ideology of realism means to engage in a cultivation of differences, nurturing a form of obscurity that in its multiple constituencies shelters that which is unrepresentable, the real, in its overwhelming ordinariness; and the fictional at the core of our reality.

In blurring the border between reality and fiction, art might create an obscurity where reality appears as always also shaped by fiction, historically contingent and thus, subject to change. This cannot happen by opposing alternative representations of reality; it can emerge, on the other hand, through a methodological speculation on it. Art might find a room for action in sustaining imagination as something not separated from reality but in profound relationship to it: if capitalist realism fills the word 'reality' with a precise meaning, art could forget for an instant its content; engaging in a systematic blurring of reality and fiction, putting these into question.

Further research will then address the following question: How can we think art as a methodological speculation on reality? A provisional answer could be found borrowing a word from Benjamin: art might make reality once again incomplete. It could create gaps in representation, making room for imagination to entangle with reality, unsettle it, disorganise it. Yet, what is left it's not a void: art fills with potentiality the gaps it creates and gathers a collectivity around an incomplete real, that could be experimented at the theatre system level and addressed collectively at the political level.

In this sense, the meantime deserves further exploration both at the structural and discourse level, as a productive entanglement between materiality and speculation, reality and fiction: can the meantime become a territory of resistance in the middle of the neoliberal mode of production and a leap towards setting up a liberated production within postdramatic theatre? As a suspension in disguise, could it fight the strict dichotomies that bind the new to tradition and oppose the fictional to the real?

The coexistence of different times, together with that of reality and fiction, opens up for performance the possibility to create a meantime, where different positions could gather together and question the notion of the future and its production. Here, performance could unfold its transformative potential not so much in terms of impact on society but rather as a carrier of the impossible possibilities within reality.

It requires passion and courage to put in place the conception of the New so that it may become an engine for the production of other new that is different from itself. In that meantime, which appears as the time of the New, it is important not to stop thinking about it, given the political, ethical and aesthetic potential that this thinking entails, and which could be triggered through a practice of joyful passions.

Reference List

Aageson, Thomas (2008): Cultural Entrepreneurs: Producing Cultural Value and Wealth. In: Anheier, Helmut K & Raj Isar, Yudhishthir (eds.): The Cultural Economy. London: Sage, pp. 92-107.
Adorno, Theodor W. (1997): Aesthetic Theory (1970 ed.). London: A&C Black.
Agamben, Giorgio (2000): Means Without End: Notes on Politics. Theory out of Bounds (Vol. 20). Minneapolis: University of Minnesota Press.
Agamben, Giorgio (2002): Difference and Repetition: on Guy Debord's Films. In: Mc Donough, Thomas (ed.): Guy Debord and the Situationist International. Cambridge: The MIT Press, pp. 313-320.
Agamben, Giorgio (2009): What is the Contemporary? In Agamben, Giorgio: "What is an Apparatus?" and Other Essays. Stanford University Press, pp. 39-54.
Baudelaire, Charles (1995): The Painters of Modern Life. London: Phaidon Press.
Badiou, Alain (2007): The Century. Cambridge: Polity.
Becker, Howard S. (1974): Art as Collective Action. In: American Sociological Review, 39, 6, pp. 767-776.
Becker, Howard S. (1982): Art Worlds. Berkeley: University of California Press.
Benasayag, Miguel & Schmit, Gerard (2003): Les Passions tristes. Souffrance psychique et crise sociale. Paris: La Découverte.
Benjamin, Walter (1985): Central Park. In: New German Critique, 34, pp. 32-58.
Benjamin, Walter (1989): N [The theory of Knowledge, theory of Progress]. In: Smith, G. (ed.): Benjamin: philosophy, aesthetics, history. University of Chicago Press, pp. 43- 82.
Benjamin, Walter (1999): The Arcades Project. Tiedemann, Rolf (ed). Cambridge: Harvard University Press.
Benjamin, Walter (2003): Selected Writings, Volume 4: 1938-1940. Elland, Howard & Jennings Micheal, W (eds.). Cambridge: Harvard University Press.
Bishop, Claire (2004): Antagonism and relational aesthetics. In: October Magazine, 110, pp. 51-79.
Boltanski, Lùc & Chiappello, Eve (2005): The New Spirit of Capitalism. Verso Books.
Bourdieu, Pierre (1980): The Production of Belief: contribution to an economy of symbolic goods. In: Media Culture Society, 2, pp. 261-293.
Bourdieu, Pierre & Johnson, Randal (1993): The field of cultural production: Essays on art and literature. New York: Columbia University Press.
Bourdieu, Pierre (1996): The rules of Art, Genesis and Structure of the Literary Field. Stanford University press.
Böhm, Andreas (2004): Theoretical Coding: Text Analysis in Grounded Theory. In: Flick, Uwe: A Companion to Qualitative Research. London: Sage, pp. 270-275
Castells, Manuel (1996): The rise of the network society. Information Age Series, 1. Oxford: Blackwell.
Cavell, Stanley (1979): Wittgenstein, Skepticism, Morality and Tragedy. New York: Oxford Uniersity Press
Chowdhury, Aniruddha (2008): Memory, Modernity, Repetition: Walter Benjamin's History. In: Telos, 143, pp. 22-46 .

Christensen, Clayton M. (2003): The innovator's solution: Creating and sustaining successful growth. Boston: Harvard Business Press.
Csikszentmihalyi, Mihaly (1999): 16 Implications of a Systems Perspective for the Study of Creativity. In: Sternberg, Robert J. (ed.): Handbook of creativity. Cambridge University Press, pp. 313-335.
Danto, Arthur (1964): The Artworld. In: The Journal of Philosphy, 61, 19, pp. 571-564.
Danto, Arthur (2002): The Abuse of Beauty. In: Daedalus, 31, 4, pp. 35-56
Deleuze, Gilles (2001): Pure Immanence. New York: Zone.
Deleuze, Gilles (1994): Difference and Repetition. London: A&C Black.
Dolan, Jill (2005): Utopia in performance: Finding hope at the Theatre. Ann Arbor: University of Michigan Press.
Dosi, Giovanni (1988): The Nature of the Innovative Process. In: Dosi, Giovanni, Freeman Christopher & Nelson, Richard (eds.): Technical Change and Economic Theory, 988. London: Francis Pinter, pp. 221-228.
Encinar, Maria-Isabel (2006): On novelty and economics: Schumpeter's paradox. In: Journal of Evolutionary Economy, 16, 3, pp. 255-277.
Fisher, Mark (2009): Capitalist realism: Is there no alternative? John Hunt Publishing.
Flick, Uwe (2004): Design and Process in Qualitative Research. In: Flick, Uwe (ed.): A companion to qualitative research. London: Sage, pp. 146-152.
Florida, Richard (2002): The rise of the creative class: and how it's transforming work, leisure, community and everyday life. New York: Basic.
Garcia, Tristan (2014): Form and Object: A Treatise on Things. Edinburgh University Press.
Garfinkel Harold (2005): Ethnomethodological studies of work. London: Routledge.
Gielen, Pascal (2003): Kunst in netwerken: artistieke selecties in de hedendaagse dans en de beeldende kunst. Leuven: Lannoo Uitgeverij.
Gielen, Pascal (2013): Institutional Imagination. In Gielen, Pascal (ed.): Institutional Attitudes. Instituting Art in a Flat World. Amsterdam: Valiz.
Giddens, Anthony & Turner, Johnatan. H. (1988): Social theory today. Stanford University Press.
Groys, Boris (2008): Art Power. Cambridge: The MIT Press.
Grosz, Elisabeth (2013): Habit today: Ravaisson, Bergson, Deleuze and Us. In: Body and Society, 19, 2-3, pp. 217-239.
Han, Byung-Chul (2015): The transparency society. Stanford University Press.
Harvey, David (1989): The condition of postmodernity. Oxford: Blackwell.
Harvey, David (2006): Neo-liberalism as creative destruction. Geographical Annuals, 88 B, 2, pp. 145-158.
Harvey, David (2010): The enigma of capital: and the crises of capitalism. New York: Oxford University Press.
Horkheimer, Max & Adorno, Theodor (2002). Dialectic of Enlightenment: Philosophical Fragments. Stanford University Press.
Hutter, Michael, Berthoin Antal, Ariane, Farías, Ignacio, Marz, Lutz, Merkel, Janet, Mützel, Sophie, Oppen, Maria, Schulte-Römer, Nona & Straßheim, Holger (2010): Cultural Sources of Newness. Discussion Paper SP III 2010-405. Berlin: WZB.

Inglis, David (2010): Before and Beyond "Creativity": Fetishization and Defetishization of the "Arts Festival". Paper presented to Creativity Culture and Democracy in Art Festivals, Bologna, November 25th-26th.
Jameson, Fredric (1991): Postmodernism, or the cultural logic of late capitalism. Duke University Press.
Kuhn, Thomas (2012): The Structure of Scientific Revolutions. University of Chicago Press.
Kunst, Bojana (2010): Prognosis on collaboration. In: joint issue of Le Journal des Laboratoires and TKH Journal for Performing Arts Theory 17, pp. 23-29.
Kunst, Bojana (2012): The Project Horizon: On the Temporality of Making. In: Manifesta Journal, *16*, pp.112-15.
Lacan, Jaques (1998): The Four Fundamental Concepts of psyco-analysis. New York: WW Northon & Company
Latour, Bruno (1993): We Have Never Been Modern. Harvard University Press.
Lazzarato, Maurizio (2011): The Misfortunes of the 'Artistic Critique' and of Cultural Employment. In Raunig, Gerald, Ray, Gene & Wuggenig, Ulf: Critique of Creativity. Precarity Subjectivity and Resistance in the 'Cultural Industries'. London: May Fly Books, pp. 41-56.
Lee, Pamela. M. (2004): Chronophobia; On Time in the Art of the 1960s. Cambridge: MIT Press.
Lehmann, Hans-Thies (2006): Postdramatic theatre. London: Routledge.
Luhmann, Niklas (2000): Art as a Social System. Stanford University Press.
Manchev, Boyan (2014): Nothing *in Common. Collaborations, Relations, Processes and the Actuality of Artistic Labour.* Paper presented to The Public Commons and the Undercommons of Art, Education and Labour, Frankfurt, May 29th-June 1st.
Martin, Courtney E. & Witter, Lisa (2011): Social or Cultural Entrepreneurship: An Argument for a New Distinction. In: Stanford Social Innovation Review, retrived from:<https://ssir.org/articles/entry/social_or_cultural_entrepreneurship_an_argument_for_a_new_distinction#>
Mouffe, Chantal (2012): Strategies of radical politics and aesthetic resistance. Paper presented to Truth is Concrete, Graz, September 21th-28th, retrived from: <http://truthisconcrete.org/texts/?p=19>.
Murray, Jon. B (2010): Post-hegemony: political theory and Latin America. Unversity of Minnesota Press
Noble, Richard (2009): Utopias. London: Whitechapel.
North, Micheal (2013): Novelty: A History of the New. The University of Chicago Press.
O'Sullivan, Steven & Zepke, Simon (2008): *Deleuze, Guattari and the Production of the New*. New York: Continuum International Publishing Group.
Osborne, Thomas (2003): Against 'creativity': a philistine rant. In: Economy and Society, 32, 4, pp. 507-525.
Phelan, Peggy (1993): Unmarked: The politics of performance. London: Routledge.
Rancière, Jacques (2014): The emancipated spectator. Verso Books.
Raunig, Gerald, Ray, Gene & Wuggenig, Ulf (2011): Critique of Creativity: Precarity, Subjectivity and Resistance in the "Creative Industries". London: Mayfly.
Reckwitz, Andreas (2012): Die Erfindung der Kreativität. Zum Prozess gesellschaftlicher Ästhetisierung. Berlin: Suhrkamp.

Reckwitz, Andreas & Koll Fabian. (2013): 'Creativity has become a kind of performance pressure – An interview with Andreas Reckwitz', retrieved from: http://www.goethe.de/ins/nz/mi/ wel/kul/mag/ges/10691034.html
Reichertz, Jo (2004): Abduction, Deduction and Induction in Qualitative Research. In: Flick, Uwe: A companion to qualitative research. London: Sage.
Nelson, Richard (1982): An Evolutionary Theory of Economic Change. Harvard University Press.
Rogers, Everette M. (2003): Diffusion of innovations. New York: The Free Press.
Rosenberg, Harold (1959): The Tradition of the New. New York: McGraw- Hill.
Saldana, Jose. M. (2012): The Coding Manual for Qualitative Researchers. London: Sage.
Schumpeter, Joseph A. (1934): The Theory of Economic Development: An inquiry into profits, capital, credit, interest, and the Business Cycle. Transaction Publishers.
Schumpeter, Joseph A. (2010): Capitalism, Socialism and Democracy. London: Routledge.
Scheer, Edward (2012): Introduction: The end of spatiality or the meaning of duration. In: Performance Research: A Journal of the Performing Arts, 17, 5, pp. 1-3.
Schneider, Rebecca (2011): Performing remains: Art and war in times of theatrical reenactment. Taylor & Francis.
Sennett, Richard (2012): Together: The rituals, pleasures and politics of cooperation. Yale University Press.
Strauss, Anselm. L. (1987): Qualitative analysis for social scientists. Cambridge University Press.
Suchman, Lucy (2008). Relocating Innovation: places and material practices of future- making. Centre for Science Studies, Lancaster University, UK.
Toufic, Jalal (2013): Distracted . Tuumba Press
Tushman, Michael & O'Reilly, Charles. L. (1996): Ambidextrous organizations: managing evolutionary and revolutionary change. In: California management review, 38, 4, pp. 215-218.
Van Maanen, Hans (2009): How to Study Art Worlds. On the Societal Functioning of Aesthetic. Amsterdam University Press.
Von Osten, Marion (2011): Unpredictable Outcomes / Unpredictable Outcasts: On Recent Debates over Creativity and the Creative Industries. In Raunig, Gerald, Ray, Gene & Wuggenig, Ulf: Critique of Creativity. Precarity, Subjectivity and Resistance in the 'Creative Industries'. London:May Fly Books, pp. 133-43.
Wilding, Adrian (1996). *The Concept of Remembrance in Walter Benjamin*. Diss. University of Warwick, Department of Philosophy.
Witt, Ulrich (1993): Emergence and Dissemination of Innovations: some principles of evolutionary economics. In: Ping, Chen & Day, Richard H.: Non-linear Dynamics and Evolutionary Economics. New York: Oxford University Press, pp. 91-100.

Appendix I

Guideline for semi-structured interviews

Introduction and warm-up questions
1. The concept of new: recognition, production, evaluation Aim: to understand the meaning respondents assign to the concept of the new, those which aspects present in the theory are dominant and explore possibilities for production.

Objective of the questions	Possible Questions
Is the idea of the new important and present?	Have you reflected on the idea of the new in your work and life? Also recently? Is it important to produce something new? Is it possible to produce something new?
What is exactly new in the perspective of the respondent?	Have you seen something new recently? (How do you recognise something new?) If yes/no, why was/wasn't it new? What is your reaction in front of something new? Have you seen something innovative recently? What's your reaction in front of something innovative? How long will this "new" be "new"? In your work, did you experience the feeling of having produced something new? Have you ever felt the urge? If yes, for you, how long will this "new" work/project be "new"? If you had to think about a definition of the new, what adjectives and characteristics would you use? (what is really new in your opinion?)
Control and deepening questions (if necessary)	Do you perceive a difference between something new and something innovative? Do you perceive a difference between something new and something contemporary? Boris Groys said that in order to be new artworks need to look alive: can actually theatre/dance/performance, look dead, being live art? When you see something that you appraise as new, do you usually recognise something familiar in it? Have you ever seen something completely new? You said your reaction is...could you tell me more about it? Do you link the idea of the new to success or to failure? And innovation?

2. Values around the new
Aim: to understand the values that drive the respondents in their work and life and whether they are connected to the new.

Objective of the questions	Possible Questions
What kind of values do respondents have and how they inform their practices in the production of the new? Is the idea of the new important and present?	What is the ethical and aesthetical horizon you refer to in this phase of your work? What are your main concerns? Do you see any kind of connection between it and the idea of producing something new? If yes, what precisely? What do you think is important in terms of values, when confronted with the process or the desire of creating something new?
How far is the concept of the new perceived as political and who can politically benefit from it? Why should people produce something new? What is the value in it?	Would you like see something completely new? Why? Would you like to produce something completely new? Why? How far would you go to produce something new? When, if you can imagine this possibility, would you stop producing art/searching for the new?
Has the new an evolutionary aspect? And if yes, how far? And what about innovation?	Do you think that seeing or producing something new is good and represents a development? In personal terms and in general?

3. The new and the contemporary landscape
Aim: to understand the particular context within which respondents act and its interaction with their practice.

Objective of the questions	Possible Questions
How the idea of new is perceived in the sector and by its actors. Who decides what is new in the sector?	Do you think there is an explicit/implicit debate in your work context/scene about the new? Who do you think decides what is new in the end?
How cultural institutions are perceived: producers of the new? Judges of what's new? Gatekeepers?	Where do you like most to perform your work? Do you think that festivals and theatres play an important role in terms of definition and production of new work? How did you feel about this in your experience of work up to now?
How this idea informs the behaviour of the respondent?	How do you feel about these "working rules" of the sector? Do they affect your way of working? And if yes, in what way? Would you try to change something? What and how?
What are the artistic conventions? And in terms of process of production?	Are there clear conventions in terms of artistic research and ways of working?
What happens when the conventions are broken/ignored?	Do you remember one instance in which these "conventions" were broken or ignored? What happened? What did you think? What did you feel?

How the contemporary context is perceived by the respondent?	Let us move to a larger perspective. What do you think of the contemporary cultural and economical context? What do you think about the attention created around the concepts of creativity and innovation? Did you ever reflect on these themes? As an artist/curator, do you feel directly addressed by this discourse?
How this perception influences the artist's everyday practices?	Given this, in which direction should we move in order to produce something new? What comes next?
Understand the complex relationship between space and time in the neoliberal context and space and time in theatre (durational performances, site-specific events) in the view of the respondent	Space and time and the way artists and curators "play" with them have been quite central in the past years, we can talk about durational performances, just to mention one example. Did you reflect on this? Going back to conventions, do you think there are precise space-time conventions, which cannot be broken even after all these experimentations? How would you break them, if you were going to??

Appendix II

Short Biographies of the Interviewees

Daniel Blanga Gubbay is a Brussels-based researcher in Political Philosophy for the Arts. He graduated in Italy with Giorgio Agamben at the Architecture University of Venice, and while working with him, he got a PhD in Cultural Studies and co-founded the theatre company Pathosformel. He currently holds the position of Professor at the Royal Academy of Fine Arts in Brussels, collaborates as dramaturge for the Kunstenfestivaldesarts, and is the initiator of Aleppo (Brussels), a research platform opening public programs in performance and political theory.

Daniel Blanga Gubbay was interviewed in July 2013 in the context of Santarcangelo Festival (Italy).

Silvia Bottiroli is a curator, researcher and organizer in the contemporary performing arts field. She wrote two books and numerous papers and essays about contemporary performing arts, focusing on collective creation and collaborative practices. She supervised diverse critical and educative projects, collaborating with a.o. SNDO in Amsterdam, Homo Novus in Riga, and Vooruit and Campo in Ghent. Since 2011, she is Adjunct Professor at Bocconi University in Milan. Between 2012 and 2016 she directed Santarcangelo Festival, one of the most relevant contemporary performing arts festivals in Italy.

Silvia Bottiroli was interviewed in November 2013 in the context of Baltic Circle Festival (Finland).

Matthieu Goeury is a Brussels-based producer and programmer of performing arts. His career led him to create a place of research for young art makers, to participate in the creation of an important museum of contemporary art, the Center Pompidou-Metz and to work as a programmer at Kunstcentrum Vooruit. He created the Possible Futures and (IM) Possible Futures festivals in Ghent. In his projects, he tries to develop an ethic based on a socio-political commitment and principles of solidarity, equity, diversity, pragmatism.

Matthieu Goeury was interviewed in July 2013 in the context of Santarcangelo Festival (Italy).

Mylène Lauzon is a poet and writer who deals with the performing art sector, where she worked as a curator, dramaturg and organiser. She co-founded the poetry magazine C'est Selon and curated multiple issues between 2001 and 2005. She has been in charge of programming, development and publishing at the CECN - Centre des Ecritures contemporaines et numériques in Mons

(BE). Since 2015, she is the director of La Bellone - Maison du Spectacle (Brussels).

Mylène Lauzon was interviewed in July 2013 in the context of Santarcangelo Festival (Italy).

Rabih Mrouè is an an actor, director, playwright, visual artist based in Beyrouth. He is also a co-founder and a board member of the Beyrouth Art Center (BAC), Beyrouth. His complex and diverse practice, spanning different disciplines and formats in between theater, performance, and visual arts, has established Mroué as a key figure in Lebanon and abroad. Employing both fiction and in-depth analysis as tools for engaging with his immediate reality, Mroué explores the responsibilities of the artist in communicating with an audience in given political and cultural contexts. His performances tour internationally and he also exhibited at dOCUMENTA (13).

Rabih Mrouè was interviewed in August 2013 in the context of Kampnagel Sommer Festival (Germany).

Giulia Palladini is a researcher in Performance Studies based in Berlin. She was a Alexander von Humboldt fellow (2012-2014), and currently teaches at the Kunsthochschule Berlin-Weißensee. Her research focuses especially on performance labor and free time, the archive, and materialist theories of artistic production. Her texts appeared in several international journals, and she collaborated as theorist and as curator to a number of critical and artistic projects (e.g. *Taking Time*, Helsinki 2013; *Experimenta/Sur*, Bogotá, 2014; *Zu ICH um WIR zu Sein*, Leipzig, 2014). She is the author of the book *The Scene of Foreplay: Theatre, Labor and Leisure in 1960s New* (Northwestern University Press, 2017), and she edited with Marco Pustianaz the collected volume *Lexicon for an Affective Archive* (Intellect/LADA, 2017).

Giulia Palladini was interviewed in Berlin in September 2013.

Mårten Spångberg is a choreographer dealing with choreography in an expanded field, something he has approached through experimental practice in a multiplicity of formats. Since 1999 has been creating his own choreographies, from solos to larger scale works, which have toured internationally. Under the label International Festival, Spångberg collaborated with architect Tor Lindstrand and engaged in social and expanded choreography. From 1996-2005 he curated festivals in Sweden and internationally, and in 2006 initiated the network organisation INPEX. From 2008 to 2012, he directed the MA programme in choreography at the University of Dance in Stockholm. In 2011, his first book, *Spangbergianism*, was published.

Mårten Spångberg was interviewed in July 2013 in the context of Santarcangelo Festival (Italy).

Appendix III

The Three Phases of Analysis

Phase 1/ Preparation and first coding cycle on all data					
Objectives (examples)	Research questions (examples)	Previous knowledge	Coding techniques	Goals
Understanding the meaning of "new"/"innovation"	What does new mean? What does innovation mean?	Yes	Analytical coding (deduction) & Memos	Organisation of data & Building analytical categories thematically
Understanding the dynamics related to the new within neoliberal capitalism in the field	What are the ethical and aesthetical concerns? What are the values connected to the production of the new?	No	Theoretical coding (induction) & Memos	Coding index & First cycle of coding: reduce data to relevant segments

Phase 2/ Transition and second coding cycles (reducing analysis to relevant segments)	
Coding techniques	Goals
Code mapping & Axial coding (first induction then deduction) & Memos	Comparison between cases
	Identification of central concepts (abstraction)
	Second coding cycle: apply axial category deductively to reduce relevant segments

Phase 3/ Third coding cycle and abductive reasoning only on relevant segments				
Objectives (examples)	Research questions (examples)	Previous knowledge	Coding techniques	Goals
Conceptualising "production of the new" Suggesting specific lines of action	What is the perception of roles/rules? What comes next?	-	Selective coding Abductive reasoning	Core concept to provide interpretation Identify unexpected connections

Acknowledgements

I would like to express my deep gratitude and appreciation to my supervisors, Prof. Dr. Volker Kirchberg and Prof. Dr. Massimiliano Nuccio, who supported me during the whole research process, offering challenging comments and valuable suggestions, encouraging me in taking brave decisions.

I am extremely grateful for the assistance and friendship given by my third supervisor, Silvia Bottiroli. Over these three years she took a very long time for travelling, walking and thinking with me about the project. Words cannot express the value of her involvement in this research: beside the interview and the insights into theatre theory and practice, she helped me in making this work relevant for today's theatre context and in taking my PhD research as a point of departure for imagining the future with commitment and joy.

This work would not have been possible without the artists, curators, and theoreticians who agreed to be interviewed for this research. I would like to thank them all for their generosity in terms of time taken and ideas shared. I hope they will find a truthful reconstruction of their reflections and some unexpected suggestions in this work. In particular, I would like to thank Mårten Spångberg for sharing his sharp critiques and passion; Matthieu Goeury and Mylène Lauzon for plotting the system's de-organisation with me; Daniel Blanga Gubbay for sharing his imaginative perspective through images and concepts which largely contributed to the final content and scope of this work; Rabih Mrouè for the insightful conversation, which constituted a turning point for the direction of this research; Giulia Palladini for combining a critical understanding of the present with the courage of taking responsibility for the future inside and outside the theatre, that brought my reasoning on performance and politics to a deeper level.

Special thanks should be given to the people who contributed to the substance of this work by questioning, discussing and practicing the ideas contained in it. In particular, I would like to thank Heike Bröckerhoff, Moritz Frishkorn, Jonas Woltemate and Jakob Klenke for providing me a terrain to experiment with theory at the theatre. These thanks are extended to Roberta Bogni, Giulia Casartelli, Federica Dell'Acqua, Ludovica Gazzè, Andrea Lorenzi, Gabriele Marino, Anna Nutini, Sarah Parolin, Robert Peper, Camilla Pietrabissa and Jeanne Charlotte Vogt, who through their very different perspectives helped me in finding, defining and nurturing the sense of my research practice.

I would like to express my deepest gratitude to the three people who patiently and caringly did the proofreading: Joachim Franz Büchner, Aisling Marks and Romilda Palamara. Besides their fundamental help with translation and language, I would like to thank them for having supported me during the whole writing process.

Among them, I would like to thank in particular Aisling Marks, whose passion and precision set up this research for publishing, for her dedication and commitment to the project that were not limited to professional proofreading but included thought-provoking inputs and theoretical exchange. I would also like to express my profound appreciation to Romilda Palamara for pushing me to do my best with lightness, optimism and love.

This work was made possible by a scholarship of "Teilmaßnahme 1.4 Graduate School des Innovations-Inkubators". I appreciate the opportunity I had to get this financial support, which enabled me to dedicate my full time and energies to research, not only as far as the dissertation is concerned, but also with regards to the possibility of attending conferences, organising research travels and participating in workshops. In this context, I would like to thank personally Eva Breitenstein and Petra Trimborn. I would also like to extend my thanks to the Sparkassenstiftung Lüneburg, in particular to Kristin Halm and Carsten Junge, who dedicated time and attention to this project, by sharing with me their hopes, concerns and reflections on the project KulturBäckerei Lüneburg. I hope that my research contains interesting suggestions for the future of this project in the context of their work.

Index

Agamben, 10, 51, 53-56, 59, 64, 77, 119, 124, 145, 159, 175
Appropriation, 8, 25, 71, 74-75, 82-85, 94, 123, 135-141, 143-145, 154, 159, 172-173, 175, 179
Art Institutions, 8, 12-13, 27, 30, 33, 50-51, 57-61, 82, 86-87, 92-97, 107, 117, 129, 132-133, 139-142, 144, 151-164, 166-167, 174-176, 178-180
Artist, 8, 11-13, 27-28, 30, 33, 35, 41, 56, 68, 70-72, 75, 77, 79-84, 87, 89, 90, 92-94, 117, 119-120, 126, 135-136, 140, 142-143, 145, 147-150, 152-154, 156, 158-159, 167, 174-175, 179
Asynchrony, 55-56, 133-134, 142, 144-146, 165, 174, 176, 179
Autonomy, 12, 64-66, 70, 74, 83, 95-96, 129, 138-140, 147-148, 153-156, 160-161, 167, 173-176
Avant-garde, 11, 55, 66-67, 69-72, 75, 79, 85, 103, 130, 152, 172
Benjamin, 10-11, 39, 42-44, 52, 58, 61-63, 65, 71, 76, 78, 120, 122, 128, 132, 135, 143, 182
Bourdieu, 10, 27, 29-34, 46
Capitalism, 7-12, 16, 20-23, 40, 64-65, 70, 73-74, 79-85, 89-90, 92-93, 97-98, 123, 135-137, 140, 143-144, 146-148, 157, 167, 168, 170-172, 181-182
Change, 9-12, 15, 18-22, 24, 26, 28-32, 35, 40, 45-46, 48, 59, 67-69, 73-74, 76, 78, 91, 94, 98, 118-119, 125-127, 135, 139-144, 147-150, 153, 170-172, 180, 182
Collaboration, 13, 25, 28, 30, 98, 134, 150-151, 155-156, 160, 174, 176, 180
Collective, 20, 24, 26-28, 30, 34-35, 82, 86, 96-99, 123, 125-126, 128, 130, 133-134, 146-147, 149-150, 155-159, 161, 166, 175, 180-181
Conflict, 13, 23, 27, 30-31, 34, 113, 129, 133-134, 150-151, 155-157, 160-161, 165, 168, 174-175, 179
Contemporary, 7, 9-10, 51, 53-57, 119, 124-125, 137, 145, 155
Creative destruction, 7, 11, 16, 19-23, 28, 35, 43, 45, 50, 65, 81, 84, 128, 171
Critique, 7, 9, 12-13, 21, 24-25, 35, 43, 46, 55-56, 71-72, 80, 82-84, 86, 92, 94-96, 140, 177
Curatorship, 14, 117, 119-120, 129, 132, 148-149, 152, 156-161, 175, 179-180
Deleuze, 11, 44-49, 52-53, 56, 60, 77, 85, 90-91, 98, 119, 123, 130-131, 141, 168
Difference, 8, 10-11, 13, 16, 22, 37-38, 40-42, 44-53, 57-58, 60-61, 96, 113, 118-119, 121, 124, 127-129, 133-134, 142, 154-157, 165, 167, 172-176, 177, 179-182
Duration, 21, 51, 56, 59-62, 66, 74, 79, 89-90, 98, 123, 129, 133, 145, 157, 166, 180

Ephemerality, 13, 59, 61-63, 74-76, 94, 96, 123-125, 130-131, 133, 136, 139, 157, 168, 171-172, 175
Eternity, 13, 53, 57, 59-63, 74, 96, 123, 125, 130-131, 151, 171-172
Failure, 23, 138, 162-164, 167, 176
Fiction, 7, 9, 11-12, 35, 57, 79, 87-88, 94-98, 180-182
Future, 8, 11, 14, 43, 46, 52-53, 56, 66, 72-73, 75-79, 91, 96, 98, 133, 136, 140, 156, 163, 167-170, 172, 174, 176-177, 182
Gielen, 9, 12, 32-33, 81-82, 86, 94-97, 140, 149, 154, 170, 175
Groys, 10, 38-41, 49, 54, 57-61, 95-96, 119-123, 154, 175
Harvey, 7-8, 11, 22-23, 25, 73-79, 84, 90, 135-136, 172
Imagination, 8-9, 11, 91, 95-97, 119, 121, 126, 154, 167, 172, 179, 182
Immateriality, 7-8, 23, 26, 28, 31, 65, 73-75, 80, 82, 85, 90, 97, 135-137, 139, 140-142, 146, 171, 176
Incomplete, 11, 13-14, 39, 43-44, 58, 121-123, 127-129, 132, 140, 143, 145, 149, 158-159, 163, 165, 167-169, 172, 174, 178-182
Indeterminacy, 7, 13, 128-129, 132, 135, 137, 139-140, 149, 157, 164, 166, 168, 172, 175-176, 179-181
Kunst, 8, 77, 91, 156, 164
Meantime, 14, 167-168, 174, 177, 182-184

Modernity, 7, 61-63, 66, 73, 76, 77-78, 80, 84, 172
Obscurity, 13, 37, 40-41, 48, 54, 95, 110, 119-121, 129-130, 142-143, 145, 148, 157-158, 172, 175, 182
Ordinary, 10-11, 13, 18-19, 28, 40-41, 48, 55, 57-60, 63, 69, 71, 120-121, 151, 155, 171-172, 175, 180
Organisation, 14, 141-145, 150, 157, 159, 161, 166, 175
Partiality, 45, 48, 68, 88, 121-122, 163-164, 172
Politics, 8-13, 30-31, 33, 35, 43, 46, 51, 53, 61, 65, 68, 71, 74, 77, 79, 82, 86, 89-91, 95, 97-98, 116, 118, 121, 126, 135, 137-141, 146-150, 152-154, 159, 161-162, 166-168, 170, 172-175, 177-182
Possibility, 7, 9, 11, 22, 25, 30, 33, 43, 51, 66-67, 70, 72, 77, 79, 94, 96-98, 120, 122, 128, 130-134, 140, 143, 145, 148-150, 154, 159, 161-162, 166, 168-169, 173-175, 181-182
Postmodernism, 11, 22, 24, 66, 68, 70, 72-79, 88, 96-97, 107, 121-122, 140, 168, 172-173, 175, 179
Potentiality, 34, 65, 91, 122, 129, 131, 135, 139-140, 156, 163, 174-176, 179-180, 182
Present time, 11, 14, 40, 43-44, 46, 52-54, 56, 64, 66, 70, 74, 76-79, 89-91, 94, 96, 98, 130-131, 140, 145, 150, 159, 163, 165, 168, 172, 174-177
Process, 7, 24, 48, 68, 71, 85, 88, 118, 161, 163-164, 176, 180-181

Product, 14-15, 24, 29, 37, 57, 80, 135, 137, 163-165, 176, 181
Progress, 11, 13, 17-19, 21-25, 39-41, 43, 48, 62, 64-65, 76, 78, 84, 98-99, 119-122, 126-127, 129, 131, 138-139, 145, 149-151, 153, 162-167, 170-174, 176, 178, 180-181
Pure means, 64-65, 138, 168, 175
Purpose, 11, 19, 21-22, 43, 64-65, 81, 126, 135, 138-140, 147-148, 151, 171-172, 176
Reality, 7, 9, 11-12, 23, 31-33, 35, 41, 46, 51, 57-58, 79, 87-91, 94, 96-98, 121, 123, 128, 132-133, 146-149, 162, 166, 170, 175, 177, 180-182
Re-appropriation, 168, 175, 178, 181
Remembrance, 11, 39, 42-44, 47-48, 51-52, 57, 76, 90, 127-128
Repetition, 44-55, 57, 62-63, 70, 85, 89-91, 96, 130, 133, 141, 168, 173
Reproduction, 7, 11, 21-22, 31-32, 40, 46, 70, 73, 75-78, 81-82, 122, 139, 141, 144, 153-154, 162, 167-168, 171, 173, 175, 178
Rules, 27-28, 30-36, 159-162, 178-181
Self-betrayal, 113, 129-130, 132-133, 141, 157-158, 165-166, 173-175
Space, 11-12, 22, 30, 33, 41, 50-51, 56-59, 65, 72-77, 87, 89-93, 95, 97-98, 105, 113-115, 122, 127-134, 140, 146, 151, 154-157, 159, 163-167, 172-176, 179-181

Spectatorship, 28, 31, 38, 92, 98, 121, 132, 152, 156, 158-162, 164-165, 175-176, 178, 180
Substitutability, 11, 19, 21, 43, 45, 50, 55, 60, 70-72, 75, 80, 95, 123, 164, 173, 178
Suspension, 113, 129, 131-133, 138-140, 149, 156-158, 165-166, 168, 173, 175, 178, 180, 182
Theatre, 7-8, 10-14, 33, 41, 47, 49-51, 56-58, 67, 74, 77, 87-91, 96-98, 116-120, 127, 131-132, 134-136, 141-146, 151-157, 165-166, 168, 170, 173-175, 177-182
Time, 11-12, 14, 22, 43, 50-57, 59-60, 72-78, 87, 89-91, 96-98, 123-124, 129-134, 142-145, 150, 156, 159, 164-168, 172-175, 177, 182
Unknown, 10, 15-18, 22, 38-41, 50, 119, 171
Value, 7-10, 12-13, 20-21, 23, 24, 26, 28-29, 40, 45, 55, 59-66, 70, 73-75, 78, 80-81, 85, 90, 97, 121, 123, 134-144, 168, 171-172, 175-176, 181
Whole, 13-14, 68, 71-72, 121-124, 128-129, 153, 155-156, 161-163, 172, 176, 180

197

budrich journals

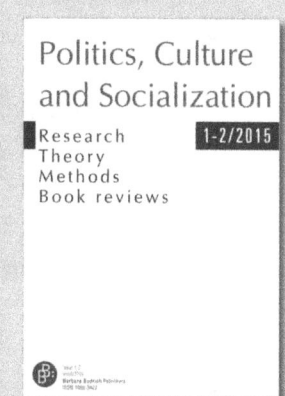

- Single article downloads
- Print + online
- Various subscription types
- Free contents:
  ToCs
  editorials
  book reviews
  Open Access contents

Barbara Budrich Publishers
Stauffenbergstr. 7
51379 Leverkusen-Opladen

ph +49 (0)2171.344.594
fx +49 (0)2171.344.693
info@budrich-journals.com

Find our journals on **www.budrich-journals.com**

IJREE –
International Journal for Research on Extended Education

ISSN: 2196-3673
ISSN Online: 2196-7423
Volume 4, 2016
Published twice a year
Pages: Approx. 120
Language: English

The International Journal for Research on Extended Education (IJREE) aims at creating international visibility and a stronger scientific profile for the research field of extended education. The Journal is published by a group of internationally renowned educational researchers and is funded by the German Research Foundation (DFG).

From early childhood to late adolescence, young people are enrolled in various public or private forms of educational arrangements. Some of them, particularly pre-school-aged children, attend kindergarten or participate in early learning courses. School-aged children often participate in school- or community-based programmes, forms of private tutoring or after-school activities such as art courses or academic clubs, or they attend all-day schools.

In as far as these activities and programmes focus on the social, emotional and academic development of children and young people and are pedagogically structured to make it easier for the participants to learn specific contents they can be summarized by the term extended education.

www.budrich-journals.com

GPSR Authorized Representative: Easy Access System Europe, Mustamäe tee
50, 10621 Tallinn, Estonia, gpsr.requests@easproject.com

www.ingramcontent.com/pod-product-compliance
Lightning Source LLC
Chambersburg PA
CBHW051546020426
42333CB00016B/2120